The publisher and the University of California Press Foundation grate-fully acknowledge the generous support of the Simpson Imprint in Humanities.

The publisher also gratefully acknowledges the generous support of the Director's Circle of the University of California Press Foundation, whose members are:

Stephen and Melva Arditti
Michael Barnard
John Geiger
David Hayes-Bautista
JAG
Donald Mastronarde
Susan McClatchy
Peter B. Moyle
Alejandro Portes
The Leslie Scalapino - O Books Fund
Sharon Simpson
Marc Singer
Lynne Withey

Handcrafted Careers

Handcrafted Careers

WORKING THE ARTISAN ECONOMY
OF CRAFT BEER

Eli Revelle Yano Wilson

UNIVERSITY OF CALIFORNIA PRESS

University of California Press
Oakland, California

© 2024 by Eli R. Wilson

Library of Congress Cataloging-in-Publication Data

Names: Wilson, Eli Revelle Yano, author.
Title: Handcrafted careers : working the artisan economy of craft beer /
    Eli Revelle Yano Wilson.
Description: Oakland, California : University of California Press, [2024] |
    Includes bibliographical references and index.
Identifiers: LCCN 2024010280 (print) | LCCN 2024010281 (ebook) |
    ISBN 9780520401556 (cloth) | ISBN 9780520401563 (paperback) |
    ISBN 9780520401570 (ebook)
Subjects: LCSH: Microbreweries—Social aspects—United States—21st
    century. | Microbreweries—Vocational guidance—United States—21st
    century.
Classification: LCC HD9397.U52 W552 2024 (print) | LCC HD9397.U52
    (ebook) | DDC 663/.42023—dc23/eng/20240412
LC record available at https://lccn.loc.gov/2024010280
LC ebook record available at https://lccn.loc.gov/2024010281

33 32 31 30 29 28 27 26 25 24
10 9 8 7 6 5 4 3 2 1

Contents

List of Figures

Preface

At its core, craft work is about making things of high quality using your hands rather than machines when possible. The people who engage in modern-day craft work use techniques that are deliberately slower and less efficient than their noncraft counterparts. They do so because they see these techniques as more authentic and thus a more meaningful way to work. In many craft breweries, for example, brewers hoist fifty-five-pound bags of malted barley chest-high to pour their contents into a steaming mash tun, sending a plume of milled-grain dust into the air. It is a messy and tiring process. Similarly, in some taprooms that offer cask-conditioned ales, beertenders use hand pumps to draw naturally carbonated liquid up from wooden kegs in the cellar. Without the aid of refrigeration or modern technology used to minimize the presence of unwanted oxygen in the beer, cask ale has only a few days of shelf life before it spoils. Producing cask ale is impractical compared to standard draft beer (which is artificially carbonated), but some say the nuanced flavors of the former make it all worth it. This is the essence of craft work.

Today, relatively few young adults aspire to become craft brewers or tend bar in brewery taprooms—at least not in the same way they might think about becoming lawyers, chemists, or even movie actors. Despite its rising popularity over the past four decades, producing craft beer remains a niche occupation focused on a type of "artisanal" work that rarely offers much in the way of prestige or pay. Those who do end up forging careers in this industry don't get there by complete accident. The reality is that some people are far more likely than others to arrive at the doorstep of the craft beer industry, often guided there by friends, family members, and prior life experiences. Many of these individuals also come to be extremely passionate about this work. I should know because I was one of them.

When I was in my mid-twenties, I worked at a craft beer bar in Los Angeles and I was at a crossroads with my career. I was staring down two distinct job paths: would I continue to work in craft beer, where I had already started to build my industry résumé and aspired to open my own brewpub one day?[1] Or would I accept an offer to head back to graduate school at a nearby university to pursue a PhD in sociology? (I had applied to the program a year earlier mainly to hedge my employment bets and keep my options open.) Brewing beer was more appealing to me at the time because craft beer was something I was *obsessed* about. As a college-educated, white-appearing man, I felt I could pursue daily tasks within breweries—such as kegging fresh beer and talking with "beer geeks" about the rotating tap list—that were endlessly interesting and personally rewarding. Plus, I loved tasting beer.

I ended up choosing graduate school, which I remember thinking, possibly in error, would lead to more stable, well-compensated work. The rest is history. But over the years, I have remained in contact with friends and acquaintances who stayed in craft beer. I have grown fascinated by the varied pathways of employment people take throughout their lives and how their personal journeys reflect a mixture of individual choices and socio-structural circumstances, with a healthy dash of the unexpected thrown in. Researching this book allowed me to investigate these very issues. What drives people toward craft work amid other possibilities? Once there, how might workers' careers unfold differently depending on their social backgrounds, and what might this reveal about the nature of employment opportunities in our changing world of work?

In this book, I refer to the emergent and layered work careers that those in craft beer forge as *handcrafted careers*. When seen at the ground level, handcrafted careers are made up of a series of loosely linked jobs, social circumstances, and individual decisions that would be difficult to predict a priori. Yet sociologists tend to bristle at the notion that individual "choices" meaningfully affect people's employment outcomes. Choice, so the argument goes, belies the larger forces shaping people's lives and constraining their ability to freely "choose" between different options (despite what they may think). To be sure, people's job opportunities are indeed framed by socio-structural contexts that bear the imprint of racism, sexism, classism, and other institutional forces within existing systems of power. This doesn't mean, however, that people's choices and actions at pivotal points in their work careers—whether to pursue one job over another or follow a close friend's career advice or not—are unworthy of sociological study. As none other than W. E. B. Du Bois put it, "sociology is the science that seeks to measure the limits of chance in human action, or if you will excuse the paradox, it is the science of free will."[2] Taking seriously the choices and actions of people who work in craft beer, as this book does, gives us a unique window to view the ongoing, everyday forces of social inequality that play out in contemporary workplaces. It also allows us to assess how people's changing relationships to work affect their work lives and identities.

Many of the individuals we will meet in the pages ahead are forging dynamic careers that are a good deal different from the creative and entrepreneurial one that I imagined for myself years ago within craft beer. And perhaps that is the point. In an industry where some workers and not others are able to express their personal passions through their jobs—and have these qualities celebrated by their peers—people end up navigating distinctly unequal career pathways over time. This book embraces the messy, unfolding realities that the lives of craft beer workers represent. Researching *Handcrafted Careers* has thus allowed me to circle back to that fateful career decision I made a decade ago, this time with a different goal in mind.

Introduction

Mike, a thirty-six-year-old white man with a neatly trimmed beard, describes "finding" homebrewing like an epiphany, something that suddenly set a new career path in motion for him. "It really started in earnest when I bought my house with my not-yet-wife at the time," says Mike. "My housewarming gift from her parents was a homebrew kit. Her parents knew that, oh, he likes making stuff and doing things with his hands—maybe he'll like brewing beer! That seemed like a good thing for them to get me," he chuckles, looking down at his hands. "Homebrewing was definitely a hobby that I was immediately interested in. It went out of control really fast. Like, brewing in the garage every weekend and stuff."

Mike and I are sitting at a wooden picnic table in a cavernous warehouse near downtown Los Angeles that, six years ago, he and three of his friends transformed into Renegade Brewing.[1] Prior to cofounding Renegade, Mike had spent his twenties working at a corporate marketing firm just a few blocks north of here. Though he liked his six-figure salary, Mike told me he knew he wanted to do something that was more creative and more entrepreneurial, something that spoke to his true passions.

"I was focusing my energies on entrepreneurship because I knew I wanted to work for myself one day. But I *definitely* didn't know it was going to be a brewery!" he says. That's when Mike met his soon-to-be company cofounders through friends of friends in the business world. The three men, all of whom were college-educated professionals like Mike, hit it off immediately, linked by a mutual love of craft beer. It was during this time that the prospect of launching a small craft brewing company began to take shape in Mike's mind.

"The early conversations were like, this guy knows marketing and advertising, he can help with that part of it. There was something different for the next guy. And the next guy. Everyone had something to contribute. Eventually, it spiraled into: well, would we all want to do this thing??" says Mike. He and the other owners decided to hire an experienced head brewer to lead the operation, luring him away from a larger and more established brewery. The company's opening team was complete: a blend of industry experts, creative types, and well-connected businessmen. Mike quit his day job and dug in.

The process of opening Renegade Brewing over the next two years wasn't easy. Mike explains that this was partly because of a drawn-out and complex permitting process. It was also because local community residents, most of whom were working-class Latinx immigrants and their families, put up stiff resistance to a brewery opening next door, which raised fears of both gentrification and public drunkenness. "I understood where they were coming from," Mike says. "But at the same time, it was frustrating because I wanted them to see that we were just a bunch of guys who wanted to do good things for the neighborhood. And we weren't going to be *that* kind of place, like, a seedy dive bar." It took a while for the company to find its footing. But by the time Mike and I met up in early 2020, Renegade had become a well-established presence in the Los Angeles craft beer scene with its splashy label art (Mike's designs) and a hoppy flagship India Pale Ale. The brewery and its leadership team had received glowing media coverage from many of the biggest news outlets in Los Angeles. While he doesn't brew for his company, Mike says he finds creative fulfillment in forging partnerships with local artists to host art and music shows for the weekend taproom crowds, the majority of whom are white men and women in their twenties and thirties.

Before we part ways, I ask Mike to reflect on what he has built here. "It was a lot of sweat equity," he says, tugging on the bill of his Dodgers baseball cap. "We did it ourselves—there's no shadow overlord here. We got loans and help from friends and family."

"And how is that working out for you?" I ask.

Mike makes a face. "Well, I didn't start paying myself until recently," he says. "Everything we earn needs to go back into the business. Somebody once told me this is not an industry to make a big fortune. It is an industry where you take a big fortune and make it a smaller one. But this is what we signed up for, right?"

SHEILA

"To be honest, I kind of fell into this," explains Sheila, a thirty-four-year-old woman with wavy brown hair and bubbly energy. "What happened was, I was waiting tables downtown at the time and I started talking to the sales reps who would come in and bring us samples of beer. I would be like, cool! That looks fun," she says. "I quickly became the server that knew the most about beer. And I could sell beer—it wasn't hard for me," Sheila explains, drawing connections between her customer-facing restaurant industry jobs in her early twenties and selling craft beer professionally for the past decade. "The other servers I worked with didn't know as much about beer, so the managers would be like, 'Sheila, for this new hire, can you train them about how to talk about beer the way you do?'"

As we talk about her career path, Sheila, who identifies as mixed race ("half white and half Persian"), leans slightly forward and waves her hands in the air for emphasis.[2] "One of my friends told me, 'Hey, I know someone who is opening this beer bar downtown, he is looking for someone to manage it—I think you'd be perfect for the job,'" says Sheila. "So I went there, got hired that day. I was running Friday night events there for a few years. That era was nonstop beer for me. If there was something I hadn't had, I would be tasting it sooner or later."

Sheila's discerning knowledge of craft beer and other "artisanal" alcoholic drinks has proven a boon during her nine-year career in the beer industry. But it is customer service that continues to anchor her day-to-day work experience. It was this aspect of her job that doubles as a source of frustration for Sheila. Sheila explains, "eventually, I knew I didn't want to serve anymore. And management wasn't moving me into the [better] bartending shifts I wanted. I was getting burnt out from stressful customer interactions and late nights." During a slow weekday shift, Sheila was approached by a sales representative for a beer distributor and offered a job. She accepted. "Working as a sales rep allowed me to still work in an energetic space, much like being behind a bar—but not," she says.

"So these days, what do you like most about the craft beer industry?" I ask.

"What do I like most?" Sheila smiles. "That's easy: beer is fun! And beer people are just like—I feel like beer is a more welcoming, opening environment."

"Any downsides?"

Sheila pauses. "Honestly, it is all still pretty male dominated. If you look at brewery ownership, it is almost all men. Distribution companies, I can only think of one owned by a woman. And merchandisers and drivers are all men." Two years ago, Sheila says she quit working for one beer distribution company because of what she would only describe as "a gender pay issue." Continuing to work in this industry has meant that she has had to adapt. "I get along very well with guys, and I've learned to pick and choose my battles. I am very outspoken, so if they say something inappropriate I kind of nip it at the bud. And they learn, *don't say that in front of Sheila.* And I'm like, 'that's right!'"

ESTEBAN

Esteban, a forty-two-year-old Latino man dressed in an oversized white t-shirt and baggy black jeans, reclines in his plush black office chair, arms behind his head. He has invited me to visit his newly renovated "office" in west Los Angeles, which is a leased storage unit with a pull-up garage door that opens onto a back alley. Inside, the walls are awash in colorful, Graffiti-style spray paint. On the floor in the corner is a pallet of aluminum beer cans still wrapped in plastic. On Esteban's desk sits a plaque: "Esteban Ramirez, CEO of Brews in Da Hood." He had it made a couple weeks ago for himself.

"I like to say, craft beer saved my life, man. Everything I do, I do all the way. That's just how I am." Esteban cracks opens a can of Hazy India Pale Ale with his brand name splashed on the front label in graffiti-style font.

He reaches under his desk for two tulip-shaped glasses and begins to pour out frothy, golden-hued liquid. I catch a whiff of ripe pineapple and papaya from across the desk.

It wasn't always this way. In his twenties, Esteban was sent to a federal corrections facility for "doing some dumb shit when I was younger" (he doesn't elaborate). He got out of prison five years later. "I've changed my life already," says Esteban. "I haven't been in jail for a long time, over eleven years now. Thank God. I got a good job—I had a good job. My kids went to great schools all around the country, my wife is a HR manager, we bought our home. But I still have the 'hood in me. I talk like that, I dress like that with my Chicano roots, bald head and everything. Everywhere I go, people are at first a little intimidated but then once they start talking to me it's like, oh fuck this guy's cool as *fuck*." A few years ago, Esteban saw his number of followers on social media unexpectedly skyrocket into the five digits after posting videos of himself casually drinking highly sought-after craft beers. Esteban attributes this to his unique presence on social media in a sea of "bearded white guys" as well as "chicks posting pictures of themselves alongside cans and bottles of craft beer."

Three years ago, Esteban decided he would try to turn his growing social media persona into a business. He had no idea how things would turn out and no formal ties to anyone in the industry. "We—my wife and I—decided to start doing something else. That's when I talked to my friend Julio and said, 'You know what? Let's fucking start making beer even though we don't have a brewery. You have a brewing license. I got some recipes. We're doing it . . . we're going to fucking start releasing new cans every month. And we'll start saving our money with that. Then, later on, in maybe another year or two, we'll be able to open something up.'"

I caught up with Esteban six months later in the spring of 2021. He had just texted me about his new GoFundMe account seeking the money from friends, family, and followers to help him launch his company. "It's going okay, man. Pretty good. Lots of people have pitched in, and a lot more have viewed the fundraiser post on social media," he explained. "But—I don't know. Shit's expensive, bro! And we still have a ways to go [to get the company off the ground]."

. . . . .

Mike, Sheila, and Esteban work in the craft beer industry in the United States, representing three of the roughly 189,000 people who are employed in over 9,000 small and independent companies that make, sell, and distribute "craft" beers. The exploding popularity of craft beer—defined as beer made by small and independent companies—over the past four decades has transformed this once-niche industry into a cultural and economic force at the leading edge of the new economy. Craft beer regularly commands mainstream media attention to go along with $28.4 billion in sales annually, representing nearly a quarter of all domestic beer sales.[3] Four out of five Americans now live within ten miles of a brewery, and city planners and local business leaders continue to push for more brewery openings to help fuel urban and suburban redevelopment efforts, giving older neighborhoods instant "cool" appeal.

Within such an aspirational industry, I was surprised to hear that having a career in craft beer was never something that Mike, Sheila, or Esteban could have predicted for themselves. Each claimed to have "found," "discovered," or "fallen into" craft beer rather than arriving there due to long-term career planning. By their own admission, something still feels unfinished about each their work lives, layered with equal parts personal drive and risk. They are hardly alone in this regard. For a growing number of Americans today, particularly young adults at the onset of their working lives, job pathways are increasingly unpredictable and nonlinear. Well-grooved career tracks bridging one's education and training into the workforce have all but disappeared, while a given worker's employment opportunities are more likely to span multiple employers and short-term job contracts than ever before. The culture of work is shifting, too. Facing a changing labor landscape, career counselors and business media outlets encourage workers see themselves as "free agents" in a wide-open market, treating jobs and employers as temporary stepping stones as they pursue careers that speak to their "authentic" selves.[4] These trends have only accelerated amid the COVID-19 pandemic, when millions of American workers either lost their jobs or left them in search of something new (the so-called Great Resignation). More so than any time in the last half century, the work careers that people are forging are less straightforward and laced with uncertainty.[5]

For many of the people we will meet in this book, seeking employment in craft beer allows them to bring their work lives together with their personal interests, whether in fine-tuning recipes for fruited Sour Ales or fostering community among mountain biking enthusiasts. In doing so, these individuals pursue custom-fit careers fueled by passion rather than economic provision. But the story isn't so simple. This is because the craft beer industry is far from immune to structural forces of inequality that afflict the world of work. Workers from more privileged backgrounds based on intersecting race, class, gender, and other social statuses continue to "find" themselves with access to more desirable job opportunities relative to their less privileged peers. Take Mike and Esteban. Both men share a zeal for craft beer and an entrepreneurial approach to managing their work lives. Yet Esteban, as a brown-skinned man with a high school education, immigrant parents, a criminal record, and no prior industry connections, could only dream of getting his start in the industry by founding a full-scale brewing company the way Mike has been able to do. Compared to Mike, Esteban's business venture—and his ability to follow his passions into this type of work—is considerably riskier to his and his family's economic livelihood. Sheila's employment history also says something about how her social background has shaped her career trajectory. While Sheila has indeed leveraged her specialized beer knowledge to access a string of job opportunities, the frontline customer-service jobs she has worked are disproportionately held by white or lighter-skinned women in an industry that remains overwhelmingly white and male. Sheila enjoys a stable tenure within craft beer, but it is not necessarily one that holds much power and prestige or offers a clear pathway toward gaining either.

Previous sociological scholarship on work and social inequality can help us understand the institutionalized barriers that minoritized workers continue to face in racialized, classed, and gendered labor settings. Research shows that managers, acting as key gatekeepers for their companies, steer the hiring, promoting, and supervisory processes in ways that often favor credentialed white men. Managers are also instrumental in assigning white women and workers of color, respectively, to subordinate roles and tasks in the workplace.[6] This draws our attention to how organizational authorities produce and reproduce workplace norms and practices that legitimize the unequal positioning of workers based on their social statuses.[7] Yet, by emphasizing top-down processes in organizations (think hiring decisions and salary offers), existing research tends to overlook how social inequality can also manifest through less overt, *microprocesses* at the ground level. Workers, for instance, bring their personal interests, connections, and ideas about employment to bear on specific workplace contexts, which can affect how they navigate key junctures in their work lives. Further, much of what we know about work and inequality is based on studies of large, complex, and hierarchical organizations such as hospitals, factories, and Wall Street investment firms. Yet these settings are increasingly at odds with the emergent, flexible, and informal labor environments that a growing number of young workers today inhabit. As a result, we have limited understanding of the contextualized barriers and opportunities that, say, Esteban encounters as he tries to launch his small brewing company or Sheila faces while moving between jobs and companies selling specialty beer for a living. The case of the craft beer industry offers a unique opportunity to understand emerging types of work in the new economy and their uneven implications for workers.

This book asks: How do people forge work careers in a changing landscape of work today? What do they seek in their work lives and how do they attempt to secure it? What does this tell us about how *microprocesses* of social inequality operate in workplaces in ways that often go unnoticed? To answer these questions, I examine the career pathways of craft beer workers in the United States. By *career pathways*, I mean the linked sequences of jobs that workers experience over time. Career pathways draw attention to how workers enter into and proceed along jobs that differ with respect to pay, power, and prestige. It is through charting the socially stratified career pathways of workers such as Mike, Sheila, and Esteban that we glean key insights into how workers navigate a changing world of work in ways that reflect, reproduce, and sometimes challenge existing social inequalities.

I argue that a complex interplay of industry structures and workers' own social connections, personalized tastes, and cultural ideas about employment contribute to the divergent employment paths that workers in this industry lead. These processes pattern the three main career pathways in craft beer: the creative pathway, the service pathway, and the hard labor pathway. These pathways are not always formally laid out, nor do they exist within all companies. Yet workers from different social backgrounds get pushed and pulled toward certain jobs and away from others at key moments along career pathways that are racialized, gendered, and classed. White men from privileged backgrounds such as Mike gain access to the creative pathway, consisting of lead brewing jobs and managerial positions that offer the most authority and prestige. Women and people of color mostly work along subordinate job pathways in craft beer that involve differently gendered and racialized work: women, especially white women, are concentrated in interactive service jobs, whereas men of color are concentrated in physical labor jobs. At the same time, within an expanding "artisanal" landscape featuring small and value-driven companies, workers' career pathways are far from fixed. This has helped some minoritized workers locate new, albeit unpredictable, employment opportunities by leveraging certain aspects of their social backgrounds.

In charting the complex work lives that unfold in the craft beer industry, I introduce the concept of *handcrafted careers*—the dynamic sequences of jobs that bear the distinct imprint of the worker doing the sculpting and the structural forces that constrain this process. Two dimensions of handcrafted careers are worth elaborating up front. First, handcrafted careers highlight the contours of career progression today that are lumpy and uncertain rather than linear and predictable. This builds on the idea of "protean" or "boundaryless" careers that are open-ended and play out across different companies amid a labor market in flux.[8] Yet handcrafted careers places greater emphasis on how the emergent employment pathways that workers navigate within a given workplace, industry, or occupational context are constrained by racialized, classed, and gendered processes.[9] In effect, the handcrafted-ness of a worker's career reflects a cumulative process of customization that is not entirely of one's own choosing because of socio-structural inequalities as well as labor market uncertainties.[10] Second, handcrafted careers involve an ongoing process of self-identity construction over the course of one's work life. This form of identity work extends beyond any one job or workplace and gets infused with deeply personal values.[11] For many of the workers we will meet in this book, building handcrafted careers that center artisanal goods and craft production are part of their broader lifestyle projects that prioritize authenticity. To be sure, the ability to curate a "project of self" through one's career has always been more available to those from privileged backgrounds.[12] Yet as more people face a world of work where jobs are open-ended and unpredictable, handcrafted careers capture something that is growing increasingly common: a process of honing who one is over time and what one seeks—but does not always find—through work.

WORK AND PASSION IN THE NEW ECONOMY

For much of the twentieth century, jobs were relatively stable, especially for white, middle-class Americans. For these workers, "standard" employment meant a 9-to-5 work schedule, livable wages, and relatively secure employment with one company—often all these things at once. Structural changes to the domestic economy during the last quarter of the twentieth century, such as deindustrialization, neoliberal economic policies, and a globalized market for labor and commodities, have contributed to the growth of nonstandard and uncertain labor conditions.[13] Today, a growing number of Americans working in the so-called new economy face job schedules, pay, and employment statuses that are, in the words of sociologist Brian Halpin, "subject to change without notice."[14] Facing precarious job conditions, employment has become an inherently short-term arrangement that must be constantly renewed and revisited rather than expected.[15] In short, more workers today across a wide range of industries are grappling with uncertainty in their work lives.[16]

Amid sweeping shifts to the economy, the dominant norms, narratives, and expectations surrounding work—or what I refer to as *the cultural logic of work*—have also changed. The cultural logic of work from decades past prioritized security and stability, whereby most workers had a reasonably clear sense of how their careers would proceed over time if they stayed the course.[17] Today, workers face a world of work where short-term employment, whether by choice or otherwise, is the norm.[18] Many workers also have less clear expectations about the *rightness* of any given career pathway for themselves. Aided by messages coming from the media and career counselors ("do what you love!" "bring your whole self to work!"), workers are told to look inward to their personal feelings and interests for clues as to what kind of work to pursue instead of outward toward traditional markers of "good" and stable employment.[19]

Having a passion for one's work—that is, a strong emotional connection or "love" for one's job—is now a dominant cultural logic of work in the United States. This "passion principle," as sociologist Erin Cech calls it, provides a justification for pursuing highly individualized labor goals and treating this pursuit as a measure of career success.[20] In effect, following one's heart when entering into the labor market has become leading career advice that embodies the new "spirit" of capitalism.[21] As Mike illustrates, workers today—especially those from socially privileged backgrounds—idealize employment that offers flexibility and the opportunity for individual expression.[22] Many value the ability to consume work by aligning their jobs with activities, social environments, and products that resonate with them personally.[23] Furthermore, workers who adhere to this relationship to work may be willing to make sacrifices in order to obtain jobs that fit their passions. While this can inspire dedication to one's career goals, it can also expose workers to exploitative labor arrangements such as working for free, accepting in-kind compensation instead of wages, or agreeing to precarious employment as a necessary foot in the door to their industry of choice.[24]

More than any time in the past century, Americans feel that work should be more than just work and that one's career should be something uniquely theirs.[25] They must balance this with the need to secure ongoing employment amid profoundly uncertain labor conditions. Complicating this matter further is the fact that access to labor market opportunities continues to be patterned by social inequalities, a topic we turn to next.

SOCIAL INEQUALITY IN EQUAL OPPORTUNITY WORKPLACES

A growing body of scholarship describes the role that today's organizations continue to play in shoring up social inequalities based on race, class, gender, and other intersectional statuses despite formal laws that make discrimination illegal.[26] Many of these organizational dynamics focus on the role of management and the top-down processes they instigate, such as how managers hire, fire, and promote people for different jobs or make decisions about how much to pay someone.[27] As sociologist Joan Acker notes, it is within organizations that "inequality regimes" continue to manifest, which Acker describes as interlocking practices and processes within organizations that perpetuate social inequalities.[28] Company managers have the power to assign men and women, white people and people of color, the more educated and the less educated, to distinct employment roles with differential access to power, income, and status.[29]

In the post-civil-rights era, inequality-producing processes within workplaces are often subtle and inconspicuous.[30] Employers, for instance, may hide their biases in ways that do not appear outwardly prejudiced yet result in discriminatory hiring outcomes.[31] As sociologist Victor Ray notes, another reason organizations continue to reproduce racial inequality is because they are fundamentally structured in ways that uphold standards of whiteness while simultaneously devaluing blackness.[32] In companies that are dominated by white people, subordinate jobs and undesirable tasks are often designated for people of color, especially those who are foreign-born and poor.[33] Company leadership may simultaneously exhibit a preference for members of the dominant racial group—especially for positions of authority—and engage in helping behaviors that benefit these workers.[34]

Some of what contributes to socially unequal outcomes goes beyond the explicitly exclusionary actions of management.[35] Many company leaders rely on intangible characteristics and personal networks to make hiring and promoting decisions in ways that disadvantage minoritized candidates. Because these kinds of "credentials" cannot be found on any formal résumé, they are harder to address and even harder to eradicate. Some managers use selective recruitment methods and other screening mechanisms throughout the hiring process to effectively reduce the "qualified" applicant pool in favor of candidates who are white and class-privileged, as sociologist Lauren Rivera's research shows.[36] They do so by seeking workers who represent a cultural fit with the hobbies and interests of incumbent workers or the company's desired clientele.[37] In short, even within well-meaning companies, key gatekeepers can reproduce social inequalities through the ways they select, promote, and evaluate workers based on white, upper-middle-class ideals.

Management, however, is only one part of the employment equation that contributes to inequitable outcomes in today's labor settings. As

Sheila's story illustrates, workers bring their own economic resources, networks, skills, and aspirations with them as they enter into and move between jobs. They engage in proactive forms of "employment management" as they navigate individualized job opportunities within an unpredictable labor market.[38] For many workers, getting a job involves tapping into personal social networks. This can enable them to expedite the formal hiring process or circumvent it entirely.[39] Yet because social ties are embedded within structurally unequal social groups, using networks to access jobs provides more assistance to some workers than others. Similarly, networks channel workers into socially coded and hierarchically situated job opportunities.[40] White men are more likely to know other white men in positions of authority, such that tapping their social connections to get jobs helps pull them into more desirable opportunities than their counterparts from minoritized status groups. Further, within a given workplace, workers are often connected to specific occupational subgroups separated by racialized and classed group boundaries.[41] This, too, can make it harder for workers in subordinate positions to access attractive jobs within their companies or industry that they might otherwise qualify for.

The employment aspirations that workers hold also affect the kind of labor market opportunities they seek and see as befitting of them. As a "self-expressive edge" of job segregation, personal aspirations are closely related, though not entirely reduceable, to one's socialization within stratified environments.[42] As Pierre Bourdieu notes, a person's "tastes" are conditioned by *habitus,* meaning the embodied dispositions instilled by one's upbringing in structurally unequal environments.[43] These include tastes for work as well as career aspirations. Sociologist Matthew Desmond, studying wildland firefighters, describes how working-class men bring their ideas about "country masculinity"—instilled from their upbringing in working-class rural environments—to their professional lives.[44] This gives their jobs both meaning and value because it fits with their preconceived ideas about what it means to be a man. One's self-expressed employment aspirations are thus framed by socially coded ideas about work, including deeply entrenched gendered, classed, and racialized norms about certain jobs in our society.[45]

Cultural framings about work can make it hard for those who don't fit the mold to feel comfortable and gain acceptance among their colleagues.

Workers such as Esteban *know* they stand out among the crowd in industry settings dominated by "bearded white guys."[46] Research shows that white women and people of color are more likely to face symbolic forms of marginalization or other kinds of microaggressions relative to their white male counterparts.[47] Women in professional firms, for instance, are less likely to fit masculinized notions of "success" in their field, often involving putting in long hours away from the home and having an authoritative persona. Instead, they contend with what Deneen Hatmaker calls a *gender-qualified* work identity: in the eyes of observers, they are *women* engineers, *women* brewers, not engineers and brewers.[48] In response, minoritized workers must learn to adapt by continually managing their differences in the workplace, or choose to leave.[49] These strategies are largely unnecessary for their more socially privileged colleagues who remain the dominant presence in their workplace.

Understanding the overlapping forces of social inequality described here goes a long way toward helping us make sense of the respective work lives of Mike, Sheila, and Esteban. Yet these workers forge careers in an industry that looks and feels very different from the corporate environments that have long been the focus of work scholarship. To clarify what this can tell us about the changing nature of work and inequality, we turn to the context of the craft beer industry today.

THE RISE OF CRAFT BEER AND MODERN CRAFT WORK

Throughout much of the twentieth century, traditional forms of craft work were in steady decline in the United States due to the rise of mass production, standardization, and routinized labor at the behest of large corporations. The "skill of making things well," as sociologist Richard Sennett describes craftsmanship, had fallen by the wayside in favor of machine-aided production methods and assembly-line labor processes. It is only in the last three or four decades that interest in craft work has reemerged partly as a counterreaction to these trends and often located in postindustrial urban spaces. Modern craft work has continued to gain in popularity among American consumers—particularly white Americans with the discretionary income to pay for these "artisanal" products. Today, craft breweries share a prominent corner of the new economy with other modern craft makers, such as artisanal coffee roasters (who hand-roast their coffee beans), tattoo artists (who treat their designs and methods as high art), gourmet butchers (who carefully source their animals and offer specialty cuts of meat), and microdistilleries (who are reviving traditional distilling methods).[50]

The popularization of modern craft work has much to do with the value specialty products gain from how they are made, served, and consumed. As sociologist Richard Ocejo notes, craft production represents reconfigured tastes among cultural elites, both those who patronize these establishments and those who work there as "masters of craft." These individuals are drawn to the idea of participating in a romanticized "urban village life," made up of small producers and a more personalized relationship between workers and customers.[51] In this sense, a key source of value of modern craft work is the "authenticity" by which these products are offered up.[52] Authenticity is not inherent in craft products—be it a pint of beer or a bag of roasted coffee. Instead, it is actively cultivated by the people who make and sell these products. Many of those who are drawn to modern craft work also appreciate what they see as the moral value of craftsmanship as well as the specialized knowledge that this work embodies.[53] Others—sometimes stereotyped as hipsters—are attracted to the coolness of the social atmospheres surrounding craft products.[54] In short, those who participate in modern craft work today engage in what Elizabeth Currid-Halkett refers to as "conspicuous production," meaning the creation of goods that gain value from making legible the process by which they are made and served.[55]

Working the Craft Beer Industry

According to the Brewers Association, a craft brewery is defined by its relatively small size of production (less than six million barrels annually), majority noncorporate ownership, and, until recently, the use of "traditional" brewing ingredients, such as hops and malted barley.[56] In 1970, fewer than one hundred commercial breweries of any kind existed in the United States. That number had been steadily declining each decade *after* Prohibition was repealed as the result of corporate conglomeration in the

Figure 1. Handcrafted spaces within craft breweries.

beer industry and a tangle of legal restrictions—homebrewing, for example, was illegal in the United States until 1978—that made commercial brewing on a small scale difficult.[57] Since then, craft or "micro-brewed" beer has enjoyed a rapid rise in popularity to go along with expanded social, cultural, and economic influence.[58] As of 2022, over 9,000 breweries are currently in business, most of them small operations. Craft breweries now make 24.3 million barrels of beer and employ around 180,000 people in the United States.[59]

Craft breweries proudly celebrate that which makes them the opposite of "Big Beer," meaning multinational corporations that mass-produce beer and often sell their brands in multiple countries.[60] Many craft breweries portray themselves as authentic rather than corporate, artisanal rather than mechanized, and locally rooted rather than globally ambitious.[61] Yet over the past two decades the gap between these two poles of the beer industry has become less clear. Big Beer companies have bought out several popular craft breweries such as Goose Island, while some "regional" craft breweries such as Sierra Nevada and New Belgium have become well-resourced companies selling hundreds of thousands of barrels of beer a year while pouring money into lobbying arms aimed at favorable regulatory changes.[62] Further, with so many breweries in operation, competition between craft breweries for local dollars has become fierce, raising fears within the industry that the market may be nearing saturation. For workers, the expansion of the craft beer industry has meant that there are far more employment options in this industry than ever before, and that jobs in craft beer today tend to be more specialized on tasks such as selling, brewing, or packaging beer.

The growth of craft beer also has other more dubious distinctions for its workforce. Many jobs in craft beer do not qualify as "good" jobs based on conventional measures of job quality, such as livable wages and relative job security. For example, brewers in the United States earn between $29,000 and $51,000 annually, and most brewers working for companies that produce under 1,000 barrels of beer annually earn toward the lower end of this spectrum.[63] Many front-of-the-house workers in brewery taprooms and brewpubs work part-time schedules and rely on tipped earnings to make a livable wage. Brewery employees of all kinds have uneven access to paid health benefits and are often at the mercy of individual employers.[64] Moreover, working in craft beer can also be hard, physical labor that differs from romanticized notions of brewery employees dreaming up creative recipes and sitting around tasting beers.[65] Despite the realities of employment within the industry, there is little sign that interest in working in craft beer is slowing down. Between 2021 and 2022—still during the coronavirus pandemic—the total number of industry jobs grew 9 percent while the number of domestic breweries in operation surpassed 9,000.[66] Jobs in craft beer continue to represent "cool" opportunities in a "hot" industry.[67]

Craft beer has long been dominated by white men, particularly those from middle-class backgrounds.[68] Sociologists Nathaniel Chapman and David Brunsma argue these demographic patterns are due to the systemic racism and white supremacy in the domestic beer industry at large, including its craft segment.[69] For instance, people of color have been all but locked out of business ownership within the beer industry owing to the difficulty of obtaining loans and accessing capital.[70] Craft beer is also less available in Black and brown residential neighborhoods—with the exception of gentrifying neighborhoods—due to a combination of racist stereotypes about the preferred alcoholic beverages of residents and calculated decisions by beer distributors to preferentially stock more affluent and whiter neighborhoods with craft and other specialty products.[71] In similar ways, craft beer is often marketed toward men and associated with male-stereotyped activities and interests, such as heavy metal music and mountain biking. This, too, can dissuade women from seeing craft beer as a possible career choice. Existing research thus describes how institutionalized forms of racism and sexism manifest in craft beer, creating barriers of entry or advancement for minoritized workers.[72]

Within craft beer workplaces, jobs tend to be socially segregated along the lines of race and gender.[73] While white men make up the majority of craft beer workers, according to recent industry demographic statistics, these individuals tend to be concentrated within the upper ranks of the industry and in creative jobs such as head brewer and brewery ownership.[74] By contrast, women—particularly white women—are overrepresented in interactive service jobs, such as taproom server or beertender, where they make up around half of all workers despite being only one out of every four workers in the industry overall. Finally, men of color, who make up less than 10 percent of the industry overall, are concentrated in low-level distribution and warehouse jobs that double as entry-level jobs.

Sociological scholarship on the craft beer industry thus remains split. Some studies expound on the cultural values of the industry, such as authenticity and artisanship, while other more critical research focuses on labor issues ranging from marginal job conditions in breweries to the structural exclusion of workers from minoritized backgrounds. By showing how these themes are deeply intertwined, this book explains how workers get channeled into socially stratified positions within this emerging setting of modern craft work. Specifically, workers' varying relationships to craft beer—and the value they see in these jobs—has implications for the opportunities they encounter in the industry. White men in this study express *pure passion* for their jobs by emphasizing their personal devotion to craft beer's specialized forms of knowledge, craftsmanship, and consumption rituals. They also idealize colleagues who hold a similar relationship to craft beer. Yet because expressing pure passion for this work—essentially, a love of "beer for beer's sake"—is constituted through social privileges related to race, class, and gender, this helps "bearded white guys" maintain a dominant position among the industry's creative class. At the same time, some minoritized workers are able to express their relationship to their craft beer jobs in alternate yet meaningful ways, such as by prioritizing community building or by championing social causes.

METHODS

Answering questions about how careers develop requires getting to know people's work lives up close. Ethnographic research is especially adept at capturing these ground-level realities. By stepping foot within a workplace and spending time talking to people who occupy this space, we gain insight into the everyday practices and subjective meanings that shape their respective work worlds, past, present, and future.

I collected data for this book in two primary ways: through in-depth interviews with brewery workers and owners and ethnographic observation of craft beer workplaces. From 2019 to 2022, I observed brewers, craft beer sales representatives, taproom workers, and delivery drivers in the workplace settings they routinely occupied.[75] I attended dozens of industry events such as brewer guild meetings, educational seminars, and local beer festivals. I also participated in three eight-hour brew days at different craft breweries, shadowing different workers involved in this process in order to familiarize myself with their respective labor routines and social interactions over the course of the workday.

I interviewed 128 people affiliated with the craft beer industry in total and followed up with nearly a third of them by the time my research wrapped up.[76] Most of the people I interviewed actively worked in the industry in some capacity.[77] These interviews helped me better understand how workers narrated their respective work careers, including both their future aspirations and what they saw as crucial turning points that led them to where they are today. Many workers I spent time with framed their job moves as a series of personal choices guided by carefully thought-out rationale. It is worth noting that I was not able to engage in longitudinal research that would have allowed me a greater range of tools to assess their career development. Instead, the data I gathered more accurately depict the career *narratives* of craft beer workers in this study: how these workers make sense of their occupational journeys, past, present, and future, as told from the present moment. These narratives are often short-sighted and faulty—sociologists have long argued that people overesti-mate their own agency and underestimate the influence of social-structural forces. But as Berkelaar and Buzzanell note: "how people talk about their work and careers matters," for it reveals what is important to workers themselves and how they make sense of their job transitions.[78]

I do not claim an insider status to workers' experiences described in this book. However, as a former craft beer worker myself a decade ago, I did have some prior knowledge of the workplace situations, pressures, and distinctly informal work culture that people would often describe to me. Further, as a white-appearing, *cis-het* man in my mid-thirties, I came across as socially similar to many of the white men in their twenties and thirties who are employed in this industry.[79] In this respect, I was just another "bearded white guy" interested in craft beer, which helped me fit in more easily during field visits. Cognizant of my social position, however, I took deliberate steps to try to understand how workers from minoritized backgrounds saw their everyday work realities in craft beer. During inter-views, I listened more than I talked, asking workers, particularly those who were white women or people of color, to narrative minute aspects of what they experienced in the workplace as if I was foreign to it all (and I probably was). During field visits, rather than assuming what was hap-pening, I followed workers as they moved through their workplaces and jotted down notes on not only what they did but who they did and didn't talk to, and the tone of voices they used to do so.

Primary data collection for this study took place in two regional craft beer industries: Albuquerque, New Mexico, and Los Angeles, California. Both are demographically diverse hubs for craft beer that have seen a rapid increase in the number of local breweries in the last decade as well as craft-beer-focused beer bars, brewery consulting services, specialty beer distributors, draft line cleaning businesses, and mobile canning com-panies.[80] Albuquerque, for instance, has gone from less than ten brewer-ies a decade ago to over forty breweries in operation today. The city is among the leading cities in breweries-per-capita according to the Brewers

Association, and its thriving craft beer scene has become a socially, culturally, and economically prominent aspect of city life.[81] In 2019, Albuquerque's mayor, Timothy Keller, made several public speeches recognizing local breweries as strategic partners in Albuquerque's urban growth, while that same year a major print publication did a front-page feature on the local craft beer scene featuring the tagline, "Craft beer creates community all over New Mexico."[82] Anecdotally, Albuquerque's craft beer industry remains disproportionately white relative to a city that is 49.8 percent Hispanic, 4.8 percent Native American, 3.2 percent Black, and 3.1 percent Asian.[83] That said, several prominent local breweries are owned or run by women and people of color, including one of the only breweries in the country owned by Native American women.

Although Los Angeles has long had one of the largest beer industries in the country, until recently it was dominated by corporate beer companies such as AB-InBev, Molson Coors (parent company of Miller and Coors in the United States), and Heineken International. The rise of craft beer in Los Angeles has been swift and relatively recent: nearly one hundred craft breweries have opened in the last decade in Los Angeles County, with dozens more in the planning stages despite the high cost of building and operating a small brewery in the area.[84] Recently, craft beer in Los Angeles has grown to the point that the city now has its own craft beer newspaper, launched in 2012 and dedicated to covering local beer news and culture. Several annual beer festivals are also currently held in the area, such as the LA Beer Fest, which regularly attracts tens of thousands of patrons. As with Albuquerque, craft beer workers in Los Angeles tend to be disproportionately white compared to city residents at large (48.6 percent Hispanic, 11.7 percent Asian, 8.4 percent African American, 0.9 percent Native American). The local industry regularly celebrates the diverse background of its craft brewers, led by Black and Latinx-owned breweries, such as Crowns & Hops and Brewjeria, and women-founded breweries such as Three Weavers.

ORGANIZATION OF THE BOOK

This book lays out a framework for understanding how handcrafted careers develop today through cumulative, overlapping processes that shape the employment trajectories of craft beer workers. Chapter 1 begins by detailing the divergent job pathways that exist within the craft beer industry, and how the racialized, classed, and gendered nature of these pathways shapes workers' employment experiences over time. Educated white men enjoy access to the *creative pathway,* which is the dominant pathway in this industry; women, especially those who are white and college educated, access the *service pathway;* and working-class men of color tend to work along the *hard labor pathway.* I show how workers get channeled along these socially stratified pathways at key stages of their careers and through engaging in *micro-transitions* with unequal outcomes. I argue that white men's access to both material and immaterial resources get systematically rewarded at each stage of the employment process. This expedites their access to the most desirable jobs in craft beer over time.

Chapter 2 focuses on workers along the creative pathway, where head brewers and brewery owners—who are mostly white men—enjoy ample flexibility and creative freedom in the workplace. These workers often have a relationship to craft beer that extends well beyond their jobs and reflects what they see as their "true" values, interests, and hobbies. This expression of *pure passion* for craft beer functions as a cultural logic of work in this industry, one that owners and employees alike idealize. Yet because workers express pure passion through social privilege, such as by downplaying financial considerations of their craft beer jobs, I show how this cultural logic of work marginalizes workers who are women and people of color and contributes to their exclusion from the most desirable jobs in the workplace.

Chapter 3 explores the blurry line between work and play for those employed in brewery taprooms and in front-of-the-house industry jobs. It is here where workers interested in *craft consumption* meet gendered patterns of service employment. Both shape careers along the service pathway. I describe how workers in this chapter see their employment as part of larger assemblages of personal values and lifestyle preferences untethered to any one type of job or company, or sometimes even industry. As they navigate contingent employment, how these workers frame their careers also varies based on the workplace they are a part of and the gendered priorities of company management.

Chapter 4 takes us to the backstage of craft beer production to examine the work lives of brewery packaging and delivery workers. These workers, who are disproportionately working-class men of color, operate in jobs that are considered less desirable by industry standards because they offer limited opportunities to enact artisanal skills and personal expression on the job. Surprisingly, some workers along the hard labor pathway are able to forge positive work identities based on the "good work" they do for, and within, tight-knit, craft-focused companies. Their careers in craft beer can also be relatively stable—sometimes spanning decades—so long as their ambitions involve supporting the white men who lead their companies establish the dominant values of the industry.

While surrounded by people who are wholly passionate about craft beer, why do some minoritized workers feel that their jobs "could never be just about beer?" Chapter 5 takes on this puzzle. I describe how white women and people of color enact a *marked professional identity* in a predominantly white and male industry. Rather than attempt to embody the racialized, classed, and gendered industry norms of their peers, some workers, particularly those who are college educated, attempt to selectively subvert these standards by highlighting aspects of their social identity while complementing company goals.

In chapter 6, the last empirical chapter of this book, I ask: what might we learn about how career pathways develop from people who do not choose to pursue them or have managed to affiliate with craft beer in other ways? I focus on the cases of three groups of industry outliers: industry consultants, amateur "homebrewers," and former craft beer workers. In highlighting career pathways less traveled, I describe the allures and pitfalls of managing handcrafted careers around an industry that is deeply entrepreneurial but also inherently unpredictable.

The concluding chapter of this book summarizes broader lessons about work and inequality in the new economy that we can glean from the craft beer industry. I draw together different components of handcrafted careers to describe how they shape complex and unequal career pathways in uncertain times. At the same time, new recipes for work are still being written within these emerging work settings.

Let us take the first step through the door.

1 Going Down the Rabbit Hole

CAREER PATHWAYS AND MICROTRANSITIONS

Not everyone in craft beer wants to be a craft brewer.

I was still thinking about the words that Lauren told me last week as I pushed open the doors to Dirty Shovel Brewing Company for a day-long visit. Dirty Shovel (for short) is a successful, Albuquerque-based brewery tucked in an industrial district with several taprooms scattered throughout the city. Lauren now co-owns the brewery after spending a decade working in, then managing, the company's front-of-house operations. Under her guidance the brewery has prospered: each of the brewery's three locations becoming lively watering holes with their own character and customer base. But it is nine in the morning now and all is eerily silent in the taproom; the smell of lemon-scented cleaner lingers in the air.

On the far side of the bar, a woman in her early twenties with pale skin and burnt orange highlights is staring at her cell phone. Seeing me, she waves. "Hey! I'm Marne. You must be Eli," she says. "They're expecting you in the back, just follow the hallway down, first door on your left." I thank her and begin walking down the hallway. The walls are adorned with a collection of pictures of Lauren and her co-owners along with what appears to be employees from throughout the years—I spot Marne with green highlights this time—as well as several glossy shots of the brewery silhouette and taproom interior.

Opening the door to the brewhouse lets out a blast of noise. Whirring engines, crunchy guitars, urgent drums over shouted lyrics ("Killing in the Name Of!"). A skinny man dressed in a black shirt and faded black jeans approaches me and introduces himself as Brad. Brad guides me on a path that weaves between steel fermentation tanks separated a few feet apart. We step over a series of thick hoses draped along the damp concrete floor, moving toward the rear of the building. At first, Brad seems unsure of how much he should be explaining to me about what goes on in a commercial craft brewhouse ("so—do you know what the main ingredients of beer are?"). When I say I used to work in a small brewery myself, he loosens up considerably. "Ah. Cool. So. I'm technically a cellarman here. But really I'm a jack of all trades." Today, Brad says he will be "doing a little bit of everything," which means helping oversee the packaging line, racking off kegs, flavoring a cider with berry sweetener, and cleaning and sanitizing fermentation tanks. "The other guys just call me 'boy,' because I come when I'm called," Brad says with a half-smile. He seems oblivious to the racial undertones of his comment.

We walk over to the packaging line where a large, automated can filler occupies the back-right corner of the warehouse. Next to it stands "Lalo" (his nickname), a stocky Hispanic man with short-cropped, slicked back hair who appears to be in his thirties. Lalo tells me that he and a couple other guys will probably begin packaging a full batch of beer within the hour and won't stop for the next four. I notice that Lalo has an earbud cord hanging from his ears. "I like to listen to music and podcasts when I work. It helps the time go by," he says. "Right now, I'm listening to this standup comedian I like."

Brad ushers me in the direction of the brewhouse, where two other men are working. One of them is Randall, who has a bushy, slightly unkept-looking beard and a pink complexion. Randall is standing atop a metal platform looking down at the steaming mash tun. He has been the head brewer of Dirty Shovel for about a year, having previously worked as an assistant brewer for another prominent craft brewery in the Albuquerque area. Descending from the platform with a series of loud clanks, he introduces himself and begins getting me up to speed on today's brew schedule.

"We began by mashing in an hour ago and I'm watching the clock to make my grain additions right now."

As we walk around the brewhouse, Randall explains more about his background. Randall was a long-time homebrewer while he worked as a dining room manager at the local branch of a national chain restaurant. "I got fed up with hospitality. Too much bullshit with customers," he says. "I figured getting a job at a brewery was my way of taking my homebrewing to the next level. I was homebrewing constantly anyway." He pauses his story to gaze into the circular opening atop the mash tun. I ask Randall what he enjoys about professional brewing.

"To be honest, *this* is my favorite part," he replies. "I love the smell of barley and hops and just watching the beer start to come together. It's magic." Randall opens an Excel document on his phone and zooms in on a variety of boxes that indicate things like "mash in temperature," "gravity reading," and "Celsius at knockout." Tapping furiously with his thumbs, he fills in several of these boxes and looks back up at me.

"I used to—" suddenly, I can barely hear Randall over the music, cranked full blast.

"HOW IS THIS, LALO?" Brad shouts. He looks in my direction. Guitars crunch angrily, cymbals crash about. "All Lalo ever wants to play is rap. Let's hear some *real* music."

"That's not true, bro! Just the other day I threw on some CCR," says Lalo, referencing the '60s rock band Credence Clearwater Revival. His earbuds are still in place.

"Yeah, and what about last week, remember?"

We settle into the day's work rhythm in the brewhouse. I shadow Randall as he continues his brewing schedule through a process of wort transfers and hop additions. Lalo is a blur of motion operating the canning line, in part because the labeling sticker keeps malfunctioning, causing multiple labels to bunch up before they stick to the beer cans. Lalo says he needs to reapply a sheet of duct tape to hold the piece snug while also watching for "low-fill" beers coming off the automated canning line. "I'm constantly fixing shit, finding a way to make things work," he says. "That's basically my job here."

Around noon, a delivery truck pulls into the loading dock near the back of the brewery opposite the canning line. Brad and another worker begin to load full pallets of beer wrapped in plastic into the truck. Meanwhile, I see the delivery driver, a middle-aged Hispanic man with a goatee, leaning against the brewery wall, half watching the loading process but more interested in smoking his cigarette. The man tells me he's been driving delivery trucks with this company—a major alcohol distribution company in the area—for fifteen years. "The job's all right, pay is decent," he says. I nod silently. "But I've been thinking about starting my own CDL license certification company, you know? They are charging $3,000 to take the test. If I start teaching that on my own, that's a lot of money, you know?" He looks up, distracted. He nods at me, puts out his cigarette and heads toward the back gate of his truck to lock it up.

Brad and I return inside to sanitize "C-clamps" near the sink. It is a welcome break from his normal work routine crisscrossing the brewery floor with quick, urgent steps. "You came at a funny time, actually," says Brad. "Today is one of my last days here. I accepted a job at the Lab[1] as a chemical analyst, which was my degree in college. I start in two weeks."

"That's great, man. Congratulations," I say.

"Don't get me wrong, I love brewing. And I like the guys and all, but—. I don't feel like I have enough control here. Plus, I've come to realize that this is really hard, physical work without a retirement or benefits. And it is not about the money, necessarily. But with my degree, I could go to a chemical lab and literally make three times what I'm making here."

·   ·   ·   ·   ·

Inside craft breweries like Dirty Shovel, the jobs that workers do seem at first glance like a loose collection of tasks, ad hoc schedules, and makeshift job titles. Workers interact casually with one another on the job, laughing and horsing around. They wear whatever they find comfortable and play their preferred music on the loudspeaker (albeit not always to everyone's liking). Part of this informality is by design, as many of the small companies in this industry strive to be authentic spaces run "like a family," as Lauren puts it.

At the same time, the specific jobs that brewery workers do differ considerably behind the scenes. They map onto an organizational and industry-wide hierarchy that only becomes clear with time and experience. Jobs in the brewhouse, in the taproom, and in distribution, respectively, come with unequal access to power and visibility in the workplace. The people who do these jobs garner unequal recognition among their industry peers as well in the eyes of the beer-drinking public. Indeed, it is mostly educated white men such as Brad and Randall who work in the most desirable, creative capacities in craft beer. Their jobs systematically differ from the manual-labor ones held disproportionately by working-class men of color such as Lalo, or the customer-facing roles occupied by educated white women such as Marne.

That craft breweries maintain a social organization of work patterned by race, class, gender, and other social categories is not altogether surprising. Scholars have identified similar patterns of socially segregated labor in workplaces ranging from restaurants and retail stores to hotels and meatpacking factories.[2] Some of the reasons for this are clear. Research shows that company management institutes policies and practices that end up contributing, either directly or indirectly, to unequal employment outcomes for workers based on their social statuses. As described earlier, management's hiring practices for positions of authority often go beyond the formal credentials found on résumés to advantage workers who approximate white, male, and upper-middle-class norms while also designating low-level manual labor or service jobs for working-class men and women of color.[3] As sociologist Victor Ray notes, these processes legitimate the unequal distribution of resources within racialized organizations whereby whiteness, along with masculinity, serves as a key credential.[4] This helps explain why workers find themselves in distinct and hierarchical roles that reflect the existing social order.

Yet this body of literature tends to frame social inequality in the labor market as a foretold outcome stemming from exclusionary, top-down company processes. This can overlook how workers experience their work lives—unequal as they may be—in a more dynamic fashion, shaped by an interplay of individual and organizational factors that unfold at the ground level over time. This is especially true in companies such as Dirty Shovel and industries like craft beer, where jobs tend to be fluid and informal. Rather than having The Boss breathing down their necks and dictating tasks, Marne, Brad, and Lalo show up for work in a setting organized more like a weekend club team with everyone pitching in. At

Dirty Shovel, how employment is linked to social inequality is far from obvious.

Examining the forces of social inequality through the lens of individual work careers can be highly instructive. For starters, the experiences people have prior to entering the labor market matter for the future direction of their work lives. Workers initially seek out jobs that reflect their personal backgrounds and using the resources they have access to. They organize their subsequent actions, including their search for new jobs amid uncertain conditions, by considering past events and future outlooks.[5] Along the way, the experiences, skills, and relationships that workers develop within a specific institutional context shape how they manage their employment across multiple jobs and employers.[6]

How, then, do craft beer workers seek to navigate handcrafted careers over time? What sculpts the moves they make into and within this industry, and how do these moves ultimately contribute to divergent career outcomes? I begin by detailing the three primary career pathways in craft beer—the creative pathway, the service pathway, and the hard labor pathway. Each of these pathways is racialized, gendered, and classed in ways that reflect the prevailing social organization of the industry. I show how workers engage in specific kinds of *employment microtransitions* as they move into, along, and sometimes across these pathways. By taking up microtransitions and career pathways together we learn about how a given worker's personal qualities and experiences interact with industry structures to craft inequality at key stages of employment.

THREE PRIMARY CAREER PATHWAYS IN CRAFT BEER

In his book *Vegas Brews*, sociologist Michael Ian Borer describes how people "move along a path" of craft beer. Borer explains that, "Drinkers become fans, fans become brewers, brewers are always already fans."[7] This indeed characterizes Randall's work experience over the years; it also matches the public imaginary of craft brewers pursuing their love of making and drinking beer as a full-blown career. But others working in the industry today do very different types of jobs for reasons that only loosely adhere to this narrative, sometimes not at all; as Lauren reminds us, *not everyone in craft beer wants to be a craft brewer.* The decades-long expansion of the craft beer industry has meant that a wide range of jobs now exists within this world of work. Many jobs focus on specialized tasks such as producing beer, packaging and distributing beer, or selling and serving beer. To be sure, these tasks are interconnected—freshly made beer must be packaged before it can be served commercially—and within smaller companies, the same person may be responsible for more than one type of job. Nonetheless, most craft beer workers I met in this study are employed along one of three career pathways. And each of these pathways are inflected with race, class, and gender characteristics, as described below.

The *creative pathway* consists of brewery owner-entrepreneurs, head brewers, and to a lesser extent, assistant brewers and shift brewers. The people who fill these roles are responsible for the craft production of the brewery, meaning they have a good deal of creative authority to create and brew their own recipes, steer brand content, and make other key decisions for their companies. Educated white men such as Randall dominate the creative pathway. According to recent industry statistics, over 90 percent of all craft brewers are men and 88 percent of brewery owners are white; only a small percentage of these companies are sole-owned by white women or people of color.[8] Because of their influential company positions, people who work along the creative pathway play an outsized role in setting the culture of the workplace and dictating its norms. This is partly why craft beer continues to be so closely associated with the "bearded white guy" image, as many industry observers have noted.[9]

By contrast, the *hard labor pathway* is composed of jobs that "grease the wheels of the company," as one worker put it, and occur largely behind the scenes.[10] Jobs along the hard labor pathway include delivery drivers, distribution workers (sometimes called warehouse workers), packaging line operators, and draft maintenance personnel. Because these jobs involve repetitive and physically demanding duties such as lifting kegs, cleaning draft lines, and feeding cans and bottles into packaging machines, they are considered undesirable to many workers in the industry. Lalo and other working-class men of color are overrepresented in jobs along the hard labor pathway relative to their numbers in the industry at large. This reflects the racialized and gendered character of these relatively low-wage

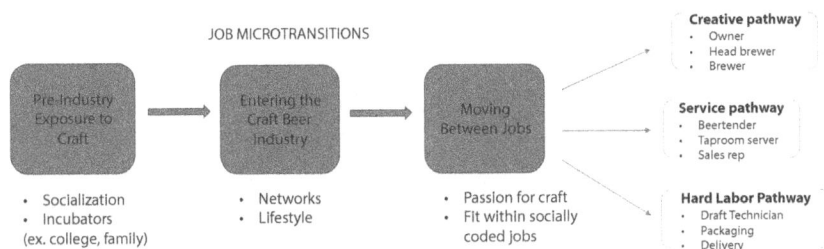

Figure 2. Diagram of primary career pathways and microtransitions within the craft beer industry.

jobs, which is similar to back-of-the-house jobs found in restaurants and other service establishments.

Finally, the *service pathway* includes taproom "beertenders," servers, and other frontline customer service and sales employees in craft beer. Workers employed along the service pathway have relatively public-facing roles in their companies and get to work closely with the specialized products made or sold there. Women, especially educated white women such as Marne, are overrepresented in jobs along the service pathway, where they make up about one out of every two workers despite representing less than a quarter of the industry overall. The feminized character of the service pathway in craft beer is consistent with other customer service jobs, such as in bars and restaurants, that prioritize friendly, nurturing, and often sexualized relations with the clientele.[11] Relative to jobs along the hard labor pathway, jobs along the service pathway are more likely to be part-time and contingently scheduled but also potentially higher earning per hour due to tips. In comparison to jobs along the creative pathway, service jobs have considerably less creative authority, though workers in both capacities get to interact closely with craft products.

NAVIGATING DIVERGENT CAREERS

As craft beer workers navigate their employment, they engage in three kinds of *employment microtransitions* at different stages of their careers.

I refer to these microtransitions as *connecting with craft, entering the industry,* and *moving between jobs.*[12] These microtransitions channel workers into and along hierarchical career pathways in the industry patterned by race, gender, and class. I describe how white, class-privileged men access the creative pathway in ways that are difficult for their minoritized counterparts to match due to the material and immaterial resources that underpin each microtransition and have value within the industry. While minoritized workers may not be overtly excluded from participating in craft beer, over time, working-class men of color such as Lalo, and educated white women such as Marne, experience expedited access to differently racialized and gendered career pathways that represent subordinate and less desirable opportunities.

Connecting with Craft

Prior to entering the craft beer industry, class-privileged white men describe being introduced to craft beer during formative years of their lives as young adults. This form of classed socialization helped them hone their own interests in "artisanal" products, including craft and imported beers. Peter, a thirty-five-year-old white man who now owns a craft brewery, recounted an early memory about the kind of adult beverages that were regularly consumed in his childhood home:

> PETER: I was observing my dad drinking craft beer. Belgian beer. He'd buy these big fancy $15 bottles of beer . . .
>
> EW: This is when you were in high school now?
>
> PETER: In high school, yeah. When it came to drinking time in college and I was going to a party, that's what I would buy. I would buy a fancy Belgian [beer] and go to a party. Everybody else would be slamming Budweiser and I'm walking around with a 750 milliliter, 12 percent [alcohol] Belgian beer, and people were like, "What are you drinking?" That's how I grew up with non-Big Beer.

Peter's upbringing in an affluent, white household by parents who already exhibited discriminating tastes piqued his own interest in "fancy" beer. Peter also learned to register these tastes as ones that carried distinct value in the social settings he frequented. Consequently, well before Peter ever sought a job in the beer industry, he began to incorporate craft beers into his own personal displays of cultural capital as well as racialized class identity.

As with Peter, early exposure to craft beer pushed other educated white men to not only familiarize with these products but to pursue them actively as personal hobbies and activities. Several workers told me that their college campuses incubated their interest in craft beer by putting them in daily contact with others who felt the same way. Clint, a fifty-year-old white man who is now a head brewer in Albuquerque, explains how he first began homebrewing:

> I started out as a homebrewer—I brewed my first batch of beer in 1988. At the time I was going to college in Vermont and I was drinking a lot of the local beer. The first homebrew I did was in Vermont because [my roommate and I] were tired of stealing his father's beer. His father had this cherry chocolate stout that he brewed himself. . . . I remember it being so delicious.

While in college, Clint was able to deepen his connection to craft beer and brewing as a consumption activity and serious hobby. It was within this classed and racialized setting where Clint's artisanal interests found both social support (in the form of his roommate, also a white man) and material support (access to a steady supply of homebrews). Many other class-privileged white workers recounted how similar college-based experiences, ranging from beer tasting groups, homebrewing clubs, and house parties, stoked their interests in craft beer, sometimes turning casual interests into sources of what sociologist Robert Stebbins calls "serious leisure." Peter, for instance, launched an "underground beer club" while he was enrolled in a graduate program in physics:

> We didn't advertise [the beer club], it was just word of mouth. For the very first one in November of 2011, the three of us who started the club just told all our friends and family, come to this party. I think we had probably fifty people that night. I say it was calm because that was probably the slowest one! [After that] I built an eight-tap draft tower out of big chest freezer that was in my basement, so we could have eight beers on tap.

Peter's experience bringing people together—albeit predominantly white, college-going men and women—to drink craft beer in an organized setting became the basis for his career aspirations. Other workers I talked to also noted the lasting impact that attending key social events where specialty foods and drinks were regularly consumed had on them.[13]

While these early experiences with craft beer were not exclusive to white men I talked to, they were often facilitated by them. For example, a white, college-educated woman who later entered the industry told me that her father used to homebrew when she was growing up. When she was a teen, he would let her try his fermented creations and guide her through the tasting process by noting the beer's aroma and appearance. It is something she now does with taproom customers. Similarly, a woman of color said she first grew interested in craft beer while attending business school at an elite university on the West Coast. At the time, a local brewpub specializing in German-style beers was a favorite hangout of her classmates, the majority of whom were white men. "It just kind of took off from there, I guess that sparked it," she explained, adding: "I had a totally different career path previously."

These stories illustrate how class-privileged white spaces can serve as *career incubators* for individuals by honing their tastes for craft beer and positioning these tastes as possible careers. By contrast, few working-class men of color I spoke with said they were exposed to craft beer through their childhood homes or because of social activities that took place within the institutions they were a part of. Manuel, a muscular, fifty-year-old Hispanic man with a high school degree recalls: "I was never a big beer guy [growing up]. But my friends, relatives, cousins, they would drink just simple Bud Light, Budweiser, nothing too specific, just generic brand beers. I never really paid attention to the brands really." Manuel's lack of proximity to craft beer through his familial and friend networks led to his indifference about craft beer well into his thirties while he worked a blue-collar job in facility maintenance. During his days off, Manuel says he and his friends spent their time repairing old cars and drinking cheap whiskey. It would not be until a small brewery opened directly across the street from his job that he tried craft beer for the first time—and at the repeated invitation of some of his white coworkers.

Bobby, a thirty-three-year-old Native American man who works as a delivery driver, mirrors Manuel's lack of personal connection to craft beer as a young adult. "I didn't know a lot about craft beer—I had no idea," he says. "Like, when you grow up on the Rez [Indian Reservation], all you drink is Budweiser or whatever they have at the bar." If Bobby's friends influenced his taste in beer, the direction of this influence was away from craft beer, which they unilaterally dismissed as too expensive or demasculinizing ("not *real* beer"). Other working-class men of color said their preindustry exposure to craft beer stigmatized these products for them. Lamar, a half Native American, half Black man with a high-school education, explained that his family members considered any job that involves alcohol to be taboo due to the racialized stigma of alcohol and the problems of alcohol abuse facing Native American communities. Consequently, prior to getting an entry-level packaging job at an Albuquerque-based brewery, Lamar had never sought to work in an alcohol-associated industry. "To this day when I go home, when I tell my relatives what I do, they are like, 'you work with beer? Okay ... yeah.' Some don't even want to associate with me," said Lamar. Men like Manuel, Bobby, and Lamar voiced an indifference or even distaste for craft beer prior to entering the industry. These forms of (dis)connection with craft beer reflect their social environments in which "fancy" alcoholic drinks hold little cultural cachet and are often less readily available anyway.[14] As a result, working-class men of color have fewer opportunities to consider craft beer as a viable option for employment—much less a desirable one.

Entering the Industry

By the time many white, class-privileged men and women began looking for jobs in the industry, they were already well acquainted with craft beer. They hung out or worked in places where it was consumed alongside friends and family and had been developing their palates for these specialty products for years (several men proudly showed me binders full of homebrewing recipes and fridges stocked with their house-made creations). In other words, these individuals participated in the same "epistemic culture" surrounding craft beer as those already in the industry.[15] Further, fitted with classed forms of cultural capital and racialized network ties, these individuals simply needed to walk through the industry doorway they already had one foot in.

Brandon, a soft-spoken white man in his mid-forties, says that transitioning into the craft beer industry felt seamless and expected even though it was never part of his career plan. Brandon recalls switching careers and leaving his previous job as a chef at an upscale restaurant to take an entry-level position in the brewhouse of a nearby brewery:

> I started homebrewing a little bit and then realized that I really enjoyed it. So I asked to volunteer at [a nearby brewery]. And I sort of just weaseled my way in until they let me go in and clean tanks, clean kegs, that sort of thing. My job just started that way. Then I got really lucky in that the owner and brewer had an accident and was unable to brew and I was the only other person in the brewery. He called me up one day and said, "How would you like to be a brewer?"

Brandon's transition into the industry stemmed from his interest in home-brewing and his willingness to do whatever it took to get a foot in the door ("I just sort of weaseled my way in"). This for him meant leaving a decade-long career and venturing into a new industry. Brandon was hardly unique among workers I talked to, particularly white men, who said they made personal sacrifices in order to get into craft beer. Some shared stories of working extra hours for free, coming in on their days off to shadow employees, and volunteering to do the least desirable tasks in the workplace—likely currying favor with management in the process by showing their devotion to brewery employment.

Other white workers were able to facilitate their entrance into the industry through consumption-focused social networks. Grant is a twenty-eight-year-old, college-educated white man with a thick, reddish beard and a laid-back demeanor. Grant said that many of his friends were already working in craft breweries or patronizing them by the time he got his first brewery job:

EW: Can you describe how you first got into the beer industry?

GRANT: I became a regular [at the brewery]. Actually, I paid to be a regular, you know: I got the membership.[16] [*laughs*]. And one drunken day, one of my coworkers—well, he was not actually my coworker at the time—he convinced me after a couple months to ask if they needed help. I had been kind of bussing tables there already anyway, just trying to help out.

Like many of his class-privileged white peers, patronizing breweries proved a key career incubator for Grant as he sought out a job in a craft brewery.

Doing so allowed him to merge his socially conditioned tastes (quite literally) and racialized network ties with his employment, all within a workplace where he was already considered a "regular" on multiple levels.[17]

Sheila, the sales representative described in the introduction chapter, was also drawn to the people, places, and activities that surround craft beer. Like Grant, her prior connection to craft beer led to her entrance into the industry. But Sheila's story also makes clear a gendered dimension to this microtransition. Unlike Grant, Sheila developed her ties to craft beer through her employment in a customer service setting that offered craft beer and other high-end alcoholic beverages. As part of being a restaurant server, Sheila got to attend daily "preshift" meetings that often involved tasting new craft beers on tap. After work and sometimes on days off, she and her coworkers would visit other restaurants, bars, and breweries to participate in a scene of craft beer consumption.[18] In other words, class-privileged young women such as Sheila are able to cultivate particular tastes in craft products and bring these tastes together with prior job experiences to enter the industry along a gendered pathway.

A small handful of workers I talked with described going directly from being avid craft beer consumers and homebrewers to becoming owner-entrepreneurs overseeing small, do-it-yourself companies. Indeed, this closely aligns with pop mythology about those who go on to found craft breweries. Yet in almost all cases, workers who made this microtransition into the industry drew on intersectional forms of privilege that allowed them to complement their career ambitions with crucial forms of capital and know-how. Recall that Mike, the brewery owner described in the introduction chapter, left a well-paying marketing career to start a small brewery with a group of four friends—all of whom were college-educated, white men like him. What Mike lacked in hands-on industry experience he made up for with economic resources along with well-placed social connections and white-collar professional acumen. Leveraging considerable personal resources helps some of the most privileged workers enter the industry in positions of immediate creative authority.

Yet race and class-coded resources don't always come together so seamlessly in helping other workers secure opportunities in craft beer. This was the case for Fernando, a heavy-set Latino man in his early forties from a middle-class family. Ten years ago, Fernando was gifted a homebrew kit by his brother-in-law. He quickly became, in his words, "obsessed" with brewing beer and, with his family's support, decided to enroll in a professional brewing school. "Once I'd graduated from [brewing school], I had applied to, I can't even count how many different postings I'd seen around … assistant brewer, cellar, everything you could think of. I probably applied for twenty different positions," explains Fernando. Fernando eventually got hired as the head brewer of a small company with a middling reputation. However, he says he got this job only after the owners, a white couple who live out of state, had posted it for a third time and were in desperate need of filling the position. Fernando's microtransition into the industry was tenuous at best. Despite his formal credentials and personal tastes for craft beer, he was not able to draw on racialized network ties to help him ease into the industry the same way white workers like Grant and Sheila have done.

Very few working-class people of color say they sought out jobs in this industry because of their prior tastes, ties, or credentials in craft beer. Instead, these minoritized workers were far more likely to enter the industry indirectly and following stints in other blue-collar or low-level service jobs. Lamar, for instance, explains the circumstances that led to his first job in craft beer:

> I was kind of just transitioning through jobs trying to find something that paid the bills, obviously, and something I enjoyed. While I was working at Lowe's [hardware store], one day my girlfriend sent me a screenshot of a Facebook post about a job. I think it was from New Mexico Beer Jobs or something like that. It was for a brewery delivery position. So, I was like, "Ah, what the hell, I'll look."

Lamar's search for employment that resulted in his first brewery job was an extension of his prior search criteria in which he was focused on finding steady, decent-paying work in any industry that would take him ("trying to find something that paid the bills"). In effect, Lamar had searched for racialized manual labor positions that did not require a college degree and stumbled on brewery work.[19]

Many other working-class men of color I talked to also engaged in similar kinds of pragmatic job searches prior to getting a job in the craft beer industry. Some had circulated for years in manual labor jobs across multiple industries. One worker, a Black man in his early thirties, told me he was a part-time cashier at McDonald's and a part-time security guard before getting a job washing kegs at a local brewery. Another Latino man was employed as a call center operator before becoming a truck driver for a water company. He did that for two years before getting a job delivering kegs for a midsize craft brewery. He compares his last two jobs this way: "I was pretty used to the work [of driving a delivery truck] when I first started at the brewery because beer kegs are heavy to load and unload—but so are water jugs." It is worth noting that few workers from race- and class-marginalized backgrounds say that they faced discriminatory hiring or other overtly exclusionary processes while trying to get a job in craft beer. Yet their microtransitions into the industry tell a more nuanced story, illustrating how the resources that aid the process—smoothing out the job search and giving it direction—are shaped by intersecting statuses of race, class, and gender.

Moving between Jobs

After entering the industry, craft beer workers transition between jobs along socially stratified career pathways that become more distinct and unequal with time. Although many workers get their start in entry-level positions, class-privileged white men are more likely than their counterparts who are white women and people of color to move into jobs along the creative pathway and continue advancing into jobs of greater authority once there. These workers do so by bringing their formal credentials, interests, and social networks to bear on industry opportunities that are already occupied by, and associated with, white men.

Drew is a thirty-three-year-old college-educated white man who typically wears a black baseball cap with a faded brim. Drew initially saw the craft beer industry as a way to fuse his "love" of craft beer and brewing with his career goals. As he explains:

> I had a business I started in college and ran for about four years. It did really well at first, then kind of crapped out on me. After I shut that down, my girlfriend and I wanted to start another business, and I had a really good friend in the oil industry back home wanting to invest. I said, "Well, I guess I'll jump on and start learning [how to run a brewery]."

After biding his time for the right opportunity, Drew secured an entry-level job in the brewhouse of a top Albuquerque-based brewery. There he began to learn the trade "from the ground up" and under the tutelage of an award-winning head brewer, a white man with over a decade of industry experience. Two years later, Drew and a business partner launched a small brewery of their own, drawing on Drew's brewing experience and burgeoning ties within the industry and his business partner's access to capital. An internal dispute between the two forced Drew to abruptly exit this company soon after it opened. However, despite this substantial setback, it took him only two months to secure another job as the head brewer of another upstart craft brewery. When I asked Drew about how he landed this opportunity, he casually explained: "I was riding back from a beer festival with the owners of Cosmic Brews and happened to mention I was looking for a job. They said, 'why don't you come work for us?' *Boom.* That's how it happened."[20]

Drew's experience illustrates how the employment bumps that "bearded white guys" encounter along the creative pathway are short-term impediments rather than roadblocks to their career mobility. Despite the unpredictability that surrounds any one job or company, the valuable industry social networks that men like Drew have ties to—especially ties to people in positions of authority from similar social backgrounds—channel them into creative jobs. These ties can also act as a career safety net pointing to new opportunities while minimizing employment risk.[21]

Personal connections and prior job experiences also help class-privileged women transition between jobs in craft beer, albeit mostly along the service pathway. For some women, customer-facing jobs in craft beer reflect a type of convenient employment they are already relatively familiar with. Ariana, a fit, twenty-eight-year-old, college-educated Latina woman, describes her initial transition into the beer industry as a lateral move between serving jobs:

> Four years ago, I was waitressing at a Thai restaurant right across from my university. And I knew the manager at the time when this brewery opened. She kind of asked me, do you want a better job—which, when you are making $30 a day—is a definite yes. Anything is better than that. [*laughs*]. So, she brought me in as a bar back where I would wash dishes and pick up trash. Later, I moved on to serving and bartending.

Ariana describes a series of job moves into craft beer and later, up the ranks of the service pathway over the past four years. She was initially motivated to search for "a better job" out of financial interest rather than enthusiasm for craft beer (though Ariana says has come to appreciate the differences in beer styles made at her brewery). Similarly, several other women told me that the allure of working along the service pathway in craft beer was principally about access to flexible schedules that could accommodate other jobs and school obligations; not all had the intention of remaining in the industry long term.[22]

In all cases, women encountered minimal resistance from management in their efforts to advance along gendered career pathways and within feminized positions within craft breweries. Some managers, such as Ariana's friend, actively encouraged such moves. Further, once there, workers understood that moving "up" could mean taking on more customer-service duties or responsibilities, including roles such as shift "lead" or supervisor. By contrast, those who attempted to transition into jobs along the creative pathway faced ongoing challenges—particularly in companies where these jobs were staffed entirely by men.

Britney, a thirty-year-old white woman with long blond hair recalls first becoming interested in brewing while observing two brewers, both white men, during her shifts at an Albuquerque-based brewpub. Britney had been working as a dining room host there for several years at the time, starting when she was eighteen:

> Because I could see the brewers [from the host stand], I would talk to them. They would come out on their lunch breaks and I would kind of bug them a little bit. But, I was eighteen—I just wanted to help. I kept asking them if I could. And then [the head brewer] left to start his own brewery, so I started bugging the other brewer every time I saw him, like "Hey, need any help back there?" And he kind of would laugh at me and be like "Little girl, you can't even lift a keg!"

After switching companies, Britney convinced her new boss to let her train as an assistant brewer. The deal was, however, that she would split time in the taproom working three shifts a week (where her boss undoubtedly felt Britney truly belonged), while spending only one shift in the brewhouse to train. Over the next few years, Britney slowly phased out her job in the taproom to work as a brewer, becoming the only woman in the company to do so. Yet her switch away from the feminized service pathway toward the creative pathway was challenged and prolonged at every step, butting up against industry expectations as well as scheduling constraints.

Unsurprisingly, both white women and people of color are highly critical of how their peers who are educated white men tend to "fall into jobs" of authority within craft beer. Jordyn, a thirty-five-year-old white woman who has been a professional brewer for ten years, explains:

> I've always approached this job as a career. And being a woman and potentially wanting kids . . . because of that reason, it's always been at the forefront of my mind that I have to plan ahead and work hard. A lot of women in the industry are actually very thoughtful and forward-thinking. But it's the men that are a little haphazard and sort of floating through things. And yet they get handed all of these opportunities all the time. And I'm just like, I'm trying to be really thinking about things and I you look over there and—*you just fell into that!*

Jordyn points to several overlapping career impediments that women routinely face when attempting to navigate careers in craft beer, particularly along the creative pathway. Because the majority of brewery owners are white men, these individuals are more likely to favor workers who are already embedded within the same race- and gender-segregated networks, as well as those who fit their socially coded perceptions of the "right" kind of workers for brewing positions. As a result, white men are not only more likely to "fall into" jobs in craft beer but fall *upward* along the creative pathway.

The employment microtransitions that working-class people of color experience outside of the hard labor pathway are also slower, bumpier, or more blocked than their more privileged colleagues encounter. Some workers blame management's inaction for this outcome rather than their actions. Josiah, a heavily tattooed, twenty-six-year-old Native American man with a high school education, got his first brewery job after responding to an ad for a packaging line operator at a midsize brewery in Albuquerque. After just two days of work, the head brewer, a white man, began to instruct Josiah on how to do additional tasks such as kegging beer and checking carbonation levels on fermentation tanks. It was work that wasn't in his job description, but because Josiah felt it indicated his boss's confidence in his abilities, he went along with it. "They just kind of threw me against the wall," says Josiah. "That's how I first got brought into [the brewhouse]."

Two months later, Josiah accepted an official move to a job where he cleaned fermenters and transferred beer between them—a job somewhere between the hard labor pathway and the lower tiers of the creative pathway. Josiah also began to aspire to join the brewers at his company, a revolving group of roughly five workers, usually white men. He voiced his interest to the owner of the brewery repeatedly. Three years later, nothing. Josiah remained in the same role with only marginally more responsibility; he left soon after to take another "cellar" job at a nearby brewery hoping that his luck would change.

The few workers of color who successfully transitioned into jobs along the creative pathway did so using networks and other resources similar to those described above. But they also faced racialized and classed barriers that limited their authority and hampered their continued employment. Anthony, a forty-three-year-old Latino man with a high school education, explains how he became a professional brewer by accident:

> I was homebrewing for about two to three years before I got in the industry. Not really good at it but I knew enough. And one day I was sitting at [the bar] and I started talking to a guy next to me who happened to be the head brewer at Power Kegs. He was lamenting that he needed help. I was like, "Right now, dude, I'm just bartending. But I can help you out one day a week." So I worked part-time as a brewer for about a year and a half.

Anthony eventually became a full-time brewer at Power Kegs and, soon after, its head brewer. However, despite Anthony's job title, the owner of the brewery, a white man, allowed Anthony limited creative control. Anthony reproduced the brewery's "core beers" based on existing recipes and had little ability to create new beers of his own. Anthony's name or picture did not appear anywhere on the brewery's website or other social media accounts, a relatively common practice for craft breweries seeking to highlight the people behind their products. These aspects of Anthony's job hampered his ability to continue building his reputation and professional networks within the local industry. When Power Kegs abruptly closed, he looked, unsuccessfully, for another head brewer job before leaving the industry entirely. Less than a year later, Anthony returned to craft beer as a shift brewer—a clear downgrade from his previous job. By comparison, no white man with comparable years of experience working as a head brewer reported being willing to accept such a "demotion": recall how Drew quickly landed his next head brewer position simply through word of mouth.

.   .   .   .   .

Examining how craft beer workers move along hierarchical career pathways helps clarify the everyday workings of inequality within this world of work. By engaging in specific kinds of employment microtransitions that bring one's personal qualities and resources together with socially coded industry structures, workers forge career pathways that are racialized, classed, and gendered at every turn without being overtly exclusionary. As I've shown, Randall, Clint, and other educated white men navigate onto the creative pathway at pivotal stages in their careers. This begins before they enter the industry, where these men develop a taste for craft beer and homebrewing through *career incubators* such as upper-middle-class homes and college campuses. These career incubators nurture specialized tastes and give these tastes value, laying the foundations for later microtransitions these workers make into craft beer jobs along the creative pathway. At each step, class-privileged white men sculpt their employment in ways that benefit from their access to privileged social networks and other personal resources valued within this industry.

White women and people of color also seek to manage their employment in craft beer amid uncertain conditions. Yet the microtransitions they engage in ultimately send them down subordinate career pathways— the service pathway and the hard labor pathway, respectively. This is because of the interplay of individual and organizational impediments that minoritized workers face when trying to access the dominant pathway, such as being locked out of white male networks or having limited exposure to career incubators for this industry. Further, these workers are more likely than their white male colleagues to "fall" into gendered and racialized career paths for which managers, colleagues, and sometimes even themselves assume they are a better fit.[23] Encountering any one of these career-channeling processes may not derail a worker's job ambitions in the short term. And in an emergent industry as fluid as craft beer there are always exceptions to the rule, perhaps even more so than other industries. But it is the accumulation of employment microprocesses over time that grooves unequal career pathways within this world of work.

At the same time, I was struck by how many craft beer workers I talked to felt like they were a part of a close-knit family in the workplace where the jobs they did were refreshingly informal and rewarding. This makes the persistence of racialized, classed, and gendered career pathways within this industry all the more revealing because the forces that uphold social inequality are largely inconspicuous. It is within these kinds of modern craft companies where social inequality gets tangled together with other social phenomena that do not feel discriminatory or unjust, such as when friends-of-friends help each other get jobs using the snug blanket of social networks, or when the personal consumption tastes of company ownership double as informal hiring metrics.

Many of these factors speak to the dominant culture of work in craft beer, which pervades all aspects of what individuals experience in the workplace. How do workers express their relationship to craft beer, and what implications might this have for the opportunities they encounter? We turn to these questions next by focusing on workers who operate along the creative pathway.

2 Careers of the Heart

In an article by *Beer and Brewing* published in 2016 called "Turning a Passion into a Career," five craft brewers were asked to describe their career paths in the industry and offer some words of advice to readers hoping to follow in their footsteps.[1] "If you're a homebrewer who wants to get into professional brewing, you have to enjoy brewing beyond the creativity of brewing. You have to really *love* beer and not just the wacky and creative beer," offered a head brewer from Portland, Oregon.

"It wasn't whimsical, but there was also no grand plan," said a San Diego–based brewer of how he got his start in the industry. "It was, like, let's see if this works and see where it goes."

"There's no growth without associated creativity," declared a North Carolina–based brewer. "And there's no reward without risk."

Each of these industry veterans talks about their jobs in ways that transcend mere employment. They suggest that while the choice to pursue a career in craft beer should be taken seriously, workers should also feel *love* and *passion* toward their jobs if they want to succeed. Indeed, one of the takeaways from this glossy magazine article is that having a true passion for craft beer is *the* key to braving a career in this often-unpredictable industry.

I heard this same sentiment repeated over and over when talking with head brewers and brewery owners. These individuals describe craft beer as "who I am" and "what I love to do"; they describe their work in this industry as a "chosen lifestyle" and a "personal passion of mine." This way of framing one's job and seeing value in it reflects an increasingly common cultural logic of work today that is not specific to the craft beer industry and its organizations.[2] Having a passion for one's work justifies why many people pursue the careers they are currently pursuing. It is also the career advice that industry veterans pass on to aspiring workers, and the rubric through which managers and employees size people up for their fit within a particular company, job, or career.[3]

In craft beer, the workers who express this sentiment most vigorously tend to be white men—just as all five of the "passionate" brewers featured in the *Beer and Brewing* article are. As we learned in the last chapter, white men tend to occupy positions in the industry that offer creative authority, visibility, and flexibility. They dominate jobs along the creative pathway relative to their peers who are white women and people of color because workers from more privileged backgrounds are able to draw on their network ties, tastes, and prior job histories at critical employment junctions to transition into the most desirable positions. But what does having a passion for working in this industry have to do with this? That is, how might the cultural logic of work in craft beer—and how workers go about expressing it—reinforce the dominant position of "bearded white guys"?

In this chapter, I show how workers along the creative pathway enact what I call *pure passion* for craft beer. Pure passion describes an all-encompassing, personal devotion to one's job. For many brewers and brewery owners, it is a relationship to their craft beer jobs that incorporates work, play, and preferred lifestyle all wrapped into one. Adhering to this cultural logic of work helps class-privileged white men justify their personal decisions to enter this line of work relative to perceived alternatives. It also shapes their views of their colleagues. Many white men treat pure passion for craft beer—essentially, expressing a love for "beer for beer's sake"—as the ideal and expected cultural logic of work in this industry, especially for those employed along the creative pathway. Yet because workers enact pure passion *through* class privilege, whiteness, and masculinity, this cultural logic of work reinforces the dominant position of white men while marginalizing workers from nondominant groups who are less able to express their relationship to work this way. As craft beer workers continue handcrafting their careers, some are better positioned than others to pursue careers of the heart that feel authentic to their individual tastes, values, and sense of gendered identity.

PRIVILEGING PASSION

The owners of the Scotland-based brewery Brewdog are unapologetic in how they express their company's passion-driven mission statement. According to the brewery's website:

> We are on a mission to make other people as passionate about great craft beer as we are. We bleed craft beer. This is our true North. We are uncompromising. If we don't love it, we don't do it. Ever. We blow shit up. We are ambitious, we are relentless, we take risks.[4]

Brewdog's mission statement declares that it is a company run by people who prioritize doing exactly what makes them happy through a heady mixture of passion, creative spirit, and testosterone-driven risk-taking. The company's mission statement, which is echoed by a growing number of businesses (just sub out the words "craft beer"), also illustrates how passion serves as a primary cultural logic of work today.

Seeking passion in one's work reflects a broader shift in how people approach their work lives in a labor landscape that is increasingly uncertain and hyperindividualized.[5] According to this cultural logic of work, workers are encouraged to let their personal interests and personalities guide them to specific types of jobs.[6] There are obvious upsides to this arrangement. Rather than a work life mired in monotony, finding a job that one is passionate about can be a source of job satisfaction and career motivation for workers.[7] Adhering to the "passion principle"—as sociologist Erin Cech calls it—means seeking employment that resonates with one's personal "habits of the heart."[8] Doing so can help some people bring their work lives together with their values and nonwork interests in desirable ways.[9] As a result, Cech notes that a growing number of young adults feel that finding a job that fits their passions is not only the mark of a good job but also a good life.[10]

Adhering to this cultural logic of work can also have mixed implications for workers. For one, pursuing a job of passion can lead workers to justify the subpar labor conditions they face, such as contingent work hours and low compensation.[11] This can end up normalizing self-exploitation on the part of workers as something that is an expected trade-off or simply a rite of passage into an otherwise fulfilling career.[12] Further, finding passion for one's work is not equally available to all workers based on their social characteristics. This is because seeking, valuing, and subsequently displaying passion in one's work life is conditioned by cultural knowledge and shaped by social location. As sociologist Annette Lareau notes, class-privileged young adults are more likely to be socialized in environments that encourage individual self-expression and espouse the ideal of embracing one's personal interests through work rather than pragmatic financial considerations.[13] Having cultivated what sociologists Aliya Rao and Megan Tobias Neely call "generalized passion," class-privileged workers are poised for success within workplaces where managers seek these traits in new hires.[14]

Workers' self-expressed job interests are also framed—and differentially valued—by gender and race.[15] Men who express a strong interest in pursuing jobs of authority are more likely to be rewarded for their "drive" and held up as "ideal workers" when compared to women who express similar interests.[16] Further, because women face greater pressure to balance work with family responsibilities, displaying unbridled passion for work can put them under greater scrutiny than their male counterparts and can hamper women's careers. In similar ways, as sociologist Adia Harvey Wingfield argues, certain emotional expressions are racialized as "whites only" in professional workplaces and valorized when expressed by white people yet discounted or stigmatized when expressed by people of color.[17] Because many workers of color navigate "institutional white spaces" in their workplaces, they are less likely to identify closely with their companies or feel they can express themselves openly as a function of their liminal social and cultural membership in these spaces.[18]

Existing literature thus outlines important ways in which passion, as a cultural logic of work, interplays with existing social inequalities to shape *who* claims to be passionate about *which* jobs and how these claims will be interpreted by others.[19] But we still have a limited understanding of how workers enact, express, and value this cultural logic of work within specific kinds of labor settings, or how exactly passion for work can end up reinforcing social hierarchies at work.[20] As we will see in this chapter, many class-privileged white men who work along the creative pathway enact *pure passion* for craft beer through complete devotion to their jobs and full participation in the lifestyles and identities surrounding them.[21] These individuals treat *pure passion* as the ideal relationship to employment in this industry—one modeled after their own—and value the expression of this cultural logic of work in others. Yet because of the way these workers enact pure passion *through* privileged social statuses of whiteness, upper-middle-classness, and masculinity, workers from minoritized backgrounds struggle to fully participate in this world of work, especially along the creative pathway.[22]

Crafting Masculinity

Researchers have long described how particular jobs are ascribed with gender characteristics that shape how workers come to see themselves. Men who operate in male-dominated work settings involving physical labor often express masculinity through their jobs, just as women construct feminine identities through jobs associated with emotional labor, such as care work.[23] These gendered work identities are also classed. For example, in his monograph *On the Fireline* about wildland firefighters, sociologist Matt Desmond notes how men raised in working-class rural environments approach their physical and sometimes dangerous jobs in ways that complement their own sense of "country masculinity."[24] By contrast, college-educated men employed within white-collar workplaces are more likely to express what Andreas Giazitzoglu and Daniel Muzio call "corporate masculinity," which builds from professional norms and etiquettes that are already familiar to them.[25]

Many types of modern craft work done predominantly by men also reinforce masculine identities.[26] For instance, Richard Ocejo describes how men who work as high-end bartenders, distillers, butchers, and barbers in New York City are "able to use these jobs to achieve a lost sense of middle-class, heterosexual masculinity in their work" by performing jobs that blend knowledge work and specialized kinds of physical labor.[27] Working craft jobs that fit their sense of gendered identity gives these jobs an extra layer of personal meaning for these individuals. Many brewers and brewery owners I met, especially men, also talk about how their jobs allow them to authentically express *who they are*.[28] Building on Ocejo's insights, I show how these individuals frame a particular kind of racialized and classed gender identity that I refer to as *artisanal masculinity*. Artisanal masculinity combines elements of authenticity, creativity, specialized knowledge, and physicality that are reinforced by the structure of work along the creative pathway.[29] Artisanal masculinity is also custom fit for white men employed along this pathway, especially those from middle and upper-middle-class backgrounds, because it allows these individuals to augment their performances of pure passion for their chosen careers. As a result, expressing "love" for craft brewing not only helps white men secure their standing within the workplace hierarchy, it also helps them shore up a social identity at work with distinct value among their peers.

ENACTING PURE PASSION FOR CRAFT BEER

Nearly all of the white men I met who are employed along the creative pathway express pure passion for their craft brewing jobs. They do so in three primary ways: through committing material and symbolic resources to their job, by downplaying formal employment conditions, and by connecting their work to their desired lifestyle. Each of these enactments of pure passion are steeped in social privileges along the lines of race, class, and gender. Further, through their actions, white men employed in positions of creative authority establish their personal approach to their careers as the dominant cultural logic of work within this setting, one against which all other alternatives are measured.

"I Was Obsessed": Committing Material and Symbolic Resources to Craft Beer

Once he started, the prospect of devoting himself wholly to pursuing a career in craft beer was never in doubt for Charlie, a forty-year-old, college-educated, white man. Charlie discovered homebrewing when he was in his late twenties and working as a grade-school teacher. Within months, he was "obsessed" with learning to brew his own beer. Homebrewing began to consume nearly all of Charlie's spare time and financial resources as he acquired a growing collection of homebrewing equipment and instruction books:

> I was a feverish reader of brewing textbooks, when I got to brewing school I'd already read all of the textbooks that they assigned us, which was nice. And again, I had this passionate group of people around me . . . we'd get together every night and just sit around and have a couple of beers together. And then on Friday and Saturday nights we would have more than a couple of beers together. We had four homebrewed beers on tap at almost all times, I was really good about keeping beer on tap. So I was brewing like twenty to thirty hours a week, and I didn't just like it. [EW: You didn't like brewing?]. No, I loved it! I fucking love it. I loved the cooking component with the extension of the fermentation aspect of beer brewing.

A couple years after first beginning to homebrew, Charlie, with the support of his wife, made the decision to pursue his passion full-time by entering the industry. Scholars note that the kind of devotion to work remains a gendered cultural ideal seen more positively for men than women.[30] Yet this does not fully appreciate how class-privileged white men bring material and immaterial resources with them to aid their passion-driven pursuits. Charlie committed his own time, energy, and resources to his future career on his days off; he received ample encouragement from his "passionate" friends and family to follow his dreams all the way.

The experiences of other white men further illustrate how symbolic and material commitments help propel them into an industry that they are passionate about. Jerry, a fifty-year-old man with salt-and-pepper hair and a pinkish complexion, explains his inspiration for switching careers four years ago:

> My wife and I traveled in 2003, 2004, 2005—any chance we had we were driving up the California coast to the Oregon coast, we were meeting with people like Peter Zion, Dale Smith or Vinnie Cilurzo at Russian River before everybody knew his name, Alan Sprints at Hair of the Dog. And all these guys had their own interesting stories and they all had their own interesting

approaches to brewing. But one thing remained the constant: they would drop everything for an hour or two and just chit chat with an overly curious homebrewer and they were open books and they would just tell you anything you wanted to hear, anything you wanted to know. And I was like, "Man, I really want to be a part of this community." I really loved it.

Jerry planned his vacation time away from his well-paying job as a scientist around visiting craft breweries and meeting brewery owners, the vast majority of whom were white men (including all those Jerry mentioned above). He recalls the passion for craft brewing that these brewers exhibited through "drop[ping] everything for an hour or two" to chit chat. It was a passion that mirrored his own. A few years later, Jerry was able to lean on his "day" job to help fund his small brewery, which he devoted his evenings and weekends to help oversee.

Workers such as Charlie and Jerry also idealize coworkers who, like them, demonstrate pure passion for craft brewing by making personal sacrifices in order to "make it." Jerry describes the traits he values in brewhouse workers:

EW: thinking about people who are working on the brew side in general, what would you say are some of the skills that really make for somebody who's going to do well in that capacity?

JERRY: It's going to be drive and passion, again. Because you're going to have to do stuff like the packaging team. It's such a repetitive job where you just do the same thing over and over every day. But if you're willing to stick through that and work hard at it with a good attitude, then you have a good chance of moving up and moving along. So yeah, definitely passion and drive. That'll get you to cellar [position] and brewhouse.

Jerry points to passion for craft beer as a core quality he looks for, particularly in brewers. He expects these potential hires to have made deliberate sacrifices—of resources, of time, and of possibly more lucrative careers—in order to work in this industry, indicating their level of commitment to craft brewing.[31] Yet what Jerry and other white men fail to see, or at least consciously downplay, is the privilege that underlies this particular career decision-making. Pursuing a job out of passion rather than economic necessity or familial obligation is already a luxury; doing so in an industry dominated by white men and their tastes, points to a more

Figure 3. Pure passion for craft: tasting from a barrel of sour beer to monitor flavor.

specific constellation of advantaged race, class, and gender traits that frame this approach to work.

"I Do This for Fun Anyway": Downplaying Employment and Playing Up Passion

Brewers who are white men systematically downplay the fact that craft brewing is their source of employment and not just a serious hobby. Many are reluctant to talk about wages or paid time off or health benefits because for them, these jobs are not primarily about any of these things. Instead, these men express what Pierre Bourdieu calls "economic disinterest" toward their jobs as a way of affirming their authentic interest in them while also highlighting the intrinsic worth of these careers.[32]

Grant, who we met last chapter, started working at a craft brewery because he liked "hanging out" there as a patron. He enjoyed talking to all the bartenders and sampling every seasonal beer the brewery made. After several months of regularly patronizing the brewery taproom after getting off work as a golf course superintendent, the manager on duty, a white man, offered Grant a part-time job bussing tables. He accepted. "For me, it's not about the money," Grant explained. Instead, he saw this as an opportunity to immerse himself even more in his preferred environment; getting paid was, in effect, a perk.[33]

The pure passion for craft beer that workers such as Grant exhibit can motivate them to leave stable, well-compensated jobs outside the industry for poorly paid positions within it. In doing so, they trade earning potential for passion potential and hope that everything will work out in the end. This same logic can also justify moving from one company to another within the same industry. For example, a college-educated white man I talked to said he got fed up with all the rules and "bean counting" involved with working as a brewer at a larger production brewery. He took a significant pay cut to work for a smaller and more "authentic" company that aligned with his ideals.

In settings where pure passion is central to why people seek jobs, both managers and workers alike point to "loving the job" as a key employment benefit. For example, Joanne, a white woman who co-owns a small, Albuquerque-based brewery with her husband, describes how their head brewer, Brandon, manages the brewhouse staff: "Brandon tells the brewers: 'guys, I know you are killing yourself twice a week brewing these double batches, but try to find the *joy* in what you are doing!'" In this sense, Joanne and Brandon both see "joy" as a job perk of working along the creative pathway, one that helps justify this career decision.

Conversely, being suspected of having a less-than-pure interest in craft beer by one's peers can register as a grave insult to brewers, a questioning of their core values. Dennis, a white man in his early thirties, illustrates this through an exchange that occurred after he informed his boss that he was leaving his head brewer job to work for a nearby brewery:

> One of the most offensive things that happened to me at Murphy's Brewing was when the owner's wife told me, "so are you just going to remake all of our beers at your new place?" And my reply was, "why would I? I have over 100 recipes that I never brewed while I was the brewer there. You think I need this? You don't seem to get it. *This is what I'm good at. Creating new recipes is why I do this.*"

Dennis felt his boss's wife's inquiry questioned his pure passion for craft brewing. Having this woman tell him not to "remake" the same recipes—a standard precaution in many industries to protect intellectual property when employees leave—threatened Dennis's identity as someone who did this work for *no other reason but* the love of innovating and creating. Moreover, in emphasizing repeatedly to me that his boss's wife "did not know anything about brewing," Dennis may have also felt his masculinity was being threatened by a woman who he perceived to be less passionate about craft beer than himself and overly concerned about her company's bottom line.

Being surrounded by workers who enact pure passion can be particularly frustrating for minoritized workers who do not relate to their jobs using this cultural logic of work. Jordyn, the brewer introduced last chapter, is critical of the group culture of her peers who are men:

> It's like a giant circle jerk watching all of these guys just congratulate each other on being so awesome, but not actually saying what they did to make them awesome. And I don't necessarily think that I'm the only one [who feels this way]. If you talk to a lot of people that have been in the industry for a long time, they would probably say the same thing. They maybe don't understand why this person is so popular when they don't project any sort of substance.

Jordyn has seen many of her white male colleagues play up their passion for craft brewing in ways that simultaneously help them signal full membership in industry circles. The way these men display their love for their jobs in abstract terms ("not actually saying what they did to make them awesome") only serves to highlight how their sense of belonging is constituted through social privilege. From Jordyn's perspective, to be seen as a passionate brewer starts with being a white man, and the rest flows from there.

Few working-class people of color employed along the creative pathway express their relationship to their jobs by downplaying their formal employment and playing up passion. Josiah, the Native American man introduced last chapter, describes this difference in stark terms. Several months into his tenure as a cellar worker, Josiah's boss asked him to help train new brewhouse hires, most of whom were white, college-educated men with limited knowledge of the hard labor involved in daily brewhouse work:

JOSIAH: When people who have college degrees and say they are into beer come through [get hired], I kind of get annoyed. Because those people are not doing the job, cutting corners on how they should do things, not necessarily following how things are done at [the brewery]. They just kind of fuck things up.

EW: so it is annoying to be a part of that work atmosphere?

JOSIAH: hell yeah. and even more annoying when you've done the thing time and time again and this person has done it for the sixth, seventh time and they still can't grasp it. You are still trying to explain to this person, and they are coming to you asking what they are doing. I was like, they told us before, figure it the fuck out. Like when I was in the marine corps: figure it the fuck out. Things not working out? Figure it the fuck out.

Josiah's own relationship to his career is best encapsulated by his expression "figure it the fuck out," which emphasizes the pragmatic job skills he uses at work. In this sense, Josiah's approach to work reflects a working-class masculinity that prioritizes physicality, dependability, and hard work.[34] His approach also presents a stark contrast with new hires who seek out jobs along the creative pathway primarily because they are "into craft beer." Unfortunately for Josiah, this is precisely the cultural logic of work that many of his colleagues who are white men value most—including Josiah's boss, who hires the men that Josiah is routinely asked to train.

To be sure, several people of color I talked to count craft beer among their passions and career ambitions. However, when compared to their white male colleagues, these individuals are less likely to downplay practical employment considerations such as money and job security. For example, Ricardo, a thirty-six-year-old Latino man, became interested in craft beer after his involvement in a Latinx-focused homebrewing club in Los Angeles—the first of its kind nationally. In the years that followed, Ricardo struggled to find a way to turn his passion for craft beer into a career:

> The beer stuff along with music, that's my passion, so how do I merge them under one umbrella and give myself a chance to make a living as well? Do something I love and pay the bills? I'm sitting here and I'm looking like, okay, I have no access to capital. There's nobody in my family that has a background in business. . . . And then my friends start actually doing it, start getting their business plans together, start raising capital, start going through the whole process. And man, they're like a year into the process and they're still not opening their doors, but they're still shelling out all this money, taking on all this debt. And so they open doors and they're like $400, $500,000 in debt right off the bat, I'm like, "I don't know if I want to do that."

Ricardo and other workers of color find themselves grappling with career prospects in the industry that they perceive to be either too costly or too low-paying to pursue ("[how do I] do something I love *and* pay the bills?"). Dennis and Grant, earlier in this section, face these same industry conditions. Yet for these white men, access to privileged resources allows them to downplay what these careers mean in terms of formal employment while highlighting how they complement their passions. What's more, expressing this cultural logic of work affirms their fit along the creative pathway.

"This Is a Way of Life": Embracing the Brewhouse Lifestyle

Many craft brewers I talked to say that a key perk of their jobs is how well it fits within the broader set of activities they engage in. This is due in part to the flexible schedules and informal work atmospheres of brewery workplaces.[35] Yet it is educated white men who are most likely to see their jobs as transcending employment and representing a chosen lifestyle. These workers assert that employment along the creative pathway is a direct expression of who they are and what they are most passionate about. This in turn helps them look past, and sometimes even embrace, the marginal aspects of their jobs.[36]

A brewer named Aaron, who is a thirty-three-year-old white man, explains that his decision to pursue a career in craft beer reflects his changed outlook on his career:

> I really flipped my perception of the narrative, you know, *go to college, put on the suit, go to the city.* There has got to be some other way to approach things! And you read a lot of things like: if it is not this big [extends his hands outward], then don't do it. Or that's not successful. And I started over a five- or six-year period, reading a lot and realizing that you really get to define what success is to you. It is not this other bigger measure of something.

Aaron rejects the traditionally masculine logic of securing a reputable career of middle-class trappings and instead opted for a career that spoke to his heart. While his choice to leave his well-paying job in corporate advertising was not easy, Aaron's justifies doing so by embracing new lifestyle priorities that are more inwardly focused ("you really get to define what success is to you"). For workers like Aaron, pursuing a career along the creative pathway reflects what they love to do with their time both on and off the clock.

Other workers emphasize the deep satisfaction they get from working with their hands to create things. These workers exemplify sociologist Richard Sennett's notion of "the craftsman"—including its gendered connotation—through their careful attention to hand-crafting material things in an exacting fashion. For instance, a brewer named Jonathan described how he was "always tinkering with things while growing up," which included breaking down old radios and motorcycle engines in order to rebuild them.[37] For Jonathan, who is a college-educated white man with fifteen years of industry experience, working in small breweries allows him to use his hands not only to brew but also to help repair the "DIY" brewhouse equipment that is constantly breaking down. All of it appeals to him. On the day I visited Jonathan in the brewhouse, he was smiling and laughing as he darted between brewing tanks pulling open valves, moving hoses, and hoisting sacks of grain into the mash tun. After his shift was over, Jonathan described to me why working as a brewer continues to be appealing to him:

Figure 4. A typical day in the brewhouse.

I was always a very mechanical person, making and creating things with my hands. More than that, I like to share it with other people. What better way to do that than eating and drinking together, right? And so I originally thought that I wanted to become a chef and I went and did a professional culinary program. After that I went to do my internships, went to work at the big Wolfgang Puck place in Hollywood, and realized that I wasn't ready to take such a huge pay cut for the next four years. I wasn't ready to put the time in to be where I wanted to be as a chef or owning a restaurant. And line cooking is fun but very, very stressful. Brewing has a lot of the qualities that the culinary arts do, but it is not quite so high pressure. And that's when I decided that I wanted to be a commercial brewer instead of a commercial chef.

Jonathan situates his brewing job within a larger set of activities he has long been passionate about, such the act of sharing freshly made food and drink with other people. He has made several career decisions—pivoting away from chef work, for example—that have gotten him closer to achieving this lifestyle with fewer downsides.

Many workers say their idealized lifestyle includes careers where they can socialize informally with others who share their interests.[38] White men I talked to are particularly likely to seek out brewing jobs in order to be closer to the specialized products they like and the people who make them. As an assistant brewer who joined the industry less than a year ago explains: "I love that I know everyone here from before [I worked here], and after I finish brewing, I can still head over to the taproom and drink the beer I helped make. *For free.*" For this man, who is white, working at the brewery is an extension of his preferred lifestyle and its constellation of craft activities, consumption tastes, and sociality.

For similar reasons, many brewhouse workers say they relish the opportunity to "hang out" in their places of employment even when they are not scheduled.[39] Spending time at their workplaces off the clock both reflects and deepens the personal passion these individuals have for their jobs. It also fosters greater connection to coworkers and customers who also spend their time there, especially when not required to. At one brewery, for example, several workers told me they coordinated a weekly "bottle share" among the brewhouse staff where everyone brought in a new beer from a different brewery to taste.[40] During these bottle shares, workers pulled together metal chairs and sacks of malted barley to sit and drink; their workplace doubled as the venue for a weekly social event where talk of beer got mixed in with sexual jokes and "war stories" about getting drunk at other craft breweries.

To be sure, women and people of color also occasionally participate in the social lifestyles of their workplaces, and few describe being overtly excluded from the off-hour activities put on by their coworkers. Yet it is also clear to these individuals who the core employees at the brewery are as well as the whiteness, maleness, and class-privilege of the workplace culture they are a part of.[41] For example, Ariana, the taproom server we met last chapter, privately expressed shock that her manager, a white man in his mid-twenties, thought it was okay to have one of the brewers dress up in the attire of a well-known Mexican festival and parade around the brewery making jokes with customers while selling the brewery's Mexican-themed beer. "It's like, we couldn't even find a Hispanic man to do that?" said Ariana, adding: "These are things that I am never *not* thinking about while I'm at work." In light of this, it may come as a surprise that Ariana still claims to enjoy her taproom-based brewery job. Yet within the "bearded white guy" space of craft breweries, minoritized workers such as Ariana routinely do not feel they are full participants in their workplace's culture. Nor are they part of the in-group of white men who enact pure passion for craft beer and install their lifestyles and interests as the default within these spaces.

FRAMING ARTISANAL MASCULINITY

> Arnold walks me through the brewery he owns with his brother. He runs his hand along the wooden bar top, twinkling from a fresh coat of varnish. "Everything you see here is handmade, by us. We did this one. Pretty happy with how it turned out." He points out a concrete wall speckled with colored glass: "That too. Those are actual beer bottles we put it there, thought it would be a pretty cool effect." Arnold gives the same treatment to the tap handles, tables, and bathroom doors. I see the only thing that isn't home-made is the brewhouse equipment. Arnold smiles when I point this out. "For that—at my own place—I wanted the very best. Figured we'd splurge on a really cool top-of-the-line model with copper trimmings."

For Arnold, a thirty-one-year-old white man with a frizzy brown beard and thin frame, it is meaningful that everything in his brewery is hand-made and carefully selected to his and his brother's specifications.[42] Arnold's brewery is built from scratch, welded together, bolted together by hand. Likewise, the beers that he creates are handcrafted in multiple senses of the word and infused with seasonal berries or dry-hopped with experimental hops that he personally adds at various stages in the brew process. These details embody the kind of man that Arnold sees himself as: someone passionate about things that are at once physical, creative, specialized, and authentic.

Like Arnold, many of the men working along the creative pathway embody artisanal masculinity. They talk about their jobs as direct extensions of their personal identities that carry pride and purpose. During my visit to North Star Brewing in south Los Angeles, the owner, Santiago, a forty-two-year-old Latino man with a graduate degree in engineering, led me on a tour of the facility:

We walk into the brewhouse—a cavernous, former equipment warehouse—stepping over hoses. Santiago explains to me that he has slowly built up his brewhouse and his collection of equipment and storage vessels, the evidence of which is now all around us. "Leading up to our opening, I used to sleep in here, you know," Santiago says, eyeing the cement floor surrounding a steel-grate drain. "This place would be a health inspector's nightmare today!" He points out a large, square vat perched on stubby metal legs. "See this? I made this kettle myself. I fashioned it out of junk scraps."

For men such as Santiago and Arnold, fashioning brewery equipment by hand represents so much more than a cost-cutting measure. It is what these workers want to be known for, how they want to be seen by others. It is a point of pride that their respective breweries do not look spick-and-span or state-of-the-art. All that matters at the end of the day is their ability to produce distinctive products that bear their own imprint.[43] In this way, these men evoke artisanal masculinity by highlighting their creative craftsmanship and authenticity infused with a healthy dose of ruggedness and self-reliance.[44]

Many other head brewers and brewery owners I talked to also describe the extent to which they have physically built, repaired, tinkered with, and jerry-rigged brewing equipment together forged from cut metal and industrial-grade rubber. These kinds of actions—as well as the act of drawing attention to these actions—speak to their core values. A brewer named Luis, who is a thirty-three-year-old, college-educated Latino man, stresses why he prefers working at his current company, a small brewpub, more than the midsize brewery where he worked previously:

Now that I'm here it's more manual. It's more of that passion again, more of that love in making sure your numbers are getting there and the flavors that you really worked on are going to happen. Not just relying on the switch that's going to rake mash in for me and extract for me and boil for me. At bigger companies it's all just a bunch of switches. Now I've got to really paddle it in, make sure my burner is working and stuff like that.

Luis conveys artisanal masculinity through the way he characterizes his relationship to his job that is deliberately physical and craft-oriented. Making his job easier and less "manual"—like his previous job—is not what Luis wants, nor is it how he sees himself and frames his identity. Luis's story captures the deeply personal relationship that many brewers have with the creative products they choose to make. Seeking this kind of authenticity in their work lives also helps these individuals justify working at smaller companies, often for less pay. Arnold, the brewer-owner described earlier, explains:

> Frankly, I would say I brew exclusively for myself. I mean, there are popular beers here, but if I don't necessarily like that popular beer, I just don't make it. I think that having a small system like what we have here, a lot of what makes a brewery good is having passionate people who work there who are excited about what they're doing. You kind of have to do things for yourself to keep a little bit of passion going in there.

Arnold illustrates how a core aspect of artisanal masculinity for many men working along the creative pathway involves staying true to oneself with one's craftsmanship at all costs. Doing so is premised on their continual access to flexible employment and creative autonomy, which can be in tension with business goals of turning a profit. Arnold illustrates this point when describing what the next few months will look like for his company:

> We're playing around with a lot of different ideas. I actually have a ton of different interests and passions and ideas. And so keeping the workload in the brewhouse limited is something that I want to do, because there are just lots of different ideas that I would like to keep time available to pursue. So, I don't necessarily want to make this full-time where I have to get more production equipment or build a space next door so I can brew more beer so that I can be even more busy with just this. I've got a handful of different ideas that I just want to play around with and some are not related to beer at all.

Arnold portrays his company as a physical expression of his artisanal masculinity. He wants to pursue a variety of activities at work while "playing around" and following his own interests. (Arnold later described his goal of building a large garden outside the brewery with herbs and produce that he could either serve to customers or use in his beers.) In this sense, class-privileged men such as Arnold treat their jobs along the creative pathway as a core part of their gender identity as well as the idealized embodiment of handcrafted careers. They cherish the flexibility to graft different parts of themselves and their interest onto their respective workplaces, reframing these spaces as desirably masculine ones.[45]

By contrast, the few workers employed along the creative pathway who do not exhibit artisanal masculinity express frustration at having to contend with unpredictable employment within small companies. Jordyn, the brewer described earlier, explains:

> I do not enjoy the many-hat-wearing of smaller breweries. It is the most frustrating thing ever, just because it seems like there's an endless supply of responsibility and the resources aren't there. Resources that would help fix things. The expectation is, especially in smaller breweries, that you will bend over backwards for the brewery because you're so passionate about it. Being in the industry for so long, I feel old. I feel old and I feel tired.

Jordyn recognizes that many of her brewing colleagues, especially those who are white men, take pride in their DIY operations. Yet the chronic lack of resources and organization within these operations rank among her least favorite parts about jobs along the creative pathway. They also play a minimal part in how she portrays her work identity. Similarly, Ishmael, a forty-five-year-old Latino man with a high school education, expresses exasperation at aspects of the industry that his more class- and race-privileged peers fully embrace. Ishmael describes coming into the industry with dreams of entrepreneurial success but little passion for brewing beer.

> I wanted to do something different with my life. I was already in my thirties, so I'm like, "I'm going to go make some money." So, I was just like, "Okay. What kind of business should I start?" I didn't really know. I landed on a brewery. I liked reading up on it and stuff, but . . . it's just a pain in the ass sometimes because I'm limited with equipment and stuff. I'm just patching things together as we go and stuff. Something is always breaking. Or I forget something. There's not a perfect brew day and stuff.

Despite participating in the industry along the creative pathway, minoritized workers such as Ishmael and Jordyn do not frame their identities in ways that evoke artisanal masculinity. In contrast to class-privileged white men like Arnold, their respective work identities are not tied up in deliberately small-scale production using makeshift equipment.

This is not to suggest that white women and people of color cannot derive pride and identity from their craft beer jobs. Yet the custom blend of authenticity, creativity, and physicality that defines artisanal masculinity closely reflects the way educated white men in this industry see themselves, further stoking their passions for careers in craft beer.

.   .   .   .   .

While finishing the last sips of our froth-laced pints of IPA, Brandon reflects on why he "still" loves craft brewing after nearly a decade of ups and downs in the industry.

> Why am I here? Yeah, the conditions suck. The money's not that good. I don't get tons of benefits, though I do get free beer. [*he pauses*] Then there's the satisfaction of knowing that everybody is on the same plane. Everybody wants to make the best beer we can because we all enjoy beer. And so I let my guys [brewers] know, you're not doing this for me, you're doing it because you can be proud of what you're putting out.

Brandon highlights the symbolic benefits he derives from his job and expects that anyone dedicated to this industry should feel the same.[46] To Brandon and many of his peers who share his views, these are careers where the work *is* the payoff.

As we have seen this chapter, it is within the brewhouse and along the creative pathway where white men express *pure passion* for their craft beer jobs—a relationship to work that encompasses labor, consumption, and lifestyle practices all in one. Adhering to this cultural logic of work helps individuals justify their career decisions and their personal commitments of money, time, and effort made toward jobs. It also etches certain social expectations into the workplace: white men such as Dennis, Grant, and Brandon idealize people who express pure passion for craft beer and can be dismissive of those who don't. Yet because workers enact pure passion *through* class privilege, whiteness, and masculinity, this cultural logic of work reinforces the position of white men in craft beer while marginalizing workers from nondominant groups who are less able to express their relationship to work this way. In effect, pure passion derives its value and exclusionary power within the workplace because of *who* enacts it and how it gets informally embedded within the industry.[47]

Additionally, for white men employed along the creative pathway, the labor of craft beer contributes to their framing of *artisanal masculinity*. It is within these small, craft-focused settings that workers who enjoy ample job autonomy portray themselves through a gendered identity centered on authenticity, creativity, and physicality. Artisanal masculinity complements pure passion for craft beer in two important ways. First, embodying artisanal masculinity, as a form of identity work, directly augments the actions and activities through which individuals enact pure passion for their jobs.[48] Many of the workers employed along the creative pathway see their jobs as both chosen lifestyles and desirable forms of identity. This helps us make sense of why these privileged workers continue to justify pursuing careers in an industry that represents neither sure-fire upward mobility nor traditional middle-class masculinity. Second, as a gendered, classed, and racialized form of identity, artisanal masculinity mirrors pure passion for craft beer in how it is constituted through social privilege. In effect, what makes inhabiting artisanal masculinity appealing to college-educated white men in this industry is their access to jobs that offer them the chance to be creative, autonomous, and authentic at work. From this perch, the more they lean into who they are and what they want to do with their time, the more they reap rewards.

Next chapter, we move beyond the creative pathway to examine the careers of those who work along the service pathway within the industry. It is here where we see how workers forge handcrafted careers in customer-focused jobs involving a very different assemblage of classed expectations and gendered work opportunities.

3   We Like to Have Fun

CONSUMPTIVE CAREERS IN THE TAPROOM

Amber, a twenty-five-year-old, biracial (Latinx-white) woman, works four nights a week behind the bar at Radiant Brewing in Albuquerque, New Mexico. It was just over three years ago, after graduating from college with a degree in microbiology, that she decided to look for a job in a brewery. "When I was younger, I had a lot of older friends that were into craft beer," says Amber. "There was a lot of popularity around it. One of my really good friends, his stepdad is the owner and head brewer of this brewery up in Santa Fe, so even growing up, the bus would drop us off and we'd just hang out in the brewery. Craft beer was something that I was always around."

As a beertender, Amber serves a wide range of customers each day ranging from parents pushing baby strollers to midweek happy hour go-ers to hardcore beer geeks. Keeping everyone happy is not easy, but Amber says that the years she spent waiting tables in college makes this task a little easier and more familiar. Recently, Amber has been focused on other aspects of her job that interest her, such as developing a better "beer palate" in order to communicate the special qualities of head brewer David's eclectic creations to customers. When off work, Amber reads up on historical beer styles and tries to seek out a wide range of beers to sample, which often involves visiting other breweries. She hopes that all of this will help her pass the exam to become a Certified Cicerone, the beer industry's version of a sommelier, to affirm her industry credentials.

As much as Amber devotes time and effort to her taproom service job, her long-term prospects at Radiant, as well as in the industry at large, remain ambiguous. During our conversation, she couches just about everything she says about her job with "right now"—*my work schedule is relatively stable right now, which is great . . . my regulars around the bar right now are awesome, which isn't always the case.* Her job also routinely causes her stress. This is the case during the slow winter months when tips dry up and management cuts back on beertending shifts or when she serves beer late at night to rowdy groups of men, "including the occasional asshole," she adds. Or, during the height of the coronavirus pandemic, when her boss required that Amber and the other beertenders function as the "mask police" (her words) to enforce the company's face mask policy for all customers and workers.[1]

"Can you try and move into management here, maybe?" I ask.

"Where would I go?" Amber replies with a shrug. "Above me [in the taproom] it is just the owners. They don't have managerial positions here. On my paystub, they actually list my title as 'Assistant to the CEO,' because I help out my boss with various things. But I'm basically a glorified errand runner. This isn't a career that's totally . . ." Amber trails off. "I make enough money and I'm doing well, but it's not totally like . . . at least I don't have to be somewhere at eight o'clock every morning, Monday through Friday."

Lately, Amber has been spending more of her time away from Radiant getting a small business of her own leading bike tours for kids up and running.

"Does this mean you'll be leaving the beer industry?" I ask.

"No, I don't think so. I don't plan on going anywhere anytime soon. I can do a lot of this job outside of my hours here," Amber says, noting that her bike tour business would take place during the day while her brewery job is evenings, allowing her to juggle the two. "Honestly, I don't know if I'll be in craft beer for the next five years. But I do love my job. The people are cool. I like the owner [a woman of color] a lot, and I'm a pretty dedicated person in general. We'll just have to see."

.   .   .   .   .

As Amber's story illustrates, taproom workers express conflicting views about their prospects of building careers in the kinds of customer-facing positions they hold within the industry. On the one hand, many of these individuals are drawn to the perks of working among "cool" people on the front lines of "fun" and informal workplaces, where the jobs they do appeal to their personal interests and preferred social environments.[2] On the other hand, Amber and her taproom colleagues, who are mostly college-educated, white women and men, contend with marginal employment conditions in small companies with little room to advance into better-paying jobs or leadership roles along the creative pathway. Workers do, of course, attempt to craft their employment to better suit them individually; Amber's foray into bike tours is one such effort. But the double-edged realities they face along the service pathway make it difficult to envision long-term careers within the industry, especially for women.

Taproom employees in craft breweries are not alone in facing a mixture of cool-yet-uncertain labor conditions. A growing number of workers in the new economy maintain similar kinds of relationships to their jobs, including those employed as fashion models, artists, high-end clothing store retail workers, restaurant servers, and cafe baristas.[3] Existing sociological research helps us understand the short-term appeal of otherwise precarious jobs from the perspective of workers themselves. As sociologist Yasemin Besen-Cassino notes, young adults working frontline service and retail jobs tend to "consume" their jobs by seeing them as opportunities to be around products, activities, and people they enjoy.[4] By threading their part-time jobs together with other paid gigs and non-work-related opportunities, these workers attempt to manage uncertain conditions by building multifaceted "portfolio lives."[5] Yet the relationship that workers have with their jobs can change over time as they weigh personal interests, responsibilities, and long-term career prospects. Some people, too, are in a better position to craft their employment to suit their needs than others because of how their material and immaterial resources interplay with organizational conditions.

How do craft beer workers such as Amber approach their employment along the service pathway, and how do the conditions that underlie these jobs pattern distinctive labor experiences along the lines of gender, class, and race? In this chapter I describe how workers in taprooms and other service contexts forge *consumptive careers* through their jobs. Consumptive careers illustrate how workers' ongoing employment decisions are motivated by their personal tastes for specialized products and their desire to participate in the social scenes that surround these products.[6] Many taproom workers say their jobs allow them to custom-fit their work lives by blurring the boundaries between labor and leisure in desirable ways. At the same time, as workers proceed along this gendered career pathway, the lack of employment stability and advancement opportunities they encounter leaves them unsure about their long-term career prospects. This is particularly true for women working in these roles who are less likely than their male counterparts to make microtransitions into roles of authority as a result of the unequal way in which workers' personal resources and cultural logics of work are valued within the industry.

WORKING THE TAPROOM SCENE

Taproom jobs in the craft beer industry involve interactive service work, which requires being friendly, cheerful, and accommodating toward customers. Interactive service work jobs continue to be done disproportionately by women in our society because of how the "skills" and dispositions associated with these jobs are feminized as well as associated with middle-class, Euro-American culture.[7] Consistent with these patterns, in the craft beer industry, nearly one out of every two workers employed along the service pathway is a woman despite the fact that men represent four out of every five workers in the industry overall. As we learned in chapter 1, women in particular tend to get channeled into feminized and lower status jobs along the service pathway because of the unequal kinds of microtransitions workers make along hierarchical and socially coded career pathways.

Taproom workers also engage in an immaterial type of work that comes with its own job requirements and social exclusivities.[8] Those who work along the service pathway help management cultivate a setting of *craft consumption* in the workplace by embodying particular kinds of classed and racialized tastes.[9] Brewery management expects that their taproom service staff will help them stage what sociologist Thomas Thurnell-Read

Figure 5. Consuming work and crafting identity in the taproom.

calls a "performance of authenticity" through their discerning knowledge of artisanal products and their ability to communicate these qualities to customers in ways that feel genuine rather than forced.[10] Taproom service workers thus function as cultural intermediaries who infuse the products and experiences they sell to customers with cultural value—what Alessandro Gandini and Alessandro Gerosa call "marginal distinction."[11] In short, the way interactive service workers in craft beer talk about, handle, and consume the products they sell *matters*, which can affect who works in this environment, what these workers experience on the job, and how their employment unfolds over time.

As Amber alluded to above, employment in brewery taprooms can feel effortless for the right kind of person, like hanging out in a familiar setting where workers can simply be themselves.[12] Yet despite having few formal rules, this setting still maintains a limited guest list. As sociologist Chris Land notes, "not everyone can combine the practical skills with the cultural performances required to *do* craft."[13] Many taproom service jobs require rudimentary tasks on paper but depend more critically on workers' cultural and symbolic proficiencies in order to thrive in these positions and make smooth microtransitions between jobs along this pathway.[14] For example, in his book *Masters of Craft*, Richard Ocejo describes a Mexican butcher working in a high-end butcher shop who was an efficient worker but whose ethnic and class identity prevented him from performing the kinds of "service education" that customer-focused craft work often requires and customers expect.[15] This points to the implicit requirements for continued employment along the service pathway: anyone can pour a beer but not everyone can convey the value of that beer to class-privileged guests who are mostly white and male.[16] And not everyone will feel like this work is for them, either.

As this chapter shows, workers employed in brewery taprooms manage an ongoing tension between the classed forms of cultural knowledge required of their jobs, the feminized nature of service work, and the constrained employment opportunities along this career pathway.[17] Class-privileged white women and men tend to find their personal interests and experiences amplified in jobs along the service pathway and reflected in others who inhabit this space. However, as these workers continue to handcraft their careers, the gendered microtransitions women and men engage in, coupled with the distinct cultural logics of work they subscribe to, end up contributing to their divergent experiences along the same industry pathway.

"I'M PERFECT FOR THIS JOB"

Many college-educated, white women and men describe how brewery taproom jobs fit seamlessly with their lifestyles. This makes it easy for them to stay with this line of employment regardless of how they first got into this industry—or how long they ultimately intend to stay there. For Lucy, a fast-talking, forty-two-year-old white woman, getting a job in a brewery taproom didn't feel like the start of a career, but rather a "fun" interim gig at first. Lucy initially took a job as a beertender at an Albuquerque-based brewery after she was laid off from her previous job in the entertainment industry, where she had worked ever since graduating from college a decade ago. Lucy explains the circumstances surrounding her job change:

LUCY: As most things go in my life, I feel like if you're just open to what the uni-
verse brings you, things just happen a certain way. I had a friendship
with [a brewery owner], who said, "We need help. Why don't you come
beertend for me while you figure out your next step?"

EW: did you see yourself staying in beer?

LUCY: I didn't. I really didn't. I thought it would be a transition. I mean, I'm a
craft beer lover and I thought it was a great gig to just come into. I'm like,
"This is perfect. I can do this while I'm figuring it out." But as I grew to
love the industry and love the people in it, *I just felt like I belonged,* you
know? So I didn't really ever have a wandering heart to get out of it
after all.

Transitioning smoothly into the service pathway, workers such as Lucy
feel like they "belong" in this labor environment and among people with
shared interests. For women in particular, this perspective can also be
consistent with how their friends and colleagues—such as Lucy's brewery-
owner-friend, a white man, who hired her—see them fitting into gendered
jobs within the industry.

Getting a customer-service job in the industry also draws heavily on a
preferred lifestyle that includes consuming craft beer. Several workers I
met said they had little work experience of any kind in craft beer prior to
getting their first taproom jobs. Mona, a twenty-eight-year-old white
woman with a master's degree in education, describes how she got into the
industry this way:

I've always liked the beer culture here in Albuquerque. It is what I did with
my friends anyway, you know, going to see live music, and eating at the food
trucks, and playing cards. Like, a lot of my social time was spent at breweries. So when I started [my job], I just really liked it. It was a really good fit.

Finding employment in brewery taprooms allows individuals such as
Mona to merge their leisure tastes with jobs that center these tastes, often
even celebrating them. This allows workers to feel that their employment
is a direct extension of the activities they already participate in ("it is what
I did with my friends anyway"). It is worth noting how this snug labor fit
is also convenient for employers: hiring people who already participate in
the social and cultural scenes of taprooms can make these spaces feel

more "authentic."[18] In effect, the workers who employers want for these service jobs are the ones who most likely consume these specialized activities anyway.

Several taproom workers also told me that their jobs complement their naturally outgoing and sociable personalities, allowing them to bring home a paycheck simply for being themselves. Sheila, the beertender-turned-sales-representative introduced in previous chapters, describes her relationship to her job in this way:

> EW: when did beer become something that you felt you could do for your career, as opposed to something else?
>
> SHEILA: I know exactly the answer to that: Beer is fun! It allows me to still work in an energetic space, much like being behind a bar. It was cool, honestly. I'm getting paid a salary to go party. I would be in a bar, and someone would be like, yeah, I'm literally supposed to have a drink. Because part of my job was to make these relationships with people so they would buy more of these craft brands. So I would be chit chatting, and making friends and high-fiving. *And how is your dog? And do you want to buy this?* So I would joke with my boss, I'm going to change my business card to say "professional friend." Because that is what I feel like I'm doing. It is not a real job, I'm just a professional friend. My boss was like, if you want to change it, I'll do it. That was honestly how I felt about my job, and how I described it to people.

Workers such as Sheila feel they are employed in capacities where they get rewarded both for their trade knowledge and their upbeat personalities. Sheila's use of the term "professional friend" to describe her job encapsulates this by portraying her ability to make friends with others in, around, and through craft beer as a coveted skill.

Like Sheila, many women enter the service pathway in craft beer from previous interactive service jobs in restaurants, bars, and cafes—illustrating the gendered nature of this kind of employment microtransition. Maya, a biracial (Asian-white) woman in her mid-thirties with a pixie-style haircut, previously worked a string of service jobs in restaurants and casinos before becoming a beertender at a craft-beer-focused bar. "I kind of fell into it, really," says Maya of her career transition. "I was young enough that taking that chance didn't seem risky. It was kind of exciting, you know?" Scholars note that it is usually men rather than women who "fall into" their careers with ease.[19] But along the service pathway in craft beer, the story is more complicated: as Maya illustrates, the prospect of "falling into" taproom jobs for women often stems from their prior employment in similar kinds of customer service roles in other industries.

By comparison, men are more likely to assert that leisure activities rather than prior work experiences initially brought them to the doorstep of employment along the service pathway. Grant, who we met in chapter 1, explains how his first brewery job represented a logical outgrowth of the activities he was already doing at the time:

> So, a couple years ago, going on bike rides, we would hit up breweries in the sense that you could hang out, have a beer or two with your buddy with your bikes, you know, lock it up, bring it in. And that is how craft beer started for me. Because I lived right by [a brewery]. So it was a perfect end-ride. And [the workers] would let me put the bike on the patio, and just go in and have a beer. Hang out, you know?

As Grant's story illustrates, men who transition into taproom service jobs do so in ways that are buffered by their status as regular occupants of this space. They describe entering taproom jobs alongside others who share racialized and classed leisure tastes and social networks. Further, men portray that their taproom jobs emerge organically from their participation in a constellation of nonwork activities that commonly include activities such as biking, yoga, and rock climbing.[20]

For workers such as Lucy, Mona, and Grant, the prospect of seamlessly fitting within jobs along the service pathway does not occur by accident but rather through employment processes that are classed, racialized, and gendered. Whereas women describe "falling into" these jobs because of their prior work history, men are more likely to have first experienced these settings as frequent and expected customers. Moreover, these distinct microtransitions tend to follow workers over time, patterning their subsequent career prospects along the service pathway. While women remain tied closely to frontline service roles that resemble the jobs that brought them into this setting, men enjoy greater employment flexibility foregrounded by their personal relationship to *craft consumption*.

"Why Would I Want to Leave?"

Prior to becoming a "professional friend," Sheila was already hooked on craft beer because of her prior experience selling these products at the high-end bar where she worked. After landing her industry job, Sheila could talk with customers about craft beer's esoteric qualities, gourmet ingredients, and the lore, or "hype," of specific breweries with little extra training needed. During the customer events that she helped organize, Sheila would personally curate menus pairing funky *saisons* with aged cheeses, and smoky, barrel-aged stouts with artisanal meats. In doing so, Sheila embodies *craft consumption,* foregrounding her tastes for hand-crafted products and her ability to communicate to customers the specialized forms of knowledge needed to appreciate these products.

Unsurprisingly, brewery managers and workers alike see craft consumption as a marker of job proficiency in places where craft beer is sold and consumed. This kind of distinction sets their workplaces apart from others that offer either "macro" products (Budweiser, Coors, Modelo) or less knowledgeable service (dive bars), or both. Some workers also frame craft consumption as a source of career development along the service pathway. Below, Maya explains how, when working as a beertender, learning to appreciate the products she sold to customers helped catalyze her career:

> I had to learn a lot about the beers because the customers would come in, the regulars would come in, they knew a lot about beer. So then I just started studying everything [about beer]. The Cicerone program had just started back then, so myself and one of the other guys that worked there started studying to take the exam. I think I just kind of fell in love with the companies that made the beer, the stories of family recipes and stuff. And how everything was so different, especially Belgian beers. *Saisons* really got me. *Dupont Avec Les Bon Vieu* [a brand of beer by Brasserie Dupont] still is my favorite beer. That beer—that one totally got me hooked. I *loved* telling customers the story of that beer. And I used to sell so much of it back then!

Maya describes her growing affinity for artisanal products and the rich stories behind them. It was something that led her to formalize her knowledge of these topics through industry credentials. For workers such as Maya, the process of getting "hooked" on craft beer and deepening her ties to her job functions as a feedback loop whereby one's relationship to craft consumption can later be deployed effectively with customers ("I loved telling customers the story of that beer").

In some ways, the language taproom workers use to describe their jobs resembles the language used by brewers along the creative pathway. Both are highly personalized and filled with emotions like passion and love. However, brewers emphasize their devotion to craft production, while taproom workers express their relationship to their jobs mostly through consumption activities. This includes regularly drinking craft beer, seeking out and procuring coveted beers, and talking about the special qualities of certain beers with coworkers and customers. For example, Jeremy, a white man in his late thirties who works as a craft beer sales representative, sees having an authentic interest in craft consumption as an important quality in taproom service workers:

JEREMY: You got to have a passion for the product, passion for the industry.

EW: what does it look like for somebody to come across as having passion for the product?

JEREMY: It can be just body language. Or a certain tone when they talk about the beer. Like, we ask strange questions like, "if you were stranded on a desert island and you could only drink one beer in unlimited supply, it just showed up, like what would that one beer be and why?" However they describe that beer, *if they really get into it*, I think that is one way [to assess passion for craft beer]. Their body language, tone of voice, that sort of thing.

Jeremy stresses that workers along the service pathway should be able to talk fluently about specific craft beer brands by drawing on stories of their own elite consumption habits that include beers that are expensive or rare. To Jeremy, workers who "really get into it" are those who succeed in jobs along the service pathway.

Among the service workers I met, men are more likely than women to emphasize aspects of craft consumption that are focused on oneself rather than focused on service work. Recall that for Sheila and Maya, their respective relationships to craft consumption remain partly rooted in developing their knowledge and skills *in order to better serve customers*. By contrast, Sam, a thirty-one-year-old white man who works as a brewery sales repre-

Figure 6. Merging work and play in the artisanal office.

sentative, explains what he sees as a general best practice for hiring service and sales workers in the industry: "So the best thing to do is send somebody [out to retail accounts] who's passionate, who loves your beer, maybe who already bartends too. If you can't afford a full-time salesperson, just have him go around the bars and just start selling beer." What Sam idealizes in craft service workers (note the gendered language he uses here) mirrors his own personal identification as an avid craft beer consumer who loves particular brands.[21] To these men, being a walking, talking, nonstop beer lover—qualities still more socially acceptable for men than women—can be a mark of distinction within the service pathway.

Some men employed in taprooms frame their continued employment decisions based on consumption preferences, such as seeking a job within one company or choosing to leave another based on the quality of beer being made there. They suggest that their personal career choices hinge in part on taste distinctions.[22] For example, Ricky, a skinny, white man in his late twenties with clear-frame glasses, used to work full-time for a brewery in Charlotte, North Carolina, for five years doing sales. "That brewery used to have excellent sours, do some really cool stuff," he explains. "Then the brewery started to cut corners. The beers started slipping as the brewery owners were spending less money per batch. It got tough to sell the beer for me when I knew the quality wasn't the same. Eventually, I quit." Ricky's new job is at a tiny brewery with a staff of five but a big following on social media. Ricky explains his decision to seek a job at the brewery: "This was the spot that I liked most. I think they do awesome milkshake IPAs and kettle sours, crazy stuff. I was hanging out here all the time. Eventually the guys asked if I wanted a job." Five months into his tenure, Ricky has been given the responsibility of opening and closing the bar himself, though he is not considered a manager there yet.

Ricky embodies craft consumption in the sense that his decision to quit working a service job at one company to join another was prompted by his desire to work for a company that aligns with his personal tastes in beer. He conveys that his desire to consume the very best of these products has been a key driver of his job moves along the service pathway. Like Ricky, men I talked with are more likely to subscribe to this approach to managing careers along the service pathway than women, though it is important to note how this kind of craft consumption is also shaped by workers' privileged class and race statuses.[23] The workers most likely to see a personalized, inward-focused version of craft consumption as a barometer for continued participation in service jobs are college-educated white men for whom these standards feel intuitive and meaningful.

Both women and men employed in taprooms who see their jobs as desirable do so in part because these workplaces represent buzzy social scenes high in symbolic value. Yet men are more likely to emphasize how these scenes are ones they personally participate in as both work and play. Below, a server named Orlando, a thirty-five-year-old Latino man, describes why he originally sought a brewery taproom job:

> It was something that was new, it was so *cool*. The beer tasted great, it wasn't like anything I'd ever had before. Just the vibes, everybody was really cool, man. It's somewhere you'd hang out even on your day off. Like I said, I was there a lot. That beer weight caught up with me pretty fast because I was just hanging out drinking after my shift! [*laughs*] Some nights I'd get off at eight and I'd be there till like two in the morning just hanging out with the

coworkers, just because they were all great people, man. It was just like, *why do I want to leave?* This is a cool spot.

Orlando says he did not arrive at his job equipped with extensive knowledge about craft beer. Rather, the primary reason Orlando pursued working at a craft brewery was in order to be among "cool" people in a workplace with a "vibe." Orlando was hired at this brewery as a weekend bouncer—a racialized, entry-level position typically held by working-class men of color. Yet in staying well after clocking-out time to continue drinking beers with his friends at the brewery, Orlando signaled his "fit" within a cool workspace as a proxy of craft consumption. He was promoted to the ranks of the primary service staff in the taproom, where he stayed for two years before getting let go by new management.[24] Orlando now works at a nearby brewery taproom in a similar service role.

Perceiving brewery taprooms as "cool" and comfortable spaces of craft consumption has a racialized dimension. Enrique, who is a twenty-nine-year-old, Latinx worker who identifies as nonbinary, draws a distinction between their relationship to craft beer and that of their colleagues, in particular white men. Enrique says, "I can't tell you how many times I'll overhear my [white] coworkers talking about staying after their shifts to do a 'bottle-share' of stuff they've brought in *themselves*. I'm like, when it is time to go home, *I'm ready*." Enrique clearly differentiates their personal relationship with work from that of their colleagues. Yet precisely because cultivating craft consumption through making extra commitments to craft consumption is such a valued practice in these spaces, workers from minoritized racial groups are less likely to feel at home in these workplaces and less able to pursue careers along the service pathway in the long run. Many taproom workers say they appreciate the products their company makes, but only a privileged subset of workers sees these products as core to *who* they are.

"I'm Here for the Community"

Unlike her taproom colleagues who engage their jobs through craft consumption, Marne, the beertender at Dirty Shovel described in chapter 1, openly admits she is not particularly interested in craft beer.

More specifically, Marne dislikes the inward-focused connoisseurship of craft beer culture—or as Marne puts it, "being into beer for beer's sake." Instead, when Marne talks to customers who saddle up to the bar, she does so in ways that deliberately avoid flowery descriptors of the products she is selling: "It's cold, not too bitter, and it tastes good. Just drink it!" Marne also couples this with an alternate vision of her job: "Beer for me is more about community. Here in the taproom, we do poetry slams, we do comedy shows, we do fundraisers. We have district attorneys, district attorneys and senators coming into our place of business, looking at us as like a hub of the community." Fostering a sense of community in the taproom and allowing patrons to treat it as a home away from home is what motivates Marne's career—whether or not she remains in craft beer.[25]

Women working in brewery taprooms such as Marne are far more likely to emphasize the community aspect of what their workplaces represent to them than their colleagues who are men. Given their customer-facing roles, being "about" community can complement their brewery's efforts to expand their customer base and establish a family-friendly brand rather than one centered on selling alcohol.[26] Yet being more about community than the beer itself can potentially bring women workers into tension with others in their workplaces or the industry at large who emphasize craft consumption, especially those who are men. It would be hard to imagine Marne, given her approach to working in craft beer, having a successful, long-term career along the service pathway within a company whose motto is something like *beer is our passion*.

Fortunately for Marne, she has found a company in Dirty Shovel that shares a similar community-oriented vision and grants her sufficient autonomy to exercise this vision in the taproom during her shifts. In an industry defined by small companies that value authenticity, variation in company leadership can have a significant influence on the work environment that a given worker encounters. Marne's boss Lauren (also described in chapter 1) explains that because every one of her company's locations has a different local clientele, she tries to adjust her taproom to match the community's needs:

LAUREN: We're very much a neighborhood bar in whatever neighborhood we're in. I want people to make it theirs. It doesn't matter what I want it to be.

EW: So, you feel like this is the neighborhood's spot?

LAUREN: Yeah. Well, I think that that's a very interesting conversation to
        have. Because there are a lot of brewers that are like, "My brewer,
        my beer." And I love that. That's great for you that you're so pas-
        sionate about it. But, rather than trying to sell people my vision of
        what craft beer is, why don't you show me what yours is and we
        can celebrate that together?

Lauren takes pride in the fact that each of her brewery's taprooms feels
different. They draw different clientele, too, from a downtown arts crowd
at one location to an older, white-collar professional crowd at another. As
a brewery owner and manager, Lauren, who is white, strives to cultivate
"authentic" craft beer experiences in her taproom, though not necessarily
by being a walking embodiment of connoisseurship.[27] Instead, she strives
to hire workers who see the purpose of their jobs as helping customers feel
that they are consuming something made from the heart, served up by
people who care.[28]

Like Lauren, taproom workers also emphasize the crafting of community around the product. They hope to create a setting where customers
are able to, as sociologist Karla Erickson puts it, "consume familiarity,"
where trying artisanal beers exists in lockstep with more authentic service
relationships. This connects craft service workers and the companies they
represent to the local neighborhood contexts they are a part of. As another
woman who works as a taproom manager puts it: "we are giving our community a place to have *experiences*."

Lauren and Marne illustrate that fostering community through their
taproom jobs can be a key part of forging careers along the service pathway. This is especially true for workers who do not align with the dominant
group of educated white men in the industry and the passion for craft
consumption and craft production they instill in their companies. Being
community-centered can help some workers transform jobs initially
obtained out of happenstance into purpose-driven careers geared toward
creating a workplace ambiance that resonates with them. It is important
to underscore that this approach does not have traction in all craft beer
companies—especially those with a reputation for appealing to beer
"geeks" interested primarily in craft consumption. Marne, for example,

notes, "I literally had this conversation with one of my regulars today. He was like, I can't stand going to [nearby brewery] because I go in there and I get treated like some fucking dumb ass that just walks off the street without like a dime in their pocket. And I'm like, yeah, I get that vibe there too." By concurring with her customer on this issue, Marne corroborates that craft breweries foster community but also that these communities are not interchangeable. By working within a brewery that hosts poetry slams instead of bottle shares, Marne aligns with a more artsy community rather than one focused on cultivating elite distinctions.

"Is This Job Enough?"

Amber remains conflicted about her future along the service pathway—whether or not her bike tour guide gig pans out. Part of this is her shifting schedule and the fickle nature of working for tips, to be sure. But at a deeper level, it is also because her vision of what her career would look like along the service pathway conflicts with the more "professional" one she had long expected for herself using her college degree. As Amber explains:

> It is something that I kind of thought about after I got my biochemistry degree. You know, you graduate and you're like, well what am I going to do now? I'm going to stay in the brewing industry and keep serving for my whole life? Or are you going to, I don't know, try and get a job at a lab or something like that. Maybe I can stay in the brewing industry and then after I learn more about beer, trying to brew or be in some sort of lab, that would be ideal. If I could be at a brewery lab, I would be so happy.

In wrestling with different career possibilities, Amber is hardly alone in expressing ambivalence toward the prospect of forging long-term careers along the service pathway. Many taproom workers I talked with, particularly class-privileged women, struggle to grapple with how to manage jobs they find enjoyable and well-suited to their interests yet appear to have little room for advancement beyond frontline service. They do not see themselves as "temps" nor "lifers" within this industry—terms commonly used to describe restaurant and retail workers—but rather stuck somewhere in between.[29] Below, a worker named Mona expresses this tension by situating her brewery service job within her own changing life course circumstances:

> The only apprehension that I have is that I am aware that my compensation is only feasible because of the lifestyle that I have now. Like, I don't have kids, I don't have a mortgage. In five years' time, will this type of job, where I am out of town two to three times a month minimum, be realistic for me? Especially with the kind of money that I am making, not having a 401k, not having health insurance through my job. Like right now, *I am under thirty, but I am not an idiot, I know this is not always going to work.* And I don't have a lot of family financial support that other people in this industry do. I know that it is not going to be sustainable financially forever if it continues to be what it is.

The dilemma of good-for-now-but-maybe-not-forever proves difficult to resolve for many taproom workers, particularly those who do not subscribe to an inward-focused vision of craft consumption to give their jobs meaning. This is due in large part to the precarious employment conditions—low wages and lack of benefits, for instance—that these frontline service jobs often entail. As Mona alludes, it can also be a lifestyle issue, in that taproom-based jobs typically involve working late hours and regularly serving and often consuming alcohol, which can be a strain over time. For Mona and other college-educated workers, embracing jobs along the service pathway means having to rethink what sociologist Elena Ayala-Hurtado calls the "achievement narrative" centered on achieving future stable employment.[30]

One possible avenue to career advancement along the service pathway involves moving into taproom management. Indeed, many of the women and men profiled in this chapter have made incremental career moves in that direction over their industry tenures, such as by accepting "lead" service roles or frontline supervisory positions within their respective companies. But these microtransitions along the service pathway are limited in nature and scope: rather than representing meaningful career growth, workers talk of nominal wage increases and ceremonial title changes. Some of this is a function of operating within well-meaning but ultimately small, family-run companies with limited payrolls and flat job ladders. Workers who seek to advance into positions of greater authority also face gendered, racialized, and classed barriers. Given the fact that the majority of leadership roles in breweries are occupied by white men, a full-scale promotion into taproom management all but requires having access to well-connected networks as well as expressing a privileged cultural logic of work to guide one's career. Put differently, while both craft consumption and service experience are important for making microtransitions along the service pathway, it is the former that carries more weight for positions of authority because of how craft consumption is embedded within the culture of the industry.

Counterintuitively, some workers attempt to resolve career stagnation along the service pathway by treating their craft beer jobs less as objects of passion and using a more business-like, opportunist approach. Bert, a white man in his thirties who was formerly a craft beer sales representative, explains the perspective he has gained on what it takes to succeed in these careers:

> From my perspective, the people who did the best are people who don't have passion in beer. People who are clever and play the system. I was very passionate about craft beer and it weighed heavily on me. I didn't want to accept money from one brand [to sell their beer] that was paying me because I'd like another brand. To people who are just trying to collect a paycheck, they play the game. I remember the people who did the best, especially at [larger company], they had really great relationships with their accounts to the point where they could say, "Hey, can you work this deal for me? I get paid $100 if I do this [sell a particular brand]." So, the account would buy it from them in cash and then credit it to another account to get a placement and there would be some sketchy deals. They played the game.

Bert articulates a "careerist" approach that he believes helps some people turn service jobs into gainful long-term careers in the industry. By "playing the game," these workers prioritize opportunities to make money through their jobs, such as through higher tips or sales commission. But he also acknowledges the inherent challenges of doing this for people like him, who turned to these jobs initially out of personal passion for craft consumption. Bert thus points to a contradiction: working craft service jobs in breweries is enjoyable because of how it aligns with one's leisure tastes, but treating this job as a career requires sacrificing some of what makes it enjoyable in the first place. Now, as a sales representative for a software company, Bert says he has reclaimed what he originally loved about craft beer, which is being a part of a "beer geek" scene focused on craft consumption (though not necessarily based on industry employment). He still goes back to visit his old coworkers in the industry, this time as a customer and not a coworker. This way, he figures, he can maintain a close relationship to craft beer without jeopardizing his upwardly mobile career ambitions.

Other workers have been able to chart new career paths along the service pathway by breaking down taproom service jobs into marketable, career-building skills. Below, a sales representative for a craft beer distributor explains his approach to advancing in his career:

> I'd be disappointed if I'm still in my same job [in two years], I can tell you that. I should be moving up. And probably headed toward beverage equipment sales more broadly. Right now, I'm doing 100 percent beer sales. I'd like to shift more toward wine and a bit of spirits. There is more money in that, and logistically it is easier. Like for wine equipment sales, there is no hot-side equipment . . . the barrels don't need special jackets, heating stuff that needs to be calibrated. It is much simpler, which makes sales easier. So, something like 60 percent beer, 30 wine, 10 liquor equipment sales would be ideal for me.

This man's approach to employment illustrates another gendered component to managing career development in craft beer.[31] He strategically positions his expertise as something not specific to either craft beer or too closely tethered to frontline service work. Where he envisions an opportunity to pivot his career away from the feminized service pathway through business entrepreneurial savvy, Amber, Sheila, and Mona continue to face a structurally limited career trajectory within craft beer and thus an ambiguous work future.

.   .   .   .   .

This chapter began by asking, how do workers employed in brewery taprooms and other craft service capacities approach their careers, and to what end? The women and men described in these pages, who are mostly educated, white, young adults, hold conflicted career perceptions about their employment along the service pathway in craft beer. On one hand, many find that these jobs appeal to their personal tastes and identities; it is work that "fits" them individually and complements what they want out of their work lives. Jobs along the service pathway also offer workers the opportunity to labor in settings where they and their peers usually "hang out," albeit this is more true for men than women. On the other hand, many of these same workers struggle to articulate where their jobs will take them in the future as they grapple with unstable hours, late nights, and other lifestyle considerations that rarely approximate linear, upwardly mobile, professional careers.

As workers such as Amber, Marne, and Jeremy illustrate, workers both move through the service pathway and frame their careers in ways that are nuanced by social distinctions. While many educated, white, young adults describe "falling into" these jobs, women are more likely to transition there from previous service jobs, owing to the gendered nature of this employment, whereas men transition into these roles mostly from being customers prior. Both arrive squarely within workplace scenes that prioritize *craft consumption,* which lends meaning and distinction to these jobs. Yet it tends to be class-privileged white men who embrace a version of craft consumption that is an immersive work-leisure lifestyle, centered on oneself and one's personalized interests. By immersing themselves within taproom social scenes that center craft consumption, these men align themselves with their coworkers in the brewhouse as well as those in positions of authority within these companies.

Women such as Marne and Lauren are more likely to see taprooms as extensions of community and hold this rationale up as the engine of their careers. For these workers, being "here" for the community while at work can be personally fulfilling; it gives their jobs distinct value that can complement a version of craft consumption that has more to do with taking care of customers. Workers feel strongly that wherever they go with their careers—Lauren with her taproom locations, Marne with her intended entrepreneurship—fostering community will be at the core. This community orientation can resonate within certain workplaces in the industry that champion these values as signs of authenticity as well as a value-driven enterprise. But especially for women from less resourced backgrounds, leaning into a community orientation toward their individual careers runs the risk of reinforcing their subordinate position within feminized roles along the service pathway. It can confine them to careers of limited growth within an industry that remains dominated by white men and the privileged cultural logic of work they espouse.

In an industry that prides itself on authenticity and informality, it is important to note that craft breweries today vary considerably in the kind of "vibe"—to use Orlando's term—they seek to cultivate in their workplaces. This in turn patterns the day-to-day experiences of workers. The superficial elements of this "vibe" may draw more public attention—a brewery's macabre-themed beers or graffiti-covered interior walls—although the way that jobs and job activities are socially coded within the workplace have a larger impact on how workers envision long-term career possibilities with these spaces. As I have noted, most taprooms incubate a workplace atmosphere built around craft consumption. While the activities associated with craft consumption are not exclusionary in any explicit sense, they stem from the tastes and interests of workers from dominant social groups and can thereby marginalize workers who do not see their jobs this way. Within this industry climate, too few companies strive to be come-as-you-are spaces that truly embody Lauren's words from earlier: *what is your vision of craft beer, and can we celebrate that together?*

We turn next to examine the careers of workers in the industry that are responsible for neither creative production nor tasked with cultivating craft consumption. Stepping onto brewery loading docks and into warehouse packaging areas, the workers we meet next navigate invisible and racialized jobs done behind the scenes. Against all odds, some of these individuals manage to see themselves, and their careers, as the glue to their company's whole operation.

4 Embrace the Shit!

PRIDE AND COMMITMENT ALONG
THE HARD LABOR PATHWAY

It is three o'clock in the afternoon and Bobby is sitting on a wooden bench near the entrance of Mountain Brewing's taproom holding a full pint of golden-hued ale. He is surrounded by other members of the brewery's distribution "team"—four other men and one woman. "These guys call me 'Distro Dad' because I'm the oldest one here. I'm like their dad," Bobby says to me. "You can call me that too, if you'd like." He smiles and lets out a soft chuckle that I can barely hear over the din of laughter in the taproom.

Before arriving at Mountain Brewing, Bobby—the Native American man who we first met in chapter 1—says that his work history had been a series of twists, turns, and dead-end jobs punctuated with the occasional bout of unemployment. He landed in the craft beer industry not by design or prior work experience but by complete happenstance. One day, when browsing an online job board, his girlfriend saw a brewery warehouse job and suggested Bobby apply. The job didn't pay much and was listed as entry-level. But Bobby recalls that it caught his eye because it advertised steady hours and didn't require industry experience or a college degree.[1] Bobby applied. "I was so nervous during the interview. I thought I bombed it," he says. "I couldn't believe it when I got the callback." Two weeks later, he began his first day on the job at Mountain Brewing.

Bobby is now one of the longest tenured employees at the brewery that is not part of management, having just made his five-year work anniversary.[2] He still doesn't describe himself as "passionate" about craft beer: "at least not like Charlie [the owner] or Alton [the head brewer] are—the brewery is their *baby*," he says. However, Bobby has come to appreciate the career he has built for himself as "Distro Dad" in other ways. "The ownership, they praise me for what I do. And they look after me. That's why I'm still here," Bobby says. "I've been in some companies where they really don't give a shit. You know, they don't care: as long as the workers do their job, they're fine. But here, Charlie always says if you have a problem, you can come to your boss. I never thought I'd be at a company where they would actually take care of somebody."

.　　.　　.　　.　　.

Each day, distribution workers such as Bobby put in long hours in the craft beer industry doing a variety of physical labor tasks that the public will never see. They perform jobs that do not get talked about in news stories and social media posts celebrating the "rise of craft beer" or the up-and-coming entrepreneurs remaking the new urban economy. Instead, Bobby and his peers quietly load heavy pallets of kegs, bottles, and cans into trucks; they drop off product orders along scheduled delivery routes and keep the packaging lines humming along without a hitch.

Working-class men of color are disproportionately employed along the *hard labor pathway* in craft beer. This is partly because, as previous chapters have described, workers engage in unequal kinds of employment microtransitions along racialized, gendered, and classed career pathways in the industry. Through this process, working-class men of color find themselves circulating among some of the least desirable jobs in this predominantly white industry, jobs that more closely resemble blue-collar manufacturing jobs than modern craft work. These jobs are undesirable not so much because of their particularly low pay or volatility relative to other positions within the industry—few workers of any kind believe they will get rich in craft beer—but rather because distribution jobs do not involve access to either creative tasks of authority, which are mostly in the brewhouse, or opportunities for craft consumption and community-building, which are mostly in taprooms. In short, distribution jobs don't possess the qualities that makes some people seek out work in craft beer.

Why is it, then, that Bobby and other distribution workers say they are committed to invisible jobs within this industry? What does employment that takes place in warehouses, loading docks, and delivery trucks offer to them? I unpack this puzzle in the pages to follow by highlighting the career perspectives of workers along the hard labor pathway as they continue to unfold. As we will see, some working-class men of color feel they have found employment that, while far from perfect, reflects what they expect out of their jobs and how they want to see themselves through their work. These individuals voice a strong sense of pride in their ability to work hard in physically demanding capacities while filling "essential" roles within their company's small-scale operations. By framing their labor—and by extension, their work identities—as distinctive complements to their white and class-privileged coworkers along the creative and service pathways, I show how distribution workers like Bobby forge careers that can be meaningful yet subordinate at the same time.

RACIALIZED HARD WORK AND WORKING-CLASS MASCULINITY

At Mountain Brewing, the distribution tasks required to keep operations running smoothly make up the "backstage" of the craft work that takes place there. These routine tasks, which include packaging beer, cleaning kegs, loading delivery trucks, and restocking retail shelves, are repetitive and physically demanding.[3] They are also considered entry-level jobs and subject to some of the lowest wages in the industry, usually only a few dollars an hour over minimum wage. In most craft beer companies, with the exception of the very smallest operations, distribution work is typically assigned to a separate team of workers, much like how back-of-the-house work in restaurants is delegated to a cadre of line cooks, prep cooks, and dishwashers.[4]

Demographically, most distribution workers continue to be white and male, which mirrors the industry overall. However, working-class people of color, especially men, are disproportionately employed along the hard-labor pathway relative to their small numbers in the industry at large. For example, while less than 1 percent of brewers are Black and 4 percent are Hispanic or Latino, workers categorized as "nonbrewer production staff," are 4.7 percent Black and 7.8 percent Hispanic or Latino—the highest proportions of either racial group in any area in the industry.[5] Similarly, among workers in the nonbrewer production staff area, just under 14 percent are women (by comparison, roughly half of customer service staff members in the industry are women). These racialized, classed, and gendered patterns of labor in subordinate jobs of physical labor are hardly unique to the craft beer industry. As noted in this book's introduction, a large body of research describes that less educated people of color are often employed in precarious jobs near the bottom of the workplace hierarchy.[6] In low-level manual labor jobs in particular, these workers also tend to be men.[7] One reason for this social stratification in the labor market is that employers, in addition to favoring socially privileged workers for the most desirable roles within their companies, look to staff low-level jobs with workers who they perceive will be tractable and thus easier to exploit. For example, sociologists Margaret Zamudio and Michael Lichter find that employers in the southwestern United States favor Latinx immigrant workers because they perceive these individuals to be "good soldiers" willing to follow job orders without making a fuss.[8] Some employers also avoid hiring workers they perceive will have a "bad attitude" toward marginal jobs, and tend to think that both Black and white Americans are more likely to exhibit this attitude.[9] This employer-led process can perpetuate racist hiring outcomes that designate people of color, particularly those from immigrant and lower-class backgrounds, for marginal jobs— should they get hired in the first place. It also compounds other existing disadvantages that workers from under-resourced backgrounds continue to face in obtaining higher quality jobs, such as acquiring educational credentials and developing professional networks.

Bobby's turbulent employment history illustrates this tangle of issues. Recall that Bobby initially sought out a job at Mountain Brewing because he encountered few other job opportunities and was tired of enduring a revolving door of precarious employment. Bobby's hard-working approach toward his job—along with the appreciation he shows toward his boss who hired him—has helped him keep his job. At the same time, Bobby's attitude toward his entry-level and relatively low-wage position also makes him an ideal worker for the type of subordinate job in the industry that many of his white and class-privileged peers would find undesirable.

Explaining why people in "bad" jobs sometimes see their work positively is a complicated story. For one, social psychologists have long noted that people tend to evaluate their own situation not in objective terms but relative to those around them and in light of previous life experiences. More specifically, workers justify their work using different kinds of "occupational rhetorics" that have meaning, including how workers subjectively understand "good" work.[10] These personalized and deeply contextual relationships to work are also shaped by social identity. As we saw in the last chapter, class-privileged white women and men tend to seek out jobs where they can consume work because these jobs fit well with their social, consumptive, and lifestyle interests. Other studies find that working-class men derive a sense of dignity from doing blue-collar jobs proficiently and reliably.[11] They affirm their version of masculinity by casting themselves and their approach to work favorably compared to others, which can include women in feminized jobs as well as more class-privileged men employed in white-collar settings.[12] Existing research thus helps us understand that a person's idea of "success" in their work life must be understood in subjective terms, and that ideas about successful careers are textured by race, class, gender, and other social identities.

Many of the workers in this chapter employed as delivery drivers, canning line operators, and draft line technicians see their jobs as part of a throughline of racialized hard labor and working-class masculinity. Their approach to their careers differs from their colleagues along the creative pathway and the service pathway who describe their careers using the language of passion and craft consumption that corresponds to distinctive identities, such as artisanal masculinity. All of this sharpens the contrast between workers in the industry and, by extension, the divergent career pathways they proceed along. Nonetheless, Bobby and his distribution colleagues continue to manage their careers in craft beer in ways that are personally meaningful, building from what they already know and what jobs in this industry offer them. Some come to see value in long-term employment with "good" companies that are small and tight-knit rather than faceless and corporatized. At the same time, these workers risk becoming further entrenched along subordinate pathways of work because their approach to work differs from the *pure passion* for craft beer evident among workers in positions of greater authority and visibility in the industry.

Embrace the Shit!

When I ask Lamar to describe what he does at his brewery, he simply holds up his calloused hands with palms facing me. "This," he says. Lamar nods to his smudged and dirtied work shirt and faded jeans for emphasis. "It takes a toll on you." Lamar, the draft technician who we first met in chapter 1, explains that he is the kind of person who can handle this work. But not everyone is cut out for a physically demanding job fixing draft beer lines and moving heavy equipment for forty hours or more a week. This is also the reason that Bobby, the worker who led off this chapter, says he has seen coworkers come and go over the years:

> There was a swinging door. People would get hired and they would leave just because it's hard work. Distribution is not a joke. Everybody thinks it's just delivering beer. But once you come here in the morning, it's fucking go. You better be ready to go, go, go, go, go. And that's what it is. And they always ask like, "You don't take a break." And I know you're supposed to take a break, but once you're on the road, you should already have a lunch or maybe snacks because if you take a break for thirty minutes, you're going to lose your window for the next delivery.

As Bobby notes, few people are fully aware of the daily challenges of distribution jobs in craft breweries—including many of his coworkers in the taproom and brewhouse. But rather than see this as a point to gripe about his job, the physically demanding aspects of distribution work make Bobby swell with masculine pride. It is *he* who is able to "go, go, go, go," not others. It is *he* who has the fortitude to endure long hours and difficult conditions at work, often in defiance of company mandated breaks and work hour limitations. Bobby's coworker Josiah (described earlier), a former distribution worker who is now a "cellar" worker in the brewhouse, shares this relationship to his job. Josiah explains, "my mentality is, *embrace the shit. Nobody cares. Work harder.* Just keep your head down. I don't really care for praise either. I just want to get in, do my job the best I can, to the best of my abilities."

Josiah and Bobby convey pride at upholding high standards of integrity on the job as well as being seen as self-disciplined and trustworthy workers.[13] These men embody working-class masculinity by carrying themselves with dignity at work, even if only they and their direct peers and supervisors appreciate these efforts. While aspects of their jobs may be "shit," it is how distribution workers deal with these aspects through grit and toughness that transforms them into sources of pride and work identity.

This sense of accomplishment in jobs along the hard labor pathway also has a material dimension. The objects that distribution workers regularly handle in the workplace are heavy to push, lift, load, unload, and dispose of. Doing so without a fuss is important to many of these workers, especially men. This was evident during my visit to a midsize craft brewery in Albuquerque called Rusty Plow Brew Works (Rusty Plow, for short). When I walked into the brewery, Jack, a white man with a high school degree and broad shoulders, was busy piling sacks of specialty malt into a heap in front of the brew kettle. As a newly hired assistant in the brewhouse with no prior industry experience, Jack was sweating through his blue t-shirt and tan-colored work jumpsuit while performing a variety of "grunt work" tasks, in his words. He explained to me that each bag of malt weighs 55 pounds. To make his point, Jack challenged me to try and pick one up to see for myself how heavy they were. When I struggled to lift a bag, he picked up two for good measure, bellowing, "They don't call me a keg gorilla for nothin'!"

Several hours later, after Jack had finished sweeping and mopping the floor, he and I went next door into the taproom to talk about his job. "I am much more of a physical labor kind of person," says Jack, who worked for nearly a decade as a metal welder. "I just like working with my hands a lot and so I've no problems working here. And being the keg gorilla." Jack draws attention to the fact that jobs along the hard labor pathway are, at their core, manual labor jobs that rely more on a pair of strong hands than formal education credentials, craftsmanship skills, or emotional labor. By claiming the title of "keg gorilla" proudly—a nickname originally given to him by his coworkers in awe of how he handles heavy kegs with ease—

Figure 7. Hard work behind the scenes at a small brewery.

Jack signals his masculinity through physical feats of strength at work. By comparison, the way Jack frames his relationship to the physical objects he works with is starkly different from how his class-privileged counterparts working as brewers relate to these same objects. While Jack takes pride in picking up and transporting kegs—working-class masculinity rooted in physicality and toughness—the class-privileged workers are more interested in carefully crafting the products used to fill these kegs and thereby asserting their artisanal masculinity.

The gendered ways that distribution workers relate to the physical requirements of their jobs is evident in other ways. For example, many craft beer companies provide workers with equipment to make the physical tasks of their work easier and safer. Yet several workers I observed, including Jack, did not use this equipment, choosing instead to deliberately handle it themselves, without assistance, as a point of pride. This unwritten standard can present problems for others, especially women. Mona, the taproom worker described last chapter, explained to me that when she was first given a tour through the warehouse, she immediately observed that many of the tools and machinery there were designed for taller and physically stronger bodies. So, too, were management's expectations for how to use this equipment. She explains her approach to doing the physical tasks of her job this way:

> I don't feel like I have to break a glass ceiling or anything, but the first brewery event I worked I made a point of dramatically moving everything by myself. To show I could do it too. Because a lot of other breweries, the way they set up kegs is so girls can move them. Or they make sure girls don't close up the brewery at the end of the night because they don't want girls to be in the taproom alone. Like, maybe not official policies, but unwritten rules, that girls can't do things, girls aren't supposed to do things. So now, that's why I made a dramatic effort to move things myself a couple of times. It was to show that I could. Because now, when other people offer help, I know they are doing it to be helpful, to be nice. Because it is a very physically demanding job.

As Mona illustrates, women ("girls") who work in and around distribution often feel they must demonstrate their physical ability when performing tasks because they perceive that this physicality is expected and even celebrated among their colleagues who are men.[14] By deliberately lifting kegs herself when setting up for events and foregoing the use of "girly" aids to make the job less physically demanding, Mona signals she can hang with the guys at work and fit into their masculine work culture. However, doing so may have come at a personal cost for Mona: after only a few months working her distribution job for a small brewery, Mona asked her boss if he would switch her out of distribution and into customer service work.

Similarly, interactions between coworkers in both the warehouse and brewhouse can also normalize physicality and roughhousing on the job. Jordyn, the brewer we met earlier, describes a situation that occurred behind the scenes in the warehouse at her previous company:

[A male coworker of mine] kept poking and poking and poking and poking and poking. And then I finally was like, "All right, do you want to do this?!" and I took him down. I can't even remember what *jiu jitsu* hold it was that basically choked him. And he was like, "Okay, okay, okay, okay. I'm done. I tap." But in order to get on this guy's level, it's almost like you have to basically either show them who you are and what you're capable of, or prove to them who you are and what you're capable of. So it's an interesting spot to be in because comparatively, my encounters could probably be considered very minor. If I wasn't who I am, they would be considered major. You know?

Jordyn feels that women are routinely called on to prove they are physically capable in order to gain, and maintain, respect in a male-dominated warehouse. By interacting with her coworkers who are men using the language of violence, toughness, and physicality ("in order to get on this guy's level . . ."), Jordyn proves that she belongs in this space. Workers like Jordyn illustrate how the physicality of these jobs goes beyond the work itself and gets wrapped into the pride distribution workers feel about their jobs that is both gendered and classed.[15] Choosing to embrace the challenging aspects of their jobs rather than minimize them can reinforce key aspects of workers' self-concept, which fits most snugly with the version of masculinity that working-class men express through employment along the hard labor pathway.

Invisible Jobs and Good Work

Sonny, a burly, fifty-six-year-old white man with a graying goatee, takes pride in his role "greasing the wheels" of the Albuquerque-based brewery he works for. Now a distribution supervisor, Sonny spends his days managing the schedules of his distribution crew and coordinating maintenance repairs for the draft systems at the company's multiple taprooms. If one of his crew members calls out sick, Sonny fills in after hours or on days off by making emergency deliveries of kegs and equipment. Much of what Sonny does for his company is invisible to both customers and coworkers alike. Filling this role is satisfying to him nonetheless:

After we got the draft system up and running last Friday, that was one of the things I enjoyed. I got the system done. It worked. And we didn't have any kind of problems with it. So, I'm good to go, right? Those are those little things where I can go: *all right, yeah, I did a good job on that.* Even if I don't get any recognition for doing that from anybody else. It's just a little self-fulfillment, I guess.

For Sonny, the joy of his job is less about accumulating splashy accomplishments like industry awards or being able to flex creativity or craftsmanship. Instead, Sonny relishes doing smaller, behind the scenes, mechanical tasks that he sees as his unique role and responsibility within the company (making sure "everything goes off without a hitch"). Setting his own schedule, Sonny fixes a tap system here, makes an extra run to the warehouse to avoid running out of a beer there. Some of the tasks he does go beyond his formal job description. Other tasks, Sonny explains, are the result of poor planning and cost-saving maneuvers done by company management.[16] Regardless of the reason, doing these tasks brings men like Sonny a sense of pride and dignity for doing good work—work that is personally meaningful because it allows them to contribute in unique ways to their company's mission to satisfy customers.[17] Sonny recalls a recent work experience that illustrates this point:

> When we were doing self-distribution and I was cleaning lines and doing deliveries, I would have a little bit more contact with customers. As a matter of fact, just yesterday I was going through the taproom and there was an elderly couple standing there. The guy says, "Hey, I just got to tell you that your beer is fantastic." He says, "We're from Wisconsin. The stuff that you guys have on right now is top notch. I can't get over how good it tastes." And then the woman asked me, "What are you doing?" I told them: "I'm maintaining the beer lines. We clean these beer lines every two weeks in order to prevent bacterial growth and keep the beer tasting good." And the guy is listening and says, "You guys got a great company. It's a great set-up. Whatever you're doing, keep it up." That was pretty cool.

Men like Sonny who work in distribution jobs stress the importance of *doing things the right way,* even if people rarely notice. The recognition Sonny describes receiving from the brewery patrons that day is noteworthy because it is the exception to the rule. It stands in stark contrast to taproom or brewhouse workers who regularly receive compliments for the service they provide customers or the beers they have recently crafted,

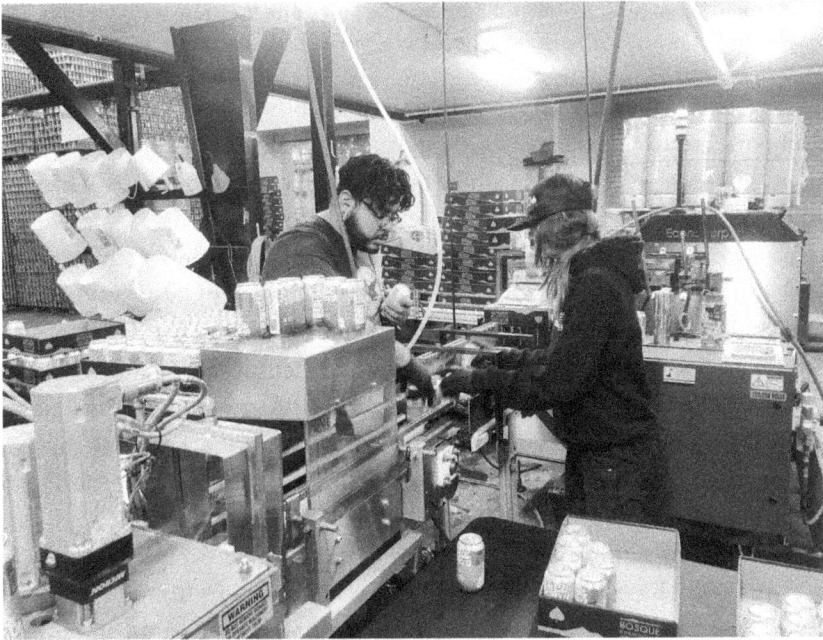

Figure 8. Workers overseeing the automated canning line.

respectively. Instead, many distribution workers emphasize the essential importance of the behind-the-scenes upkeep that they perform for their companies each day, such as cleaning beer lines. These men affirm a quiet-yet-tough, working-class masculinity by dismissing the need for praise for doing good work, not seeking it out.

Other distribution workers share Sonny's perspective toward jobs that are less visible and accorded less authority in the workplace. Daniel, a Latino man in his late twenties employed as a distribution worker at a Los Angeles–based brewery, describes what he likes about his job:

> I'm working two positions not only managing the warehouse and its day-to-day operations, but also doing the delivery driving for them. I think at the end of the day, I feel accomplished, for sure, because I was able to do that, and I was able to do this, and nothing is left undone. Nothing is incomplete. I've been told that my work is appreciated. Is that enough? Yeah, sometimes it's enough to be recognized, like, you are a vital person right now, maybe just for right now. Not to say I'm not replaceable, but for right now, for this

moment, I am pretty vital and I am getting shit done for them with no com-
plaint. I come in with a good attitude every day. Let's say that.

Workers such as Daniel take pride in their ability to work hard for their
companies until the job is done. In the quote above, Daniel places emphasis on how he goes about his job rather than what this job entails. This, he
perceives, makes him more "vital" to management and less replaceable.
Other working-class men of color I talked to share Daniel's commitment
to doing the job "the right way."[18] Paco, a Hispanic man in his mid-fifties
with a high school education, says that he has built his entire career based
on this principle, a career that spans over two decades.

When Paco lost his kitchen job in the mid-1990s, a friend suggested he
apply for a job in a brewery. His friend told him that the work was similar
in nature to cooking in that it involves following recipes and procedure,
using his hands, and maintaining rigorous cleaning standards. "I didn't
know anything about brewing beer back then, didn't even know what a
brewery was," he explains. Despite having no formal training in brewing
beer, Paco proved a quick learner. He eventually moved into the brewhouse under the tutelage of his company's head brewer and owner (who is
a white man). To this day, Paco tries to impress the principles of being an
industrious, procedure-oriented worker onto new hires:

> What I learned in restaurants was that most cooks have bad habits, okay?
> They're going to come in and try to do things their way. But as a chef or a
> sous chef, no—you have to stifle that immediately. You're not there, you're
> *here* now. You are going to learn it our way and unlearn bad habits.

These days, given his senior position at the brewery, Paco sits in on hiring decisions for both entry level-jobs in the brewhouse and in distribution. The blue-collar qualities Paco values in new hires are the same ones
that he attributes much of his own career success to: discipline, attention
to detail, and commitment to hard work. For example, when I asked Paco
who he admires in the industry, Paco immediately answered by describing
a working-class Latino man named Javi with a similar background in
racialized physical labor:

> That guy has an incredible work ethic. It's funny what got him in the brew-
> house: he applied for the cleaning position we had available and I'd watch

him work. When he'd clean the pub, he would move the tables from one side of the pub itself and sweep underneath the tables and everything. Mop underneath them. Clean up and move the tables to the bar side over, sweep, mop the floors. Do that every day. When he would go out to the patio and clean the patio, he'd do the same thing with the patio tables, sweep. We had two guys that did it, it was Javi and another guy. The other guy would sit there with a water hose and push it up from under the tables in the patio and stuff. Javi would move the tables and sweep.

To Paco, Javi is the kind of worker who would rather keep his head down and do the job he is asked to do without being told twice. He is the kind of "good soldier" who takes pride in doing a job the right way even if no one is watching, taking on more work as needed.[19] Further, Paco reasons that these qualities hold special importance in an industry like craft beer that is full of people passionate about what they do but sometimes with shoddy attention to detail behind the scenes.

It remains the case that working-class men such as Paco receive far less attention and accolades within the industry than their bosses, who are most often white, class-privileged men. Yet the former are able to frame themselves as integral to the success of their companies, because in their minds, they are the ones taking care of essential, invisible tasks that would otherwise go ignored. In this way, workers such as Paco feel they have found "good work" in supporting roles within their workplaces: positions that are less about hefty paychecks or creative autonomy and more about the meaningful roles they play in relation to their jobs as well as their colleagues.

Other distribution workers find opportunities to appreciate what their jobs offer them relative to past employment experiences in relatively low-wage, racialized positions. A good example of this is Daniel, the distribution worker described earlier. Daniel's first warehouse job was working for a toy distribution company in his early twenties, where he had to inventory, receive, and process stuffed animals for carnival games. He did this job for seven years until he and his girlfriend decided to move to another nearby city. Daniel says he searched job ads for another distribution position, eventually finding one at the craft brewery where he currently works. There, Daniel works among in a team of five men—two Latino and three white—in a warehouse facility separated from the primary brewery and taproom; at the warehouse, most of the delivery workers from other companies he comes in contact with are Spanish-speaking, Latino immigrants. "It's funny, I don't consider myself fully fluent in Spanish—like, I'm more comfortable speaking English—but when I talk to those guys, I slip into Spanish full time. I'm just rattling off things in Spanish, you know?" says Daniel. Describing his distribution coworkers, he notes: "most of the other warehouse guys, they just want to go home to their families after they are done with work, not come here [to the taproom]. And if we want a drink, we have it over there."

A real eye-opening experience for Daniel occurred when he decided that he would head to his brewery's taproom for a free "shift beer" each day after clocking out. While this put him at odds with his distribution coworkers, it also added new value to his job in the form of exposing him to craft consumption. Daniel explains: "It wasn't until I actually came to hang out here in the tasting room and meet the brewers that I got my first taste of, oh, *this* is what this business is like!" After several months of post-shift drinking in the taproom, Daniel has learned to appreciate the wide range of products his company makes and has even gotten to know some of his coworkers responsible for innovating these products. This has deepened Daniel's appreciation for his distribution job in craft beer in ways that break from his past experiences in these jobs outside the industry.

Some workers who do eventually leave their companies do so with reservations. These reservations, in turn, illustrate their approach to their careers and what they value. For example, one man, who is biracial (white and Latino) and has a high school degree, describes the brewing company and his boss he previously worked for this way:

> The owner actually took pretty good care of me over there. He gave me insurance, he even gave me money to go check out other breweries and stuff like that. It wasn't very much, but it was enough to go try some beers and stuff like that. And I never asked for anything from anybody. I never asked for a raise, and it just wasn't—it's not my style. If they say, hey, you've been working your ass off, here's a raise. I'm like, cool. I'm not going to ask them and if it's a place that doesn't do that, then I shouldn't be working with people like that.

This man began as a general "assistant" to the head brewer and then later moved into a formal role as a brewer. Despite this title change, he describes working behind the scenes at his former company with little formal recognition and marginal wages ($16 per hour), even for the craft beer industry. What he did have was more important to him: access to health benefits, daily job perks as well as a boss who he felt genuinely cared about him. In his view, it was these traits that kept him loyal to this company for more than five years. When I asked about what caused him to finally leave, he described a changed relationship with his former boss:

> He's got a lot of shit going on, he's balancing all kinds of shit. So he wasn't always really paying attention because I was just under the radar and he's like boy, you keep the beers going, you're working your ass off all the time. It was just time to move on. And I'm happy that I did.

As the quote above illustrates, many of the distribution workers I talked to say they contribute to their companies by working hard and doing good work. Much of this labor goes unseen. When it also goes underappreciated by the people they work for, workers look elsewhere for employment as they try to find a new opportunity that allows them to realize their particular career vision.

Growing with "Good" Companies?

Toward the end of our conversation, Sonny made a comment that stayed with me long afterward. I had just asked him about whether he had any plans to open his own brewery—after all, I reasoned that Sonny had worked nearly a decade in a variety of positions for a successful brewery, including in distribution management.

"I have no passion to brew beer. So no, I'm not interested in opening my own place," said Sonny without any hesitation. "But I *do* have a passion to work for a good company, one that continues to grow while taking care of its employees."

Sonny's use of "passion" to refer to the company he works for rather than his personal love of craft beer took me aback. In talking with dozens of head brewers and brewery owners, the prospect of being passionate about a "good company" along the lines Sonny describes rarely came up. Brewers, particularly those who are class-privileged white men, were far more likely to talk of pursuing their self-centered pure passion for brewing. This often required moving to *different* companies to do so rather than staying with just one. By contrast, Sonny voices a career logic more common among his colleagues employed along the hard labor pathway and from less-privileged backgrounds. It is a career logic that decenters craft beer—the opportunity to make it or consume it—as the key criteria of a meaningful career.

For example, Jorge, a twenty-three-year-old Latino man with a high school education, describes his current distribution job in relation to his previous jobs outside of the industry.

> I'll say over and over again, this is the only company that I've felt it is almost a family.
>
> At [the water distribution company], everybody they just did their work. They would talk to you in the aisles, because it was a big warehouse, but everybody generally kept their head down and did their work. Which I'm fine with, that's how I've made my money. But here [at the brewery], everybody is really open. They've embraced me. The first day I walked in, the taproom manager comes up to me like, "hey! How's it going?" We started having a conversation, and I tell her that I'm looking for Sonny. And she's like, "oh, you're the new guy!" And that's how the company has been, they've been really open and laid back. At my previous two companies, there was always this question in my mind, would I be able to do this until retirement? I couldn't say that. They did pay me good money but it was like *you work for us, you do what we need you to do.* You were expendable. If you didn't do the work, somebody else would.

Working in a friendly and communal atmosphere at the brewery has changed Jorge's perspective on his work life and career expectations. He draws attention to how he is treated by his company rather than the specifics of his job tasks and evaluates his current employment positively in light of his past labor experiences.

Like many other working-class men employed along the hard labor pathway, Jorge's career remains firmly blue-collar and characterized by low-skill physical labor that is racialized, classed, and gendered. But working in craft beer has also textured this experience. Rather than loading products onto a truck in a large and anonymous warehouse environment, Jorge now does these same tasks in a setting where he is one of only three people in his company with this responsibility. Plus, Jorge now has a relationship with his coworkers who appreciate the role he plays within the company. After clocking out, he sees his coworkers heading to the tap-room to hang out for a "shift beer" rather than going their separate ways ("everybody kept their head down and did their work").

To be sure, Jorge's glowing assessment of his job at River Bend may have been shaped by the fact that he had been there only two months by the time we talked.[20] He was quite possibly in a "honeymoon phase" with his job. Yet Jorge is not alone among distribution workers who make posi-tive comparisons between their current jobs along the hard labor pathway and past ones they've held outside the industry that involve similar types of hard labor on paper. For instance, one delivery driver, a white man with an associated degree, drew a contrast between his company's culture to his previous work experiences in the restaurant industry:

> It is a complete and total revolution of how we are able to just be a family. And it's because when you love what you do and you're happy with what you do, it is just different. Like, the head brewer could say to me, *Hey man, we need you to stay until 5:30 to knock some of this stuff out.* No problem, bro!
>
> I genuinely felt with every other job I was at, no matter how good I was, if I got into a car accident and I passed away, they would be like, "Oh, no. That sucks. Okay. We need somebody to cover. What are we going to do? How are we going to work?" I genuinely feel like if something happened to me here [at the brewery], not to be weird, but it feels nice to know that my boss and my coworkers would all be like, "What the fuck? How do you replace that?"

As the quote above illustrates, some distribution workers cherish working for small companies in this industry that they feel are genuinely interested in taking care of their workers in both material and immaterial ways. Doing routine physical labor on the job may not necessarily stoke their personal passions for craft beer or evoke their "love" for their jobs. But clocking in at a workplace that is tight-knit and supportive can inspire them to work hard and remain loyal to their employers. Within this con-text, and inscribed with a working-class career approach, these workers find other ways to find meaning in their jobs, such as taking pride in being the kind of person who will respond to requests from their boss with an unconditional, "No problem, bro!"

·   ·   ·   ·   ·

Seen from one perspective, working-class men of color who are disproportionately employed along the hard labor pathway contend with racialized, classed, and gendered employment that is perpetually low wage, invisible, and structurally subordinate within their companies. Much of their daily labor involves low-level and physically strenuous tasks, which, in the eyes of their more privileged coworkers, make for distinctly undesirable careers. Yet as sociologist Vicki Smith notes, how workers come to feel about their jobs is often a more complicated matter, one that can be better "explained by their own occupational trajectories—where they have been, where they hope to go, and what they perceive as possible."[21]

Unlike many of their colleagues, especially those employed along the creative pathway, distribution workers such as Paco, Daniel, and Jorge do not seek out jobs in this industry out of pure passion for craft beer. Instead, they prioritize finding jobs that offer relatively stable employment consistent with what they already know and how they see themselves. Through expressing pride in hard work instead of pure passion for their jobs in craft beer, these individuals assert a working-class masculinity. It is within workplaces like Mountain Brewing and in relation to workers who approach their careers differently where working-class men derive a sense of responsibility, identity, and purpose through jobs along the hard labor pathway. While landing in craft beer may have been arbitrary at first (though often consistent with a longer trajectory of racialized and gendered employment), navigating employment in this industry can also shape their subsequent career perspective in unexpected ways. Working for relatively small "good companies" guided by values like authenticity and an ethos of passion for what they produce can be eye-opening. As Jorge and others note, it can be a welcome contrast to what workers see as their precarious employment options within companies that tend to treat workers as "expendable" (to borrow Jorge's words).

As much as working-class men in this chapter are able to make long-term employment along the hard labor pathway their own, jobs along this pathway can also be exclusionary toward women. This is because of how workers play up physicality, roughness, and sometimes even violence in ways that augment their sense of working-class masculinity. Among the small handful of women I met with experience in hard labor jobs, most felt they must approach their jobs in a similar way in order to fit in, such as Mona and her heroic efforts to move heavy kegs all by herself to prove a point. Mona's departure from her distribution job to a customer service job is also telling. In response to a distinctly gendered, as well as racialized and classed, workplace subculture in which they represent an ill fit, some workers find themselves pushed and pulled into different jobs, while others may choose to exit the industry entirely.

Distribution workers remain segmented away from the dominant workforce within the industry with limited ability to advance up company hierarchies beyond the hard labor pathway. This is in part because of the way the routine tasks of distribution work play a supporting and largely invisible role to craft production and customer service. It is also because of how the dominant cultural logic of work in this industry reinforces the position of class-privileged white men while framing other approaches to work as second fiddle. As much as workers along the hard labor pathway take pride in their ability to put their heads down and work hard, this remains an industry that idealizes people who express pure passion toward the artisanal products at the center of it all. For this reason it is worth noting that many of the working-class men of color who express enthusiasm for their distribution jobs are relatively young and new to the industry. This may make them more likely to focus on the perks of working for a small, family-like company relative to more corporate settings where they would do similar jobs. Some will inevitably follow workers like Paco and Sonny into gendered, working-class careers along the hard labor pathway. Others may struggle to justify their employment over time in the face of stagnant mobility and perpetually invisible work.

Which brings us back to Bobby, who, about an hour and a half into our conversation at Mountain Brewing, begins to recline against the wall, his eyes slightly glossy. "This one's on me," he says, a slight slur to his speech as he tells our server—a brunette woman with fair skin and a sleeve of tattoos on her left arm—to bring us another round of beer. "You have to try this new one that the brewers came up with. It's some new barrel-aged beer. I can't explain it. Tastes *bomb* though. And high in alcohol, which I like."

I ask Bobby if this is what he wants to be doing the rest of his career. The swiftness of his answer surprises me, like it is something that is never far from the front of his mind.

"I know I gotta get back home to the reservation. That's where my heart is. That's where my family is." Bobby isn't sure what he will do for work on the "rez." Except that it probably won't be in the beer industry given limited distribution channels coupled with the ongoing stigma of alcohol in his family. "But," he adds, perhaps remembering our earlier conversation, "I'll be here until then."

As I leave for the evening, I linger on Bobby's sentiment. *He will leave a good company to get closer to who he is.* There is a certain irony to this, given that many of his college-educated, white peers enter craft beer precisely to align their careers with who they feel they are and what they love. Does this always need to be a zero-sum trade-off for people like Bobby? I turn to this issue next chapter, where we examine how some minoritized workers, facing an industry replete with social and cultural standards of whiteness, class privilege, and masculinity, find new ways to make their careers speak to who they are and the issues they stand for—issues that go well beyond craft beer.

5 "It Could Never Be Just about Beer"

Arturo, a thirty-two-year-old Latino man with a penchant for fedoras, is determined to make Urban Roots Brewing succeed. Arturo cofounded the Los Angeles–based company with two friends a decade after they started homebrewing together. Back then, Arturo had just graduated from a prestigious public university in California and was still trying to figure out what he wanted his career to be. "I like working with my hands. I like getting into it," says Arturo. "I think brewing offered me that outlet of doing something that was very involved, not just mentally but physically as well." The creative process of developing recipes and then brewing them himself also appealed to him. "There's style guidelines that are set forth by the BJCP[1] that are like, *an IPA should be this, a stout should be that, and a Pilsner should be this*—that's if you really want to get technical and submit things for competitions and things like that," explains Arturo. "But in craft beer, you also have creative freedom to incorporate your own twist, your own culture, your own wants, your own flavor into that particular style. It may no longer be to style, but whatever! It's your creation, it's your idea."

"What's an example of that?" I ask.

"We're like, what can go well with stout?" he says. "Stouts are chocolatey, rich. What about *mole, pipian,* and things like that? Because our background is Mexican, Guatemalan, and Cuban, we're like, 'let's add some *guajillo chiles*, some *pasilla, ancho*, some dark chocolate to the beer,' some of those main ingredients in creating *mole*. The stuff we grew up with, you know? We do a *cafe de olla* brown where, in the boil, we'll add piloncillo, star anise, clove, orange peel, cinnamon, a lot of the ingredients in *cafe de olla*. And then we'll add coffee as well. We've had people drink it that didn't necessarily know what it was say, "Oh, this tastes just like *cafe de olla!*" I was like, *yeah, that's what we're going for!* That tells us it works, right?"

As much as Arturo and his cofounders take pride in the distinctive beers that Urban Roots produces, this alone is not what drives their company. Arturo recognizes that Urban Roots is among a small but growing number of Latinx-founded breweries in an industry that continues to be mainly white, especially among the ownership class. This awareness has directly influenced his approach to building a career for himself and his company:

> I feel like there's always this sense that we owe it to our community to bring them with us, right? I think people of color, or minority owners, are a lot more intentional about that. We owe it to them. Like *each one teach one*, right? If I'm getting this capital, I'm going to share it. I'm going to spread it too, because I want to open resources and spaces for others that might not have had access to those spaces before. I want to make it accessible. And I think minority-owned businesses are a lot more intentional about making things accessible and not necessarily foreign or inaccessible to the community.

·   ·   ·   ·   ·

Arturo's story about founding Urban Roots Brewing feels very familiar in some respects. As we've seen in previous chapters, many craft beer workers cherish the ability to express their personal values, authentic identities, and distinctive tastes through their jobs. Brewery owners proudly infuse their companies with motifs that reflect who they are, such as mountain biking gear or heavy metal insignia; brewers craft recipes using an ever-changing array of unique ingredients and new techniques; and taproom workers refashion their workplaces as sites of craft consumption and camaraderie for like-minded customers.

Arturo is also keen on these aspects of working in craft beer, but there is more to his story. As a brown-skinned Latino man, Arturo, along with his two other Latinx company cofounders, is attempting to carve out a place in an industry where his social characteristics inevitably make him stand out from the crowd. This both complicates and enriches his experience. Being surrounded by mostly white people (men) at craft beer events—where everyone always seems to know each other—makes Arturo hyperaware of his outsider status and the myriad challenges this could pose for him, his company, and others who look like him and aspire to enter the industry. This same reality has also given Arturo a sense of purpose of what he is trying to do with Urban Roots and with his own career: he wants to run a company that suits his interests while simultaneously giving back to his community.

This chapter asks: how do minoritized workers such as Arturo negotiate their work identities and creative career aspirations in an industry that remains predominantly white and male? Answering this question starts with recognizing that workers of all kinds do not experience their labor environments in universal ways but rather as a function of their intersecting race, gender, and class statuses, as well as that of sexuality and age.[2] A large body of research shows that minoritized workers often struggle to identify with, and advance within, workplaces associated with members of dominant social groups. They must instead learn to operate in settings where the very notion of what it means to be "professional" or be considered an ideal employee is closely associated with whiteness and masculinity.[3] As sociologist Adia Harvey Wingfield notes, workers of color employed in these environments often end up shouldering a disproportionate amount of "racialized equity labor," such as by becoming the de facto point people for conversations about diversity, or being tasked by management to lead nonwhite client interactions.[4] For similar reasons, women working in highly masculinized professions such as engineering must adapt a blend of coping strategies and impression management techniques to navigate everyday interactions with colleagues in an attempt to frame respectable work identities.[5]

This research deepens our understanding of minoritized worker experiences at the intersection of race, gender, and class within workplaces and industries. Most existing studies on this topic focus on large organizations with a hierarchical power structure and uniformly white leadership.[6]

However, this overlooks how variation and change at the organization- and industry-level context may influence how minoritized workers are able to frame distinctive work identities and navigate unique career moves. For instance, there is some evidence that smaller and more flexible organizations have greater potential to improve the employment experiences of women and people of color, as do work contexts in which the gendered and racialized valuation of work is less fixed.[7] This would imply that in settings such as the craft beer industry, work norms and values may be more customizable than in their highly corporatized counterparts, making it potentially easier for people from a wider range of backgrounds to feel they belong. Yet in other ways, the overwhelming presence of educated white men and their privileged expressions of pure passion for craft beer may limit the range of work identities and career possibilities available to workers in the long term.

This chapter also offers critical insights into the ground-level experiences of minoritized workers in their places of employment at a time when diversity, equity, and inclusion (DEI) workplace initiatives are gaining rapidly in popularity. Many workplaces today, including those in the craft beer industry, claim to champion DEI efforts and do so by hosting company-wide conversations, employee trainings and contracted workshops, and public messaging. While these initiatives may not be new—organizational efforts to support diversity go back decades[8]—the prominence of these efforts, especially set within small, flexible, and "authentic" organizations, shape the context within which minoritized workers navigate their careers in this industry.

As Arturo's story illustrates, many of the craft beer workers featured in this chapter construct work identities that reflect their ambivalent identification with industry standards as well as their minoritized status within industry spaces. By threading parallel objectives in their work identity that selectively engage their race and gender identities, I show how these workers express what I call *marked professionalism*.[9] Marked professionalism contrasts the normative and idealized relationship to work espoused by members of dominant social groups, including the expectation that workers should exhibit *pure passion* for craft beer above all else (see chapter 2). Instead, some minoritized workers in this industry construct racialized and gendered work identities that strategically extend beyond being "just" producers, distributers, and servers of craft beer.[10] As we will see, workers attempt to expand what it means to be a craft beer professional by drawing more attention to social causes while selectively highlighting aspects of their social identities that align with business goals. Moreover, enacting a marked professional identity complements other efforts by individuals to forge employment along a possible *social equity pathway*, one in which job opportunities draw explicit attention to minoritized social identities and related social issues.[11] However, the long-term viability of the social equity pathway remains fraught due to the limited number of such positions available in small and fast-changing companies, as well as the fact that, for workers, navigating this pathway relies heavily on the entrepreneurial efforts of individuals who must simultaneously grapple with their marginalized position within the industry more generally.

SOCIAL CHANGE ON TAP?

In recent years, the social homogeneity of those who participate in the craft beer industry as workers and consumers has been the subject of growing critique.[12] Fueled by a larger nationwide conversation about social injustice in US society, many craft breweries have engaged in formal and informal efforts to make their industry and its workplaces more inclusive of women and people of color.[13] These new initiatives have received overwhelming public support from breweries, industry observers, and consumers alike.[14] Between 2020 and the first half of 2021 alone, over two dozen DEI initiatives were launched within the industry and in support of workers from underrepresented backgrounds.[15] These include the "Road to 100" initiative, which seeks to support 100 women in pursuit of a Cicerone certification, which is similar to a wine sommelier certification; the Michael Jackson foundation, which offers brewing education scholarships for Black and brown workers; and "CraftXEDU," which aims to promote equity and inclusion through offering educational opportunities to members of underrepresented groups. The sheer number and variety of DEI initiatives in the craft beer industry has generated cautious optimism from observers about the prospects of improving demographic diversity within the industry. As beer journalist Beth Demmon writes, "Though far from perfect, the grassroots spirit of craft beer has made it a model for the drink industry's larger push toward diversity and inclusion."[16]

Seen from a different angle, the fact that predominantly white and male breweries and industry associations seeking to maintain a positive public perception have devoted considerable resources to DEI efforts should surprise no one. Further, research shows that the efficacy of company DEI initiatives for improving the employment experiences of minoritized workers has been mixed.[17] Organizational sociologist Elizabeth Gorman notes that specific actions that organizations take, such as diversity recruitment programs for potential workers and diversity training programs for supervisors, can improve the opportunities that underrepresented groups face within these settings.[18] While some types of diversity efforts have been shown to increase opportunity for women and people of color—the groups most commonly targeted by diversity initiatives—they can also promote backlash from supervisors and coworkers.[19] One study finds that mentoring and networking initiatives helped women navigate the organizational landscape otherwise dominated by men but did nothing to reduce managers' biases toward these workers.[20] Similarly, Kaiser and colleagues find that company prodiversity programs can lead workers from dominant social groups to presume organizational fairness and dismiss further claims of discrimination by minoritized workers.[21]

Indeed, some critical scholars argue that "diversity ideology" within mainstream organizations largely upholds existing social hierarchies and power structures.[22] As sociologist Joan Acker notes, many DEI-focused projects within organizations fail because they do not address the fundamentally gendered, as well as racialized, social systems and their associated beliefs that the organization is founded on.[23] With the root cause of inequality left intact, change agents hired at the behest of upper management—like the initiatives they champion—often fail to achieve their stated goals. From this perspective, it is *through* diversity discourse rather than in spite of it that decision makers perpetuate cultural ideals of whiteness and masculinity within organizations. In these settings, the rules, culture, and identities circulated by management and among employees reinforces the position of members of the dominant group, which in turn makes it difficult for women and people of color to not only access upwardly mobile opportunities but also identify with the organization.[24]

In light of changing conditions in craft beer, women and people of color employed in these settings face ambivalent pressures that signal their value within the company while simultaneously maintaining their "otherness" in different ways.[25] I now show how minoritized workers in craft beer enact a marked professional identity in three distinct yet overlapping ways: (1) by using their roles within the industry to support social causes meaningful to them, (2) by seeking to expand the definition of industry professionalism to go beyond that of beer-focused expertise, and (3) by strategically highlighting parts of their social identity that align with company goals. In each case, the way these individuals assert their work identity strategically incorporates their social identity in ways that resonate with their companies and can potentially lead to opportunities for their individual careers.

Brewing for a Cause

Chandra and Ty, both of whom are Black, college-educated, and in their mid-thirties, have come to see their participation in the craft beer industry as inherently political. The fact that they are often the only people of color operating in the respective spaces of employment shapes their daily work experiences. Chandra recalls one such moment while visiting a brewery for work: "There was this one [Black] guy I met out in the Thousand Oaks area. And I was like, 'how is it for you out here?' And he's like, 'honestly, it doesn't matter.' *But he got really excited to see me at a brewery.* We both geeked out with each other for a while. We were excited to have an opportunity to talk beer and just be excited that there were other people [like us] who really love it." Chandra conveys a sense of surprise at seeing a fellow Black person working in craft beer, something that led to a bonding moment. Ty puts things in more blunt terms. In recounting the challenges that he and his brewery cofounders, all of whom are men of color, faced in opening their small, LA-based brewery, Ty notes, "we have to be good politically. We have to get good at what we're doing. Because honestly, it's not meant for us. The whole entire brewing industry isn't meant for us. It's not built for us." While Ty did not elaborate further on this comment, later in our conversation he noted the challenges that he, as a Black man, has had securing loans to fund his operation, which is a racialized barrier to access in this industry as well as many others. For Ty and Chandra, operating within institutionalized white male space within the craft beer industry has brought their minoritized race and gender statuses into sharp relief.[26] It also continues to affect the way they enact their work identity by attempting to develop ties within the industry while grappling with constant questions about their belongingness.

Ignacio, a thirty-nine-year-old Latino man who recently launched a brewery with several other members of his family, tries to use craft beer as a platform to support social causes relevant to the community he grew up in. Before entering the craft beer industry, Ignacio worked for a decade as a community organizer in East Los Angeles, a heavily immigrant and Latinx area of the city. During this time, he developed an interest in homebrewing, which became more serious after he joined an all-Latino homebrewing club in the area. In deciding to cofound a small brewery along with several of his family members, Ignacio strives to integrate his love of craft brewing with his long-standing career vision of supporting social justice and community building. "[Starting my own business] was something I wanted to do. It was never necessarily about beer. But once beer came about and fit within all these things—or I could at least make it fit within all these things—and people liked it, it just kind of kept going, you know?"

For Ignacio, starting a small brewery near where he grew up in a heavily Latinx neighborhood represented an entrepreneurial opportunity that could "fit within all these things," rather than a wholesale switch of his professional identity and career. Retaining his passion for social equity issues was an important factor in Ignacio's decision to open a craft brewery of his own. For instance, Ignacio and his co-owners recently launched a series of beer releases in which half of the proceeds are donated to a local charity that supports members of marginalized groups in need. His brewery's most recent release partnered with a nonprofit celebrating the labor of undocumented Latinx workers in Los Angeles. By engaging in what sociologists Jody Vallejo and Stephanie Canizales call "social entrepreneurship," the value-centered business norms of craft beer have given him the flexibility to build his company how he sees fit.[27]

Ignacio's friend Esteban, the social media influencer-turned-brewery-owner described earlier, also uses his growing platform within craft beer

Figure 9. Los Car Washeros: a benefit beer for undocumented car washers, made at a Mexican-American-owned brewery near Los Angeles.

to highlight the culture and lifestyle he grew up with—one that he says has little in common with the existing "white bro" culture of craft beer:

EW: Tell me about the kind of stories that you want to try to prioritize for #BeerGangster. Are there some things that you want to showcase on that platform, IG [Instagram] or whatever, over other stories?

ESTEBAN: Yes. People know me by chugging beer but that's not just it. #BeerGangster ain't just about chugging beer, man. That's what it started as, that's what got us on the map a little bit because the chugging beer thing, the videos and everything. But I just want to showcase my community. I want people to know that, hey man, it's cool to come over [working-class neighborhood where Esteban is from] and enjoy beer. And we're good people too.

Esteban recognizes that his status as a prominent "beer influencer" stems in part from the novelty of seeing, in his words, a "Cholo"—loosely defined as a Latino man who dresses and acts like a gang member—deliberately chugging some of the most sought-after craft beers in viral social media video posts. Esteban's decision to chug beer instead of sip it in small quantities is deliberate. Chugging craft beer subverts norms for "expert" evaluation of beer, which, according to a leading certification program for beer professionals, involves systematically assessing the aroma, color, mouthfeel, flavor, and aftertaste of the beer from specialized glassware befitting of the beer style, such as snifter for stouts and tall and narrow glasses for pilsners.[28] Instead, Esteban trades in these standards in favor of capturing what for him is a more authentic relationship to beer and beer drinking. He rejects conventional standards while celebrating his working-class Latino identity as well as the neighborhood of south Los Angeles where he was born and raised. As Esteban's "beer influencer" status has grown—his number of followers on social media is now in the five digits—he has expanded his brand to incorporate collaboration beers with local hip-hop artists, professional athletes of color, and Black and brown craft brewers. "I see myself as a bridge, not a divide. I'm all about bringing new people and cultures together using craft beer," he explains.

The notion of "bringing people together" through craft beer can sound generic, a slogan that nearly all brewery owners would agree with in principle while in practice upholding the status quo. Instead, the distinction is in the details. For workers such as Carly, a forty-three-year-old, college-educated white woman with short-cropped blond hair, her commitment to advancing social justice in her career is evident in how the business she helped to found is fundamentally structured. Carly explains:

There's a lot of generous breweries who try their best to connect with their communities and donate what they can. We are different in that our purpose for existing is to be a community-based brewery that is choosing instead of keeping its profits to reinvest them in our communities. So that's really where the line is.

Like Ignacio, Carly spent years working as a community organizer prior to entering the craft beer industry. By founding her brewery using a social enterprise license instead of a traditional business license, Carly planned a company model from the ground up that returns profits to the local organizations she partners with.[29] As Carly puts it, social justice aims are "baked into" her company by design. "For me, it was always about how do we get people invested in their community? How do we make sure that when people come in contact with [the brewery], they can understand they are part of this community?" says Carly.

Workers such as Esteban, Ignacio, and Carly assert their marked professional identity by using their visible positions within the craft beer industry to advance social agendas. They approach craft beer as a means to an end rather than the end itself, leveraging the flexibility of operating small businesses in an industry that emphasizes authenticity in the process. Instead of shedding their social identities in order to participate in an industry associated with whiteness and masculinity, they draw on aspects of these very identities as points of distinction to shed light on social issues they care about.

"It Could Never Be Just about Beer"

Derrick, a college-educated Black man in his mid-fifties who owns a craft brewery in New Mexico, did not initially think that publicly supporting Black and brown causes would be a part of his professional identity or career goals. It is not that Derrick did not care about these issues personally, but he wanted to own a company that was known for making great craft beer *first*. His perspective shifted as he gained more experience in the industry. Derrick notes that he had to continually confront his race when among his white industry peers. These experiences informed not only his daily strategies of "microresistance" but also his business approach moving forward.[30] His customers, many of whom are Black, called for him to offer lighter and sweeter beers to go along with traditional Southern fare. Derrick eventually shifted his business model. Upon opening his second brewery taproom, he deliberately chose to locate it in an underdeveloped part of the city home to a large Black community rather than in a predominantly white area with an established craft beer customer base.

Derrick also offers up his brewery space to local community groups, free of charge. "For me, it could never be just about beer," says Derrick, reflecting on his decade-plus of experience in the industry.

Derrick's use of "just" in his statement above is significant. He constructs a marked professional identity forged through craft beer but also *in reaction to* its dominant social and cultural associations. For someone like Derrick, identifying as an industry professional in a predominantly white industry always comes with a qualifier. By contrast, being "just" about beer—that is to say, singularly devoted to craft beer and brewing—is something Derrick says he often sees in his white male colleagues.

Other workers of color also frame themselves in reaction to racialized and gendered norms within the industry. Jerome, a college-educated Black man employed as a taproom manager, explains: "From the very beginning of me accepting a position in the craft beer industry, I said, *'just because I love drinking craft beer, I hope you know that I am not a beer guy.'*" Jerome makes a deliberate point of differentiating himself from "beer guys" in ways that go beyond drinking preferences and evoke social distinctions about who tends to be interested in working in craft beer. It is this relationship to the industry that those on the margins are all too aware that they do not, and perhaps cannot, fully embody.

Not all minoritized workers arrive in the industry with fully formed ideas about how social advocacy will factor into their job duties, identities, and career paths. This becomes clearer with time and experience within the industry. Jerome, for instance, says he did not have a "passion for DEI" at his job prior to the events of June 2020, surrounding George Floyd's murder at the hands of police and the protests that followed. Says Jerome:

> In our senior leadership meeting, our organization [initially] said, you know, we don't really get involved in politics. That's not our thing. And through tears over Zoom, I just said, after listening to everyone speak on the topic, to be a Black man in the US at this time, I have seen plenty of companies that have said something. And it may easily come across as cliché or just marking a box, for many others. But being who I am, I certainly take note of the companies whom I've given my time, attention, and money. Rather than stay silent. That led to our company starting to open their eyes more.

That day, speaking to his predominantly white leadership team at the brewery, Jerome found a meaningful way to contribute to the conversation as well as a new way to frame his own career purpose. Jerome could not have predicted the confluence of events that led to this moment. But the shift in his perspective was notable all the same. As a case in point, a few weeks before I spoke with him, Jerome had organized and led a professional workshop for brewery owners on how to make taprooms more inclusive and welcoming for people of color.

Many other workers who assert a marked professional identity stake a claim in the industry that expands beyond beer expertise. Like Jerome, this expertise can stem from personal experiences in craft beer that ultimately reshape their sense of career purpose. For instance, Yareli, a queer Latina woman and one of Arturo's cofounders of Urban Roots Brewing, says that a light bulb went off when she realized what made patronizing craft breweries comfortable for her: it was about *who* she brought with her into these spaces. Yareli explains:

> [When I would go to breweries] I was surrounded by my community, like, lots of folks of color and queer friends and partners. It was just very diverse. So when I was experiencing these spaces I was never alone. It was always with *my* community. That helped to shape my understanding of what these spaces could be.

Similarly, Erica, a thirty-one-year-old Latina woman, explains her perspective on her job as a manager at Desert River Brewing Company:

EW: what is the experience that you're trying to cultivate at Desert River? Has that changed over the years?

ERICA: I think that it's become much more community-minded, about relationship-building. Whether that's coworkers with each other internally, coworkers and customers, community partners and coworkers. Before, it was like, "What does our logo look like?" and, "How do our cans look?" Those are all important, and they all feed into this monster that is Desert River. But now it's a lot more relational. There's this personal sense of: how can we all be Desert River? . . . I want everyone who's involved in any way to be adding to that story. Storytelling and story-building is also at the forefront of my mind, too, and making sure that we're highlighting the people who work here and not just the beer and amazing opportunities in the community to find out more about New Mexico or water rights. I think storytelling [is] almost being, I don't know, a space for learning, for hard conversations.

Erica's initial strategy of managing her brewery's brand was business-first and value-free ("how do our cans look?"). Yet this is exactly what has changed for her over the last couple years, which coincided with her move into company ownership. At Erica's insistence, Desert River has taken deliberate steps to promote and invest in DEI in the workplace, making the brewery's clientele aware of these social initiatives in the process ("we lost a few regulars during this time," Erica admits). Both Erica and Yareli now assert that building gathering spaces of inclusivity and new kinds of "storytelling"—and educating their clientele about the value of doing so—are high priorities for them in their respective companies. It is a newfound voice that speaks to these workers' sense of purpose within the industry. "How will you know when you've succeeded?" I ask Erica. "It should just be a feeling when you step in the brewery, like, the feeling that, 'I belong. I feel comfortable here.' We are not there yet, but we are working on it," she replies.

White women and people of color also say they face an assumed lack of authority and expertise in their work settings.[31] This comes at the hands of both industry coworkers and customers. In response, some workers have sought to bolster their formal industry credentials to "prove" they belong. One woman of color in her early forties told me that her decision to pursue Certified Cicerone credentials—which requires passing a rigorous examination about beer styles, brewing technique, and beer service protocols—was her effort to signal her expertise to those who might otherwise be skeptical about whether she belonged in a position of authority in craft beer. To be sure, acquiring professional credentials is a common way for workers to build their professional pedigree in hopes of advancing in their careers. Yet minoritized workers were more likely to place heightened importance on the value of formal credentials relative to their colleagues who were white men. Given that women and people of color are already "marked" by their nondominant status, shoring up formal credentials can be one way to tilt a discriminatory playing field back their way, at least on an individual basis. As Chandra explains: "I have two master's degrees. Black women are some of the most heavily educated people because you kind of have to in order to open doors. Like, John [Chandra's boss, a white man] even said, I took this interview because you have the most amazing résumé. I'm like, thank you! [laughs]." Further, Chandra and Erica both perceive that their peers who are white men enjoy informal authority and assumptions about their expertise in craft beer in ways not granted to them. Their pursuits of professional degrees within the industry are efforts to hedge their careers within a system slanted against them.[32]

The inverse can also be true: the *absence* of industry credentials raises more eyebrows for minoritized workers than for white men. According to one brewery owner who is a white woman, soon after she accepted her first general manager position in the industry a decade ago, she was accidentally forwarded an email chain in which several brewery owners and head brewers in the industry had traded tongue-in-cheek remarks about who she had "slept with" in order to gain such a promotion. Proving that she had done no such thing to acquire her job required immense personal and professional resolve. It required not only becoming a professional with craft beer expertise but also a thick-skinned businesswoman able to navigate demeaning and offensive microaggressions from her industry colleagues. Facing systemic sexism in the industry emboldened her to build up her own brewery's culture in ways that would prioritize being more socially inclusive, particularly for women.

Selective Identities and Double-Edged Opportunities

The majority of workers we have met so far express racialized and gendered dimensions to their work identities that are formed largely in reaction to their underrepresented status in the industry as well as how they are perceived by their white male colleagues.[33] However, not all workers see this as a clear disadvantage for their individual career prospects in craft beer.[34] By representing "diversity" while also upholding existing professional standards in the industry, some minoritized workers enact marked professionalism in ways that align comfortably with their company's business goals. Doing so can also buffer these workers' personal microtransitions along the social equity pathway in ways that are tethered to specific company contexts and stop well short of contributing to industrywide change. Marisol, a thirty-year-old Latina woman who works as a brewer at a midsize brewery, illustrates this point. Marisol describes how she first got her job:

I think it helped that I am female. I'm not big into the female empowerment, but I know that was a big draw—although it wasn't a big deal to Brian
[a white man who was the previous head brewer and hired Marisol]. I do
know that [the brewery] likes the sound of it. Because when I became the
first female lead brewer for [the brewery], that's all it was, I did not have a
name anymore. I was called the first female lead brewer for [the brewery].

Within the context of an all-male leadership team, Marisol recognizes her
rapid promotion to head brewer may have had something to do with the
cachet the company gained by being able to say they "promote diversity"
through her hiring. Marisol generally downplays her gender and racial
status at work ("I'm not big into the female empowerment"), which may
have contributed to her ability to advance within a company that is otherwise run by white men. At the same time, Marisol also alludes to the double-edged sword of being the company's first *woman* brewer.[35] As a token
of diversity in her workplace, it is worth noting that few other women or
people of color have followed suit in advancing to higher roles in the company, especially along the creative pathway.

Other workers seize on their minoritized status to seek mentorship and
other kinds of career opportunities facilitated by well-connected colleagues from more privileged backgrounds. Luis, the Latino brewer
described earlier, emphasizes how key connections with white men in the
Los Angeles craft beer industry have helped him cultivate a unique professional identity in the industry:

LUIS: I've experienced white brewers and owners giving me an opportunity to
        bring a different perspective to the brewing process. With me, my experi-
        ence with the whole Hispanic and white community and the whole
        industry, I hate to say it, but I've enjoyed working with more white brew-
        eries than Hispanic breweries. I know there are plenty of stories where
        Hispanic brewers tried and it was a different story. But what I experi-
        enced was being Hispanic was a plus.

EW: What do you mean by that?

LUIS: Because I showed them that we're hardworking, we have creative flavors,
        creative techniques, and they saw me as a positive part. I can bring diver-
        sity to their brewery. They saw me as another option for adding new
        beers and more flavors. They saw a market that they never tapped into?
        At first, I was kind of like, "Oh man, they're just using me. I'm just the

token Hispanic." But it was nice because they gave me the recognition, the white breweries like [names two breweries], the ones I've worked at that are white. Then I go to [Latino-owned brewery] where it's more Hispanic, diverse and I'm like, "Oh, I'm finally going to fit in. I'm going to be with my other people. This is going to be great," but it was completely the opposite. They expected everything from me. They were, "You're the Hispanic, you just brew and make me money and do this," and blah, blah, blah.

Luis notes the relative ease with which white men in craft beer were able to support his own career development, specifically by linking him to opportunities along the equity pathway that leverage his distinct ethnoracial and cultural background. In Luis's view, it is in this industry context where "being Hispanic" is seen as a "plus." By highlighting aspects of his identity and culture rather than attempting to whiten them, Luis performs "biographical work" by mining his background as selective source material for his marked professional identity.[36] Doing so makes him and the beers he makes unique—just as it makes the white-owned company Luis now works for more marketable.

Some minoritized workers in craft beer are critical of what they perceive to be a growing movement to overly emphasize social identity over conventional standards of professionalism in the industry. While these individuals may acknowledge existing race and gender disparities in the industry, they stop short of pointing to structural sources for these patterns in their own companies, or the implicit whiteness and masculinity of industry norms and standards at large.[37] For example, Sheldon, a thirty-four-year-old Asian American craft beer sales manager, explains:

EW: Right now, in the beer industry, there's some local breweries [in the area] that are proudly talking about their race and their culture. What is your take on all that?

SHELDON: So yeah, I have a pulse on that, I see what is going on. Do I necessarily believe it is right or wrong? Diversity is great, yes. Forced diversity? Probably not as great. Like, if you are going to consciously make an effort to be diverse. It isn't natural, natural growth. So, there is nothing blocking Asians, Blacks—there is no one that has a fucking sign up that says, "you can't work in beer because you are Black." There is nothing like that. And especially in craft beer, it comes

down to your passion, your drive. In my opinion, very little of
it comes down to your race or ethnicity, color or skin tone. It has
everything to do with your attitude, your work ethic. But that is
just my personal perspective on life. [*laughs*]

Raised by a single mother in a "lower-middle-class" household, Sheldon
uses his own career experience in craft beer as a baseline. He emphasizes
how his personal ambition and drive to succeed in a system premised on
colorblind professionalism have contributed to his steady rise in the company ranks.[38] In doing so, Sheldon engages whiteness and maleness to
frame himself as suitably professional, or perhaps more accurately, suitably professional and safely diverse in a predominantly white setting.[39]

One thing that workers such as Sheldon, Marisol, and Luis share is that
their individual careers have received a boost through their proximity to
white workers in positions of authority as well as their personal belief in
the underlying value in existing cultural standards within the industry. In
stark contrast to Derrick's sentiment, for these individuals, keeping things
"just about beer" at work has worked out well enough. So, too, has their
ability to perform diversity through their marked professional identities in
ways that are strategically advantageous for themselves and aligned with
the interests of the companies that employ them.

.   .   .   .   .

The workers highlighted in this chapter are crafting careers that require
carefully managing their industry credentials alongside their minoritized
social statuses. Many feel they do not have the privilege of doing otherwise
in an industry dominated by white men and default assumptions
about employment coded in whiteness and masculinity. Yet, by selectively
incorporating aspects of their social identities into their work identities,
I have described how these workers enact a *marked professional identity*. This occurs in three distinct ways: (1) by using their roles within
the industry to support social causes meaningful to them, (2) by seeking
to expand the definition of professionalism to goes beyond that of
industry-focused expertise, and (3) by strategically highlighting parts of
their race and gender identity that align with company goals. Each of
these strategies can be individually rewarding to workers—giving their

careers a sense of purpose—just as they can sometimes open new job opportunities.

Forging marked professional identities also remains an inherently fraught process for workers from minoritized status groups, one that embodies agency asserted amid intersecting, social-structural constraints within the industry. This helps explain why not all white women and people of color engage in this form of identity work, and those who do vary in their use of different strategies.[40] To be not "just about beer"—to paraphrase Derrick's words—means standing apart from colleagues committed to just that logic, including many of those who occupy positions of power along the creative pathway in the industry. Importantly, I find that the white women and people of color most likely to enact marked professionalism are those who are already operating from positions of relative authority and visibility within the industry or are able to draw on other kinds of classed credentials such as college degrees to buffer their career prospects. It is this relatively privileged subset of workers, rather than their working-class peers in invisible jobs along the hard labor pathway, who can present themselves *through* social difference in ways that can help them access career opportunities along a tenuous social equity pathway.

The specific industry context of craft beer shapes how workers enact marked professionalism in their work lives. Despite the whiteness and masculinity evinced in many breweries, other aspects of these work settings may allow workers to forge alternative work identities and career paths. A key dimension of this is the value placed on authenticity and community within companies that are more flexibly structured compared to their corporate counterparts.[41] In the former industry context, owners may see workers who express marked professionalism as assets to their company's socially conscious ethos, just as consumers are likely to view workers' assertion of their social identities on the job as signs of authenticity.[42] Erica's experience serves as an exemplar here, whereupon gaining a leadership position in her company she successfully pushed for greater investment in social justice causes.[43] Furthermore, the expanding number of opportunities in the craft beer industry designed to support minoritized workers with funding, mentorship, and skill development could represent the expansion and diversification of the social equity pathway in this industry. The long-term viability of this pathway for workers hoping to forge careers in craft beer, however, remains tenuous. This is because many opportunities along the social equity pathway are limited in number (a lone DEI officer within a company) or temporary in nature (a three-month "diversity" fellowship or a marketing campaign on social inclusion). More so than in jobs along the creative, service, or hard labor pathways in craft beer, navigating the social equity pathway relies heavily on the entrepreneurial efforts of minoritized workers as they grapple with their marginalized position within the industry more generally.

One the most consistent themes among all types of craft beer workers is the unpredictable nature of their career paths. With this in mind: what more can we learn about these varied career paths and the social forces that shape them from workers who are connected to this industry but are not directly employed in it? In the last substantive chapter of this book, we search for answers by examining the experiences of former workers, industry consultants, and amateur homebrewers who operate along *alternative pathways* of work in craft beer.

6   Paths Less Traveled

SIDE PATHWAYS, HOBBYIST CAREERS,
AND DEAD ENDS

Alfred, a thirty-five-year-old head brewer with over five years of industry experience, has conflicted feelings about his role as a formal mentor and brewery consultant. He wants to support his current clients, who are mainly white, college-educated men and women in their thirties and forties looking to make a career transition into the industry or shore up fledgling business operations, but Alfred's own career in craft beer has left him feeling increasingly exhausted and disillusioned.

"The people who say they want to get into the industry, they are not stupid about it," says Alfred, scratching the back of his faded baseball cap absentmindedly. "They think there will be a pay cut to work in a job that is a lot more enjoyable than their current jobs. But what they don't realize is that the work is super repetitive and the pay is literally one-third of their current salaries. They are stunned to learn the craft beer industry is *that* low earning. Like, one woman I met with just a couple weeks ago who is currently an accountant, she just sat there trying to process what I just said."

A few weeks after our initial conversation, Alfred left the industry entirely. Offering advice to others, he later explained to me, was part of his last-ditch attempt to breathe new meaning into his career in craft beer.

But eventually he found himself unable to offer honest career advice to prospective brewers and brewery owners when this advice could not save his own career. "It was particularly hard for me because brewing was what I was *most* passionate about in life," says Alfred. "I still love the pure act of brewing. But I got chewed up and spit out by the industry part of it."

.   .   .   .   .

Many people who are employed in craft beer, or who aspire to be in the future, feel that building careers within small companies dedicated to things they love will bring their work lives in line with personal interests, values, identities, and preferred lifestyles. Of course, as previous chapters have shown, not everyone can engage their careers this way, and minoritized workers often get channeled into subordinate career pathways that offer fewer opportunities for creative authority and visibility. Yet, Alfred's story highlights a side of handcrafting careers in emerging settings of the new economy where passion and precarity can sometimes go hand-in-hand.[1] Despite enjoying access to the creative pathway, Alfred could not escape marginal employment conditions. This ultimately caused him to change the course of his work life in ways he could not have anticipated.

Thus far we have followed workers who are continuing to build careers in craft beer (albeit along hierarchical and socially stratified career pathways). What these individuals share is a relationship to their jobs as seen from *within* the industry. From an organizational standpoint, this offers a limited perspective on the forces that push and pull a given worker's career over time because it doesn't reflect the experiences of individuals who leave the industry or find other ways to participate in it. This is especially important to understand given the volatile nature of work in settings like the craft beer industry, as well as the highly individualized careers that many workers attempt to lead. Workers want jobs that "fit" them, but where these jobs will be located can change over time and sometimes from company to company. This chapter asks: what can we learn about the process of handcrafting careers from those who maintain alternative roles and relationships to this industry?[2]

In centering the stories of former workers, industry consultants, and amateur homebrewers, this chapter lays out three alternative career pathways in craft beer. I refer to these pathways, respectively, as the *exit pathway*, the *side pathway*, and the *hobbyist pathway*. Each of these pathways is distinct from one another as described below. Yet in all cases, I find that workers weigh the prospect of employment in craft beer against what they perceive as the pitfalls, risks, and barriers to building long-term careers in this industry. These alternative pathways provide us with further insight into what it takes to manage careers amid uncertainty and structures of work that are racialized, classed, and gendered. I show how workers featured in this chapter negotiate their *symbolic affiliation* with craft beer alongside the *material realities* of these careers. As these individuals reconcile their personal passions for craft beer with the precarious employment conditions they face, workers such as Alfred end up managing their relationships to their careers in ways that are distinct from their counterparts directly employed in the industry while also being shaped by one's access to privileged resources.

ALTERNATIVE CAREER PATHWAYS IN CRAFT BEER

Craft beer has expanded well beyond the confines of small, localized breweries and specialized bars and "gastropubs" of decades past. Today, with over 9,000 craft breweries in operation, a wide assortment of business suppliers, consultants, industry guilds, and professional organizations make up the world of craft beer.[3] Correspondingly, a growing number of people navigate craft beer along *alternative pathways* and in roles that do not involve direct employment in companies that make, sell, and distribute craft beer. I lay out three alternative pathways below before elaborating how individuals experience these respective pathways in ways that require reconciling their symbolic affiliation with craft beer with the material realities of employment in this industry.

Former industry workers such as Alfred constitute the *exit pathway*. Having previously spent years or sometimes even decades employed in craft beer, these individuals have seen firsthand the day-in, day-out work along existing career pathways within the industry.[4] They are also very familiar with the cultural logic of work in craft beer, including the expectation that workers will (and should) express pure passion for their jobs.

For this reason, leaving the industry—and with it, their professional net-works, skills, and titles—holds deep meaning for many of these individu-als. Charting the perspectives of former workers thus reveals the dark side of what it takes to forge long-term careers in this industry and what con-stitutes key tipping points toward career exit for some.

Workers engaged with craft beer along the *side pathway* are employed in capacities that support the expanding infrastructure of the industry. They operate as consultants or find jobs with mobile canning companies, brewing equipment manufacturers, specialized business law firms, and label design companies. People building careers along the side pathway provide services to core companies within the industry—breweries, mainly—that may not be able or willing to do them in-house, such as can-ning large amounts of beer or strategizing next spring's marketing cam-paign.[5] Some of these individuals resemble what organizational scholars Stephen Barley and Gideon Kunda call "itinerant experts," meaning peo-ple who possess specialized skills and professional networks that allow them to forge custom careers on their own.[6] Yet because the skills needed to do this job continue to fluctuate, workers are forced to adjust or risk becoming obsolete. For this reason, workers who hope to remain employed along the side pathway must retain a close relationship to the business dynamics of the industry and those who make these decisions.

Finally, individuals who operate along the *hobbyist pathway* engage with craft beer in ways that are decoupled from the commercial aspects of the industry and the formal employment paths that exist within it. For amateur homebrewers and beer competition judges and organizers, this sets their experiences apart from others described in these pages. Yet those along the hobbyist pathway do share what sociologists Rodgers and Taves call an "epistemic culture" with their professional counterparts, one that celebrates craft beer as a blend of art and science.[7] Both amateur homebrewers and craft brewers, for instance, expend considerable time and effort toward creating specialty products that emphasize quality and creativity, and many craft brewers get their start as homebrewers. As will be described below, serious hobbyists treat craft beer as a meaningful source of social engagement and creative stimula-tion, one complete with well-organized gatherings and events.[8] This allows them to connect to craft beer in ways that are highly symbolic in nature while maintaining a middle-class profession status and avoiding the industry's uncertainties.

Dead Ends and Career Exits

> Talk of a "fun place to work" is out of touch with [the
> brewery's] actual culture of chaos, stress and mistrust.
> —Jonah, former head brewer

Many former industry workers say that marginal employment conditions are a problematic norm in craft beer. In their view, facing these employment conditions has, over time, made it impossible for them to continue managing work careers *despite* their personal affinity for craft beer and brewing. Troy, a thirty-five-year-old biracial (white-Latino) man with a graduate degree in chemical engineering, explains his frustration with the career limitations he faced while trying to find work within a brewery:[9]

> Speaking to my exit from the craft brewing industry, I realized that even the owners of craft breweries don't make that much. Even though we put out volume [at my last brewery], our margins in package beer just aren't that great. Like, 80 percent of our volume made up 20 percent of our margins. So that means that the brewers don't get paid much. *Nobody does.* And as a chemical engineer graduate, I realized there just wasn't that much room for growth. The owners probably made less than the brewers did, full disclosure.
>
> And I was starting to become more expensive too. I was making $45k as an operations manager that oversaw $3 million a year in beer sales. But because that was one-sixth of our total sales, that was a big deal for the company.

What initially drove Troy to craft beer in his early twenties was the prospective of putting his chemistry skills to work to make better beer, something he loved spending time doing. This fueled his career for years. Eventually, Troy said he began to realize that "there wasn't a way to make money in craft beer." When he began comparing what he was making at his brewery relative to what he could make using his graduate degree in chemistry in other industries, his career in craft beer seemed less and less desirable. "We can't live on Nut Rolls alone!" says Troy, referencing the nut-based candy that often comes free with deliveries of malt from a lead-ing malt company that makes both these products. "In this industry, you can throw a Nut Roll at somebody [and they'll be happy]. You can't do that at General Motors. So there."

Many former workers say that forging careers in this industry eventu-ally clashed with their aspirations for upward mobility and stable work. They eventually became disenchanted with having to make "trade-offs" that involved long-term compromises to their finances or career pros-pects. Jerome, the former sales representative we met last chapter, explains the tension he felt before quitting his brewery job: "My attitude was, I know what I'm worth, what I bring to the table. I want to get paid for that." What Jerome believed he was worth was increasingly at odds with what craft breweries were willing to pay him. Further, Jerome asserts that his mentality is the opposite of how most workers in the industry approach their careers, where accepting jobs regardless of negotiating compensation and benefits is the norm.

Former workers I talked to who are from race- and class-privileged backgrounds are both more likely to say they initially entered the industry because of their passion for craft beer and quicker to note their personal struggles to stay in jobs that prove to be relatively low-wage, uncertain, and with limited advancement opportunities. Put differently, it is privi-leged workers for whom building precarious careers in craft beer repre-sents the greatest deviation from middle-class career expectations.[10] For example, a college-educated white man who left the industry after six years, texted me shortly after leaving his job as a brewery sales representative:

> I LOVED working in craft beer. But unless you own a brewery . . . the money just isn't there. I started working for my friend's marketing business quarter four last year and after they promoted me, wife and I made the move [to a new city]. I greatly enjoyed my time in LA and all of the wonderful people I met [in the industry]. But it was time to move and save some $.

This sentiment embodies what former workers, especially those who are white and from middle-class backgrounds, express about craft beer: it is work that they personally "loved" that ultimately proved unsustainable as a career. This perspective also shapes how former workers look at those who stay in the industry. Below, Jerome discusses what he think motivates workers who are still in craft beer and contrasts this with his own perspective:

JEROME: I still see some guys around, like, *how do you even keep the enthusiasm?* I think it is because this is still the dream job for them. A lot of younger sales reps [are] coming into it with a passion. But I feel [for me] being in the industry was something that was taking the joy away from something I love. I was like, I have to get away from this before it breaks my fucking brain!

EW: Yeah. So who do you think are the kinds of people who are succeeding, or at least staying in craft beer distribution or sales?

JEROME: I believe they are very committed to craft. These are people that I saw their enthusiasm remain even when they moved around to different companies, though they didn't move around too much. Also, everybody I know that is like that is still in the clubs: all the brewery clubs. They still go to the festivals, like GABF, even if they aren't getting paid to go. The dudes that will line up and trade beers online. It is one to one: those who are still doing it from those of us who have moved on. Like, we still enjoy a good beer, but I don't know any of my friends that are fed up with beer who will do any of that anymore.

Jerome surmises that one way to remain committed to careers in this industry is through being fully immersed in the industry culture— something he himself struggled to do over time as his career priorities have shifted. For him, continued access to the immaterial perks of the job is no longer enough.[11] Troy, the former worker described earlier, also notes how being closely tied to industry social networks can help workers remain enthusiastic with their careers:

For brewers, there is an Instagram channel called Wortwranglers. And when I see these guys post, it reminds me of that camaraderie you see with military guys. They are taking out their frustration through laughter, through building those types of social bonds. And I really see that a lot in the craft beer world. People who are still in craft beer may be underpaid and underrespected but they really love what they do. That's what keeps people in it, that camaraderie, that commonality among each other.

Reflecting on his own experience, Troy now sees that many of the homosocial bonds he formed in the workplace based around an "in this struggle together" mentality functioned as a commitment device for his career—something that kept him in it longer than he should have stayed. Still, walking away from the industry can be extremely difficult for workers. Jonah, a white man in his late thirties who spent over a decade in craft beer, explains his perspective after quitting his head brewer job several weeks ago:

> I'm not ready to invest emotionally in that journey again. And I have some personal stuff, like, I lost my mom last year. So that kind of thing wore on me. I also had some depression that kind of went into that. I now want to find a thing where it's kind of the opposite of most people that get into the industry, because they want to have their job be their passion. I've done that for so long. I'm looking for the opposite. I wanna find a job that can just be my job, and then I can find my happiness and my passion somewhere else.

As Jonah indicates, finding a way to be *less* passionate about craft beer, or at least able to compartmentalize one's passion from one's employment, may be the best way for workers to remain in the industry long-term. Other workers go further to indicate that this kind of willful disentanglement can be strategically useful for long-term career success in craft beer.[12] Bert, the former sales representative introduced earlier, explains:

> EW: how would you describe the skill needed, even the characteristics needed to do that job well?
>
> BERT: Yeah, that's a good question, and I don't know. From my perspective, the people who did the best are people who *don't* have passion in beer. People who are clever and play the system.

Bert paints a picture of his former colleagues still in the industry who go about their careers without emotional attachments in order to capitalize on advancement opportunities. Doing so was a challenge for him personally because he never could disassociate his passion for craft beer from his job. By contrast, a brewery sales rep named Paul is proud of being able to "play the game" in ways that Bert describes. Paul, a white man in his late thirties, is a self-described extrovert who is also "fluent in craft beer speak." This he says has contributed to his success selling beer in his region and, more broadly, his rapid series of promotions within his company. But Paul draws a line at becoming too taken-in by the consumer culture of craft beer in ways that might interfere with one's career ambitions:

> I'm not waiting in line [at a beer festival] for shit. I'm not enamored by brewmasters or owners of breweries or anything like that. I do love this industry and I do love the products that we sell. But the pomp of all of that does not appeal to me in particular. I know, and have known at least, a lot of reps who are beer nerds, who think because I love this product I think I should sell it. Those people usually don't last for that long.

Paul exhibits a strategic form of detachment from the object that he is trying to make a career of selling. He sees this as a sharp contrast to brewery workers who consume their work, such as by treating it as an extension of their hobby or by spending off-work hours doing the same things they are paid to do.

Other workers deliberately try to distance themselves from the cultural logic of pure passion for craft beer in order to improve their career prospects. Santiago, the brewery owner with a graduate degree first described in chapter 2, is critical of what he sees as his colleague's "non-professional" behavior:

SANTIAGO: To me, this is a business at the end of the day.

EW: Do you feel like other people are in this industry for a different reason?

SANTIAGO: Yes. I think the more traditional approach is like: "beer is my passion. I want to bring beer to the people." No, motherfucker! This is a *business*. But at least that's how I see it because it is a business. Because I need to eat every month out of it. I need to support my family. I don't want to be here all the time. It's like there's another brewery in Inland Empire that opened and we went like a year before the pandemic and the owner was trashed behind the bar. We had had like four beers and he was trying to add and he was struggling, so he was just like, "Ah don't worry about it."

While Santiago has remained in craft beer, he understands the perspective expressed by former workers who have grown disenchanted with the lack of economic opportunity in the industry as well as the passion-as-compensation culture surrounding these careers. By actively pushing back against this approach, workers like Santiago and Paul attempt to manage their careers with business savvy designed to maximize career advancement opportunities while avoiding employment uncertainty.

Side Paths of Business Opportunity

When Henry, a white man in his mid-forties with an MBA degree, looks at the craft beer industry today, he sees a growth industry with expanding business opportunities. None of these opportunities, however, involve starting a brewery, which he says is because of the challenges these companies have in turning a profit. Instead, Henry is one of a growing number of individuals who operate along the *side pathway* of the industry by building careers as contractors, consultants, paraprofessionals, and other kinds of specialized industry suppliers. The careers these workers forge prioritize entrepreneurial business opportunities that draw directly from their existing industry credentials and personal resources while also offering workers the chance to participate in an industry social scene they personally enjoy.

Henry recalls first drawing up his business pitch that would eventually become a mobile-canning business as a capstone project for a business school:

> I was really interested in business plans and had a couple different ideas. One was for a distillery, not for mobile canning. I ended up winning the competition. I wanted to move forward with that but I got a call from a brewery, a friend of mine that I've known for years that was interested in getting into packaging beer. As soon as I heard that I had a flashback to college where I had friends who used to do the mobile bottlings for the wine industry. So I was like, well, if they can do this for wine, we should be able to do some sort of mobile processing for beer! I looked into it and I think a month later I had a new business plan. Within a couple weeks, I had financing. I ordered my first canning line and bought a truck and got all the gear ready to start the mobile business.

With a brand-new mobile canning business in tow (literally), Henry quickly developed working relationships with several small breweries in the southwestern United States that were not able to package their own products themselves. To grow his company, Henry leveraged his personal interests, social connections, and business experiences all at once. He explains his ongoing relationship to the industry by pointing to a blend of personal interests and entrepreneurial savvy:

> Packaging is a very difficult aspect of the brewing process and, I think, one of the hardest. But I think a lot of breweries don't necessarily think about the packaging arm when they get into it. For me, that's the entrepreneurial piece. It's not that we don't love beer and we don't love products—we do *for sure* and we love being in the brewery scene—but I don't think any of the owners of the mobile canners ever thought they'd be brewers. We were all involved, like, I had restaurant experience and bar experience, that kind of stuff, but I never saw myself being a brewer opening my own brewery necessarily. I saw an idea and I knew, as an entrepreneur, it's just a matter of trying to conquer all the pieces that go along with that.

Like other class-privileged white men working as brewers and brewery owners, Henry enjoys a seamless fit within the craft beer industry. Yet in contrast with these individuals, workers such as Henry forge entrepreneurial careers along the side pathway by helping *other* people pursue their passions—and strategically avoiding the financial risks of doing so in the meantime.

Samesh, a twenty-eight-year-old Indian American man with an engineering degree from a prestigious university, describes his journey to founding one of the first data services companies for craft breweries in similar terms as Henry. Before running his company, Samesh was working for a large technology company. He found the work monotonous and constraining. "You are totally replaceable," he says, "and you rarely get to see how your work contributes to the end product." After attending a job fair, Samesh decided to accept a job offer at a craft brewery doing systems management. The company had few formal procedures in place at the time he arrived, which gave him some ideas for starting his own company to offer these services. Two years later, Samesh founded his own company that offers data and operational insights to craft breweries, naming it, "The Missing Factor." Samesh explains his thinking:

> If you have somebody who's very passionate about craft beer, they might have some blind spots, just like the yin and yang of art and science. And I think the idea is that if you were just to be passionate about [brewing beer], you wouldn't have consistency, you wouldn't have quality, you wouldn't have

the metrics that you're tracking. Right? So even if you have the passion, I think you're not getting anywhere without the data side of things. And that's really where The Missing Factor started as a consulting company that focused in on going to breweries and checking out how I could help them on the process side. The missing factor is data.

For Samesh, founding The Missing Factor blended his interest in achieving more hands-on control over his career while simultaneously keeping him involved with an industry he was drawn to for its informality and freedom. Importantly, like Henry, Samesh portrays himself and his company as a *complement* to the people who found craft breweries out of passion for craft beer ("Just like the yin and yang of art and science"). This allows him to participate in the industry culture, albeit from a less risky position.

Workers who operate along the side pathway must also evolve to fit changing demands within the industry as well as in their own lives. Gustavo, a college-educated Latino man in his early forties, embraces an eclectic career wearing multiple hats: he fashions himself as an independent salesperson, a brand ambassador, and a small business owner wrapped into one. Gustavo spent most of his twenties and early thirties doing a combination of sales and brewhouse work for several craft breweries in New Mexico. He saw an industry that was rapidly growing: within a decade, a dozen local breweries became thirty, then forty. His family was also growing at home, which meant he needed his work to produce a larger paycheck each month. Gustavo saw a business opportunity to transition his career toward something he refers to as "beer brokering":

> These days, if you don't have someone like me advocating for you, you're dead. Dead in the water. The only thing that's going to change that is if you've got huge brand recognition and momentum in the market. Then [corporate distributors] are motivated, right? Because their customers are asking them for your product. If you don't, you're done. Distributors probably have 50 percent of brands over there that don't have a rep—don't have someone like *me*. Somebody telling them how or teaching them or training them how to sell the beer? It's not going to happen.

Gustavo now works with several small breweries doing his beer brokering work. He has also started another side business doing professional servicing for draft lines and has gained steady contracts with bars, restaurants, and breweries in town. Like other types of self-employed professionals and industry contractors, Gustavo recognizes the entrepreneurial career he leads along the side pathway lacks stability and exposes him to risks during possible economic downturns.[13] But he also feels he has developed a buffer to this uncertainty with his business sensibility, industry knowledge, and extensive professional connections.[14] He remains part of the industry while also standing apart in other ways. In this sense, Gustavo's career efforts mirror those of other modern craft workers described by sociologist Richard Ocejo, who stretch their occupational identities across multiple roles (such as consultants and brand ambassadors) to help them advance their careers.[15] "There was a lot of experimentation early on to say, where should I allocate my time?" explains Gustavo. "My strength is that I hustle, and I have a nose for 'Okay, well that's not working. I'm going to shake the tree over here and see what's gonna happen if I do this.'"

For workers along the side pathway, knowing which tree to shake is more than a matter of luck: it often draws directly from one's prior experience and connections within racialized and gendered pathways of work. Francine, an outgoing, college-educated white woman in her mid-forties, knows what services she can provide to brewery owners because of her decade-long experience working in brewery taprooms. A few years ago, Francine says she grew tired of working on her feet engaged in customer service. Without a clear next step for her career along the service pathway, it took several months to figure out how to transition her career while remaining tied to the industry she knew well. Francine eventually found a way to leverage her insights into how to run a successful taproom:

> People around me kept saying, you gotta stop giving people this free information. This is pretty specific skill set. Like, *you could make a career out of this.* There are consultants that come in and do corporate consulting or something like that.
>
> I realized: most brewers start off as homebrewers, right? So, it's not a business—that is just a hobby. I wanted to be very clear that if you have gotten to the point where you've filed for a business license, *this is not a hobby anymore.* [My company] was born from that idea: we are a business and we have to treat it as such.

Francine, Henry, Gustavo, and other workers forging custom-fit careers along the side pathway combine their entrepreneurial savvy with prior knowledge and connections within craft beer. Equally important is what motivates these efforts. Each of these workers capitalizes on business opportunities that are directly informed by the practices, perspectives, and shortcomings of those employed in craft breweries, especially along the creative pathway. In doing so, these workers navigate entrepreneurial careers less centrally defined by pure passion for craft beer and more on the ability to leverage opportunities enabled by others who follow this cultural logic of work.

"Who is making money in craft beer today?" I ask Henry toward the end of our interview. Henry's newest business venture, about to launch a few weeks after I met him, involves a partnership with another business owner to open a production-sized brewery that will brew beers for other companies (sometimes known as contract brewing) for a charge.

"Well," he pauses. "Think of it this way. It's like during the gold rush: it's the people selling the pickaxes, you know what I mean?"

Symbolic Affiliation and the Hobbyist Pathway

When I arrive at a private residence nestled in a middle-class suburb of Albuquerque, the garage door is open with the rock band AC/DC blaring from a scratchy stereo. In the middle of the garage sits a three-piece steel contraption rigged with multitiered, 10-gallon pots, a makeshift pulley system overhead, and a gas burner at the base. Kenneth, a retired army sergeant in his early sixties with a crew cut, emerges from the house dressed in a mechanic's jumpsuit. "Welcome to my paradise! I built all this myself," he says, eyes lighting up. Kenneth turns around and beckons me forward with his hand before suddenly stopping in his tracks. "Oh, I almost forgot. Want a beer? I got three on tap right now: a chamomile Saison, a barrel-aged quad—that came out really nice, been aging nearly six months—and a hoppy pale ale."

Amateur brewers like Kenneth love the pure hands-on activity of homebrewing. They are passionate about the creative process of *crafting* beer from scratch and tinkering with equipment and recipes to their own specification. By this measure, these individuals share much in common with professional

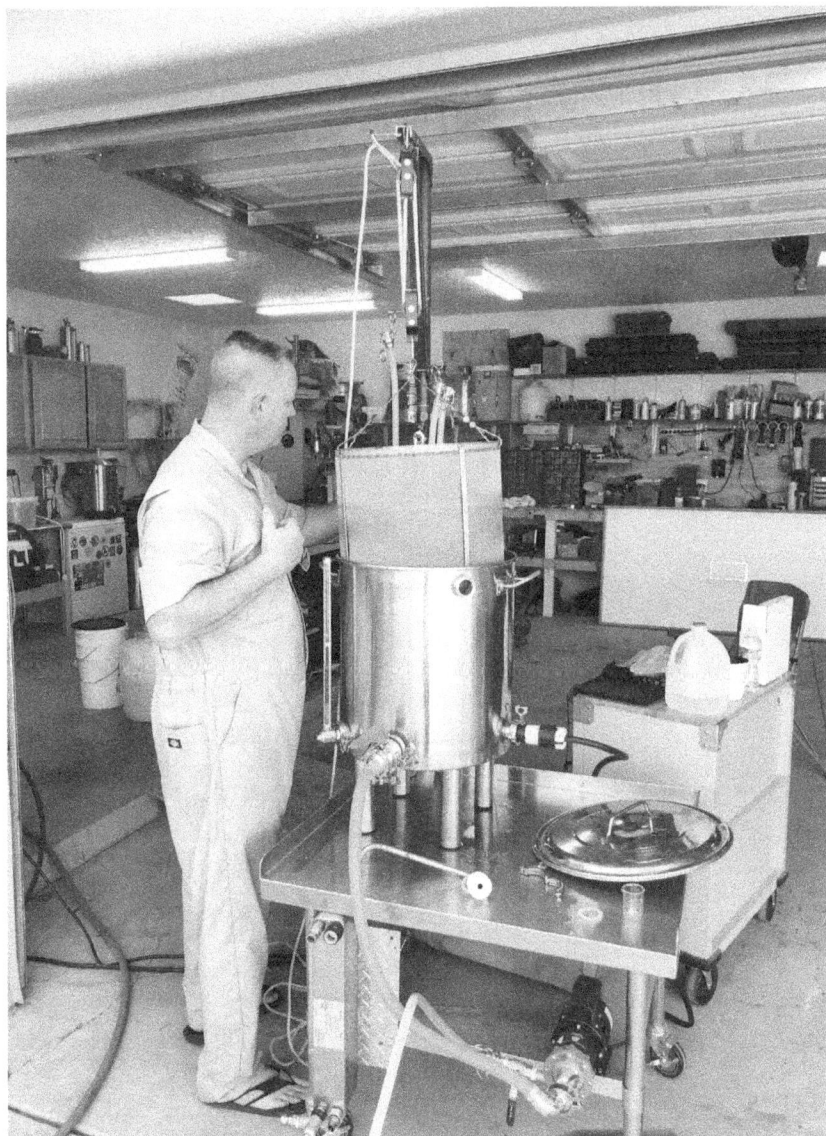

Figure 10. A Homebrewer with his DIY brewing system, including a customized pulley and welded table.

brewers, including the fact that, statistically, homebrewers are disproportionately white, college-educated men. There is one key difference: Kenneth has never had an interest in pursuing craft brewing as a career. He is not alone. In fact, less than half the homebrewers I talked to said they had any interest in formal employment in a craft brewery, let alone owning one in the future. Instead, homebrewers seek *symbolic affiliation* with craft brewing in terms of shared values of artisanship, creativity, and authenticity. By keeping their "day jobs," they minimize their exposure to economic risks, unpredictability, and monotonous work routines that come with pursuing craft beer as a long-term career. In this sense, for people like Kenneth, homebrewing serves as an exemplar of middle-class leisure rather than a career that also comes with marginal economic rewards and an unpredictable future.

Homebrewers such as Emmett, a twenty-nine-year-old white man employed as an engineer at a large science laboratory in Albuquerque, frame their journeys along the hobbyist pathway as an effort to *preserve* their passion for craft brewing. Emmett explains his perspective:

> I thought about [entering the industry as a brewer], and a few people have suggested I should. But I think I prefer the freedom I have with it just being a hobby. My size of creating stuff is much smaller as a hobby; it will remain small and I think that remains in a controllable quantity. If brewing was a real job for me then I would have to expand everything and change all of these processes. Then profit is always the goal. I can't be losing money all the time and then I might decide, well let's cut corners on this and quality would go down.
>
> EW: Yeah. That makes sense, but one might say, you've invested all this time and money, you're making hopefully a great product, wouldn't you want to be able to sell that kind of thing?
>
> EMMETT: No. I don't know why not. [*pauses*] I guess I wouldn't want it to ever become a job and be stressful or unenjoyable.

Emmett contrasts the "freedom" he has as a homebrewer with the inevitable compromises he feels he would face in order to brew professionally or run a business. For him, passion for craft brewing is the goal, not profit and *certainly* not added stress. Others share Emmett's perspective by emphasizing their un-work-like relationship with craft beer. Quinn, a white woman in her fifties, describes her homebrewing style as one of "anti-routine," by which she means an expression of her individuality and personal creativity. She explains her preference for continuing to home-brew over pursuing a career in craft beer:

EW: Could you ever see yourself going that route of opening a brewery and entering the industry?

QUINN: No. It's not for me. I would not enjoy it anymore. It would be work. By that, I mean, say you have great recipes, and yeah, you have some great beers as a professional, but you've got to live up to that and be able to replicate it over and over and over. Come up with new stuff. And take into account, "Well, how much can I get with this?" And it's stressful. It's not fun at that point, for me.

EW: And just to clarify, how is that different from what you do [as a home-brewer]? Because clearly, this is something that is a lot of fun, that you are doing for pleasure. So what's the key difference there?

QUINN: The key difference is that *it's on my own time*. It's when I feel like doing it. When I have great ideas, or when we have great ideas, "Hey, let's brew a beer." Or you try something new and you're like, "Hey, I want to replicate that. Do you think we could make that?" "I don't know. Let's see."

Homebrewers like Quinn and Emmett feel they can maintain a more authentic relationship to craft beer by staying amateurs rather than "going pro."[16] In their view, engaging craft beer along the hobbyist pathway allows their brewing activities to be focused solely on passion-filled discovery rather than commercial production demands. Unlike industry contractors such as Henry, the aspects of craft brewing that hobbyists view as most rewarding are the aspects that are least compatible with treating this activity as a formal work career or business enterprise.

Many homebrewers also view brewing beer as a continual process of learning that is deliberately distinct from their work lives. For these individuals, homebrewing represents a heady mixture of art, science, and experimentation that few say experience in their day jobs. Additionally, homebrewing appeals to gendered interests in tinkering with gadgets and machinery, especially for men.[17] I sat down with two longtime homebrewers, both white men in their fifties, to talk about their relationship to homebrewing.

"I like being able to play scientist," one explained. "Last homebrew club meeting was a thumbprint beer, where they give us the ingredients and we each are trying to make the same beer style but with our own thumbprint on it. Last year, they gave us the grains, the hops, the yeast, so we had to brew using the same ingredients. We could change how much water we could use, the temperature of the water, the mash time."

"This year, they once again gave us a base malt, hops, yeast and said you could add one specialty grain," added the other homebrewer. "So this one came out with a *lot* of variation. We chose to add Black patent malt [which turns the beer a dark brown color]. Another group added Carapils [a very light malt in terms of color and flavor]. Another group made a sour IPA. Everyone did a bunch of weird things, like use a whirlpool. That was pretty cool."

"I'm curious, what do you think made homebrewing so interesting for you both?" I asked.

"*I think it is because we had a problem that we couldn't solve,*" the first homebrewer replied. "First of all, we wanted to brew bigger beers. That meant that we needed bigger mash tuns. That means we needed a bigger kettle. The same kind of thing. One thing led to another, you know?"

As these men illustrate, homebrewers often say they enjoy a process that has both tactile and intellectual components that don't need to be resolved or mastered. This allows them to treat homebrewing as an individualized puzzle with endless possible variations rather than a commercial product that needs to be consistent. For example, one homebrewer keeps a thick binder of recipes that he has brewed in the past ("I never brew the same beer twice"), while another has retrofit an entire room of his house with shelves for fermenting beer and a draft system built into the wall for pouring these creations.[18] Minimizing their formal commitments to craft beer allows homebrewers to embrace their passion for the creative dimensions of this activity more fully. As Quinn aptly notes, "I'm brewing for me, so let's just try it out! That's always my attitude."

As I was shown pictures of customized brew systems, handed elaborate recipes, and given tours of extensive homebrewing setups, I couldn't help but note how much time, effort, and money these individuals have sunk into homebrewing—not unlike the career investments that many workers in the industry make. Yet, the former feel that the commitments they exert toward homebrewing are categorically different from those oriented toward a work career. Quinn's homebrew day, for instance, is a social occasion on weekends that involves cooking lunch and lounging on her outside patio with her husband and usually several friends. It is not, as she speculates, about punching a time clock, brewing to pay bills, and otherwise worrying about getting all the steps of brewing perfect.

Quinn, Tom, Norman, and Kenneth all differ in their approach to homebrewing—and perhaps that is the point. Their distinct relationships to this craft activity embody the freedom and tinkering that they say a hobby encourages and professional brewing would squash. For these otherwise stably employed, college-educated men and women, choosing to remain along the hobbyist pathway also involves a pragmatic assessment of the precarity of these careers. Despite their love of brewing, none of these individuals is interested in disrupting stable, professional careers outside the beer industry.

Even homebrewers with ambitions of selling their creations to paying customers recognize the risk of moving further in the commercial brewing direction. As one homebrewer explains:

> Right now, we—myself and two partners—are kind of at a crossroads. Trying to figure out what to do next and trying to get on the same page about it. *It is hard because we all are doing well in our respective careers.* Like, I just got a pay raise, [one of my partners] just became a school principal. And the other gal is doing really well as the GM of the taproom she works at. So it is like—we all understand that we would be taking a pay cut, giving up a lot in order to start a brewery. And we are prepared to do that for the most part. But when I think about contract brewing to start out, with the slim margins, it's tough . . .

For this homebrewer and his would-be business partners, the prospect of launching a career along the creative pathway involves nontrivial personal sacrifices and economic risks. By contrast, remaining a homebrewer—while holding down other kinds of jobs and careers—is less risky while still allowing them to be creative and flexibly engaged with this preferred activity. The fact some homebrewers continue to entertain the idea of entering the industry at all speaks to the powerful allure of careers that center individual passions rather than sideline them.

·　　·　　·　　·　　·

		Career Commitment	
		HIGH	LOW
Symbolic Affiliation	HIGH	Industry workers	Homebrewers
	LOW	Consultants and contractors	Former workers

Figure 11. Varying relationships to craft beer among those on alternate pathways.

In a taped interview for the magazine *Brewbound* in the spring of 2022, a former brewery owner turned industry consultant named Kelly Rowe claimed that he doesn't personally know any craft brewers who have managed to be profitable in today's business climate.[19] "People always want to know, well, what's the secret to making my brewery successful? But that's the thing—right now, with the industry the way it is, I don't see how this is possible. There are things that help, sure, and I try to speak to that."

To varying degrees, many of the former workers, contractors, and homebrewers in this chapter echo Rowe's sentiment about the bleak prospects of building long-term careers in a volatile industry. Yet their perspectives and experiences also speak to the enduring appeal of forging handcrafted careers in other ways. This chapter thus illustrates how individuals attempt to manage their *symbolic affiliation* with craft beer alongside the uncertain material conditions that come with these careers. A worker's access to privileged resources and networks can certainly make this process easier in the form of a wider range of available employment options. Yet it can also create new tensions for these same workers as they make sense of parallel concerns about socioeconomic status.

Former worker such as Troy and Alfred say they now understand that pursuing their highly social and passion-driven careers came with substantial downsides. In taking the exit pathway, their stories reveal the hidden costs of the commitments of time and energy that many industry workers make to jobs that are often of marginal employment quality and limited career mobility. By contrast, industry contractors such as Gustavo and Francine prioritize a business-savvy, entrepreneurial angle for their careers along the side pathway. These careers allow them to minimize risk to their work careers while maintaining strategic ties to the people and activities that make up the scene of craft beer. Finally, those along the hobbyist pathway such as Kenneth and Quinn stoke their personal passions and symbolic affiliation with craft beer without making any formal career commitments.

The purpose of this chapter has not been to paint a portrait of the unilaterally poor quality of careers in this industry or the illogic of people who opt for these careers. Clearly, many workers I talked to are forging long-term employment in craft beer that is personally meaningful and stable "enough." Yet, the nuanced experiences of those along alternative pathways complicates our understanding of how people manage the pressures and uncertainties they face in their work lives in craft beer and other similar settings of the new economy. For instance, why do some former workers from privileged backgrounds, such as Troy and Bert, express dissatisfaction with their careers in ways that many of their colleagues do not? Research suggests that some workers may be able to "re-enchant" their careers by switching positions or finding new places to do the same thing.[20] From this view, former workers may have simply failed to pivot their work lives successfully (or locate a viable side pathway for themselves within the industry). Another possible explanation for career variation is rooted in workplace dynamics. In an industry where company structures vary widely, workers who find employment within companies that stoke their personal interests while also providing relatively stable, livable employment could make it more likely that they will stick with their careers in the long term.

Yet another way of approaching this issue is to observe differences between those who maintain a nonprofessional relationship to craft beer—which I have called the hobbyist pathway—versus those who work within the industry, especially along the creative pathway. As I have described, members of both these groups share social similarities and seek symbolic affiliation with craft beer while deprioritizing its economic considerations.[21] Yet the distinctions between these groups illustrate conflicting ways of managing middle-class careers alongside individualized interests. Whereas homebrewers seek to preserve their pure passions for craft beer from the safe perch of middle-class hobbyism, industry workers bring their pure passions together with a handcrafted outlook for their careers. The former strategy is invariably less risky in that it preserves a conventional distinction between work and leisure. But it is the latter that offers greater insight into how today's workers choose to navigate—no, *must* navigate—a world of work that is both less predictable and more atomized than ever before.

Conclusion

ESTEBAN

"This is it! This is our new home, dog!" Esteban exclaims, arms out-stretched and pointing upward at the rafters of a cavernous warehouse in south central Los Angeles.

Much has changed for Esteban since I first met him nearly three years ago. Back then, he was filming videos of himself chugging rare beers in his home kitchen and posting the footage on social media for thousands of followers; his career path into craft beer seemed as improbable as his future was uncertain. Today, Esteban and I are standing in the middle of his soon-to-open brewery. Or at least half of it. As Esteban explains, "The owner for this spot [a Latino man] actually approached me because he knew I was looking around. He asked whether we wanted to split this location. He opened this place during the pandemic and has never really been able to fill it up like he thought. And that's what *we* do, man! So I think it works out really well for both of us."

Esteban hopes to have his new company up and running by the end of the year.[1] Along his journey, Esteban says he has gained valuable insights into the business side of the industry from a small network of Latinx entre-preneurs who have established themselves in the local scene. He recently posted a picture to his Instagram page of a pending "notice to sell alcohol" sign at the future site of his brewery, along with the caption: "It's starting to feel real. We have worked our butts off for the past 4 years to make this a reality. We still need the community's help for as little as $100 bucks you can be part of this dream (prayer hands)." The post was liked by over 1,200 people, with dozens of encouraging comments ("congratulations brother . . . well deserved!!"). And yet, Esteban does not have much room for error since he is relying on a patchwork of crowdsourced funds to finance his operation. His family, meanwhile, is subsisting entirely on his wife's modest income. As Esteban continues to forge his own career pathway in an industry he never expected to enter, the stakes are higher than ever.

SHEILA

Nearly two years after we first spoke, I caught up with Sheila again in the spring of 2023. She had recently turned thirty-six and given birth to her first child. She had also transitioned to a new role within her company doing remote sales work from home. "I don't even know what my current job title is these days," Sheila said with a laugh. "Assistant to the CEO? Senior brand manager? Account specialist? Let's go with the first one." When I first met her, Sheila was interested in working in craft beer not as part of any grand career plan but because beer was fun and working jobs along the service pathway complemented her previous customer service experience in restaurants. But even then, Sheila had hinted to me that pouring beer at festivals and attending late night events at bars couldn't last forever. "I'm getting too old for that stuff," she says firmly. "Sometimes I'll attend those beer functions. But only as a patron. Like, work is still *work*, you know what I mean?"

Sheila's career has stabilized over the past few years as she has moved further behind the scenes and away from the face-to-face action of selling craft beer. She is into her sixth year working for the same craft beer distributor. "The pandemic hasn't been too bad for us, to be honest," she says. "People still want to drink, and they are just doing it at home instead of at bars. Our sales are up, which keeps me busy."

"Any difference in how you see your career now?" I ask.

"I'm still in craft beer—which is a blast. I know that I have this beautiful, golden position with my company that is different from a lot of other people in the industry," Sheila explains. "These days, I'm sitting at a computer instead of being out in the field like before. This is my life now." She pauses. "I guess I've just found a way to be able to be in this industry without letting it consume me."

MIKE

Mike's company, Renegade Brewing, hasn't fared so well over the past two years since I last visited him at his buzzy brewery. The company was crippled by the pandemic-related mandatory closure of its taproom for much of 2020 as well as a bad lease deal signed years ago. The nature of running a profitable craft brewery in Los Angeles had also changed. Nearly 100 breweries have opened in the Los Angeles area in the six years since Mike's brewery poured their first beer. During that time, craft beer's share of the domestic beer market has all but flat-lined, meaning that more small companies have to share the same slice of the industry pie.

In the spring of 2022, Mike and his co-owners announced they would be shutting down Renegade Brewing for good. In a statement to a local beer publication, the owners wrote, "Starting off in a garage, to what it has become is truly amazing. Our staff and our customers have become like one big family and it's one of the most rewarding things about [the brewery]." Then, citing business challenges during the pandemic: "even though packaged distribution was going well, our on-premise distribution levels were significantly down and there wasn't any sign of that changing anytime soon." During my final visit to Renegade, things were eerily silent. Fermentation tanks sat empty, plastic-wrapped kegs were piled in the middle of the taproom, and the hoses that once zigzagged across the cement floor hung wrapped up in tight loops against the wall. The brewhouse had a "For Sale" sign taped to it. As I walked around still taking in this sudden development, I ran into Mike, who was waiting for a meeting with potential buyers. Mike says that the next chapter in his career will most likely be out of craft beer. "It is funny you should visit today," Mike tells me. "I just talked with my former boss in marketing about getting my old job back. It's just—" he trails off, his face slightly scrunched. "It is kind of surreal thinking about heading back into an office and having a boss after all these years working for myself."[2]

· · · · ·

As the respective stories of Esteban, Sheila, and Mike illustrate, forging handcrafted careers embodies the promises and perils of employment in the new economy. Many craft beer workers lead highly customized careers that do not follow set paths with clear start and finish points. Instead, workers are pulled and pushed across emergent job pathways that are at once shaped by industry structures and etched by their own social connections, personalized tastes and interests, and cultural ideas about employment.

In making sense of the still-evolving careers of craft beer workers, this book helps us understand how overlapping forces of social inequality pattern divergent employment trajectories for workers. These trajectories take shape within an industry landscape that, like many other settings of work today, is in flux. For this reason, rather than assuming that systemic forces of oppression bear down on workers in predictable ways, I have examined what career opportunity looks like at the ground level and over time. This gives us a unique lens with which to view the unexpected twists and turns that workers experience at key moments in their careers—such as Esteban's patchwork assemblage of a company or Mike's quick rise to the top of the local industry before his unexpected business failure. When viewed in isolation, these employment experiences may seem idiosyncratic. But taken together, they reflect the live-wire tension between privilege and precarity that characterizes the work lives of many Americans today.

In the section that follows I underscore the main findings and arguments of this book and specify how they contribute to scholarship on careers dynamics in the new economy, cultural narratives about work, and the complex forces of social inequality that operate in today's workplaces. I conclude by suggesting several ways to lay the groundwork for higher quality, sustainable employment not only in craft beer but other similar industries where workers pursue handcraft careers that offer them meaningful work and identity but not always equitable opportunities for career growth on their own terms.

RACIALIZED CAREER PATHWAYS

As this book affirms, what people experience at work is fundamentally shaped by their social backgrounds with respect to race, class, gender, and other statuses. Examining the *racialized career pathways* of workers in craft beer showcases the ways in which intersecting social statuses affect how workers navigate employment that is uncertain, individualized, and entrepreneurial. These career pathways are not clearly laid out for workers, and jobs along them are only loosely linked together. Nonetheless, within a given industry, differently racialized—as well as classed and gendered—career pathways exist in hierarchical relation to one another such that traversing one or another has material consequences for workers' lives.

Three primary career pathways exist in the craft beer industry: the creative pathway, the service pathway, and the hard labor pathway. We've seen that the experiences of class-privileged white men in this book systematically diverge from their colleagues from minoritized backgrounds at critical junctures in their respective careers. Specifically, the employment *microtransitions* that white men engage in—connecting with craft, entering the industry, and transitioning between jobs—are shaped by their privileged resources, which facilitate their access to rewarding careers along the *creative pathway*. As chapter 1 explained, workers like Mike are socialized in ways that bring them to the doorstep of craft beer. Their connections to friends and colleagues familiar with the industry subsequently buffer their entrance into and along the most desirable career pathway.[3] "Bearded white guys" deploy their varied resources in workplace settings where a particular expression of middle-class whiteness and masculinity is idealized.[4] This allows them to advance upward by default while also partly shielding them from the jagged edges of employment uncertainty. To be sure, the career outcome of any one worker in this industry remains far from certain, as Mike's story indicates. Yet the expedited access to the creative pathway that class-privileged white men enjoy allows them to engage their ongoing work lives as meaningful sites of—as sociologist Scott Land puts it—"autonomy, self-realization and sociality with high-quality products that contribute to the common good."[5]

The careers that Sheila and other college-educated women engage in share an affiliation with those along the creative pathway in that their jobs are highly visible and center a close relationship with artisanal products. Jobs along the service pathway appeal to class-privileged, white women and men because they allow these individuals to align their values and consumer identities with their work lives.[6] Service pathway jobs also involve feminized types of work, which in turn shapes how women and men engage these jobs differently. Many educated white women in the industry, such as Sheila, transition into customer-facing roles in taprooms from previous interactive service jobs—types of work linked by emotional labor and customer care. Meanwhile, educated white men working along this pathway are more likely than women to arrive there because of their focused interest in *craft consumption,* which involves specialized cultural knowledge about artisanal products. As a result, while both men and women employed in service jobs build careers along a structurally subordinated pathway within the industry, men more easily plug into a workplace culture dominated by their personal interests and their expressions of masculinity.

Working-class men of color have less access to either the creative pathway or service pathway because of the ways these pathways are, in different ways, etched with class privilege, whiteness, and feminized labor. Should men like Jorge, the former water company truck driver, find work in this industry, they mostly find themselves channeled into racialized jobs along the *hard labor pathway* working as delivery drivers, canning operators, and facility maintenance. These are jobs that, despite existing within a craft-focused environment, resemble low-level, blue-collar labor that is often racially outsourced to men of color in our society. While some working-class men of color do make headway outside the hard labor pathway, their microtransitions are often slowed, blocked, or liable to setbacks relative to their race- and class-privileged colleagues. At the same time, some of these individuals come to see unexpected value in building careers along the hard labor pathway. What men like Jorge and Anthony (introduced in chapter 4) say they want is decent, stable work for a good company rather than the opportunity to realize a passion-driven career. By this measure, working in small companies for bosses wholly dedicated to their jobs may not result in better pay or enhanced prestige, but some workers say it offers them a newfound sense of satisfaction in knowing their careers have meaning and their specific role within the company is valuable to those around them.

The notion of racialized career pathways makes several contributions to the study of social inequality in contemporary settings of the new economy. First, following Joan Acker, Victor Ray, Adia Harvey Wingfield, and critical scholars of work, I find that the employment advantages that workers from more privileged backgrounds enjoy flow from racialized, classed, and gendered organizational structures. Organizations make policies and institute practices that marginalize workers from nondominant groups, and these practices contribute to social stratification within craft breweries just as they do other kinds of workplaces.[7] At the same time, the case of craft beer illustrates how inequality-producing dynamics can also occur in ways that are less overtly exclusionary than in the past.[8] As craft beer workers navigate highly variable employment contexts across multiple stages of their work lives, they bring their material and immaterial resources to bear on specific employment opportunities.[9] These cumulative dynamics reshape the nature of the career climb itself and whether it portends advancement or otherwise.[10] By detailing the *employment microtransitions* that workers make along *racialized career pathways,* this book captures ground-level dynamics of social inequality that have been largely overlooked by scholars of racialized organizations. It is the interplay of workers and their industry and workplace structures that ultimately adjudicates racially stratified work careers.

The experiences of craft beer workers illustrate how social networks and cultural resources help race- and class-privileged workers transition into and along desirable career paths that are otherwise ill-defined and precariously constituted.[11] Minoritized workers, such as white women and people of color, may not necessarily find themselves barred from entering the workplace outright, but over the course of multiple employment microtransitions, many find themselves diverted along subordinate career pathways that do not offer the same degree of autonomy or authority.[12] I suggest that the overlapping social forces that contribute to social inequality over the course of one's career have an outsized impact in work settings such as craft breweries that are less dictated by formal credentials and instead draw from a loose assemblage of social memberships, lifestyle experiences, and other immaterial qualities.[13] In elite corporate settings, candidates perceived to be a social fit with colleagues may help break a tie among similarly qualified applicants, as sociologist Lauren Rivera's research has shown. But in the craft beer industry, demonstrating a prior affinity for artisanal products and social ties to the "community" of people working and playing in the industry can be *everything.*[14] In effect, what limits access to dominant career pathways in this corner of the new economy is the fast-tracking of certain people who seek out highly specialized jobs by drawing on aspects of who they are, who they are connected to, and how they want to live their (work) lives.

PURE PASSION AND THE NEW CULTURAL LOGIC OF WORK

Expressing or "having" passion for one's job is not necessarily a bad thing. It can make one's work life personally enjoyable, meaningful, and motivating. It is only when we consider the social implications of expecting workers to relate to their jobs through passion where we see the problematic dimensions of this approach. As the dominant *cultural logic of work*— meaning, the way people think about and value work—in craft beer, workers draw conclusions about who is a good fit for the most desirable positions of creative authority based on the passion they evince for these jobs. Specifically, craft beer workers idealize their colleagues who express *pure passion* for craft beer, an all-encompassing relationship to one's job that incorporates aspects of work, play, and preferred lifestyle. As I have argued, pure passion reinforces the position of "bearded white guys" in craft beer because of how this relationship to work is expressed through privileged tastes, values, and identities closely associated with whiteness, class privilege, and masculinity. Those able to express pure passion get pulled to the front of the employment line—especially for desirable jobs along the creative pathway—which in turn locks women and people of color out of these job opportunities.

Educated white men such as Mike enact pure passion for craft beer in three primary ways: by committing material and symbolic resources to their pursuit of jobs in this industry, by downplaying concerns about formal employment, and by consuming the lifestyle of craft beer. As a result, these workers approach their jobs in ways that transcend work and seem custom fit for them personally.[15] Alongside the personal resources and structural conditions that incubate their employment microtransitions along the creative pathway, the ability to express pure passion for craft beer legitimizes their dominant position within this industry. Put differently, educated white men continue to be held as "ideal" and deserving workers for jobs of creative authority based in part on how they are able to approach their jobs.[16]

As Victor Ray notes, more research is needed on "how the emotions of Whites shape the daily operation and distribution of resources within organizations, or what types of group-based solidarity White organizational inclusion may foster."[17] Identifying pure passion as a dominant cultural logic of work in craft beer answers this call by specifying a key cultural process that upholds social inequality in contemporary workplaces.[18] Moreover, the racialized and gendered effects of this shared emotion in the workplace often go unnoticed. Industry participants who idealize pure passion look like they are merely celebrating people who share a similar "love" of craft beer rather than trying to force out those who don't. None of this is specific to the craft beer industry. Pure passion as I've described it here is likely to be embedded as a dominant cultural logic of work in labor settings that place a high value on authenticity and personal "tastes" for specialized forms of work.[19] Indeed, recent research indicates that other modern craft jobs such as artisanal bartending, craft distilling, and gourmet butchery are dominated by white men and similarly coded in masculinity, class privilege, and whiteness. A promising extension of this research could investigate whether pure passion still holds sway within labor settings that are racialized, classed, and gendered in different ways, such as the feminized craft labor of Etsy producers, or the working-class masculinity of vintage repair work.[20] Given differences in labor context and socially coded workplace structures, even if individuals were to evoke passion for their jobs, this may not have the effect of helping white men shore up their positions of authority.

The value of pursuing pure passion for work may also resonate with a growing number of people today who seek personally meaningful opportunities in their work lives. This is especially true of workers willing to sacrifice economic stability or forgo familial responsibility in order to prioritize a career that feels "authentic" to them.[21] Indeed, searching for a job one is passionate about is thought to have fueled the so-called Great Resignation, or the "Great Reshuffle," in the wake of the COVID-19 pandemic, where millions of American workers left unsatisfying and typically precarious jobs in search of new employment. Toward this trend, this book offers a cautionary tale: overly celebrating those who enact pure passion for work will likely result in a labor market "reshuffle" that ends up reproducing very familiar social hierarchies when all is said and done.

Finally, it is worth noting that engaging one's work through pure passion can potentially exacerbate other employment issues workers face. Prioritizing how a job fits with one's consumerist lifestyle while also choosing to downplay formal employment conditions can be a difficult way to approach one's work career in the long term for all but the most socially privileged workers. The widespread expectation that workers will be passionate about craft beer can make it difficult for these workers to engage in discussions about decidedly *nonpassionate* things like benefits, raises, career advancement, or even workplace harassment. This is precisely why people like Brent, the former craft beer sales representative, assert that workers who do their job best in the long term are not as passionate about them, or are at least able to compartmentalize their passionate interests from their employment requirements. In short, pure passion can end up blinding workers to the realities of their marginal employment conditions that only grow more pronounced as workers proceed further in their careers.

MARKED PROFESSIONALISM AND THE EQUITY PATHWAY

Expressing pure passion for work, especially directed toward artisanal production, may be the dominant cultural logic of work in craft beer, but it is not the only one expressed by workers today. As chapter 5 described, Derrick, Ty, Erica, and other minoritized workers in this industry are forging work lives and identities that are less dictated by the values and social norms set by the dominant group of workers. Instead, these individuals construct work identities that strategically extend beyond the producing, distributing, and serving of craft beer, and the kind of whiteness, class-privilege, and masculinity that pervade these labor settings.[22] By threading parallel objectives into their work identity that selectively engage their race and gender identities, these workers express what I have called *marked professionalism* through their careers.[23]

Enacting marked professionalism is in part a response to default—that is, *un*marked—work identities fashioned by members of the dominant group in this industry. Some minoritized workers make it a point to express differently racialized and gendered relationships to their jobs, such as by voicing social justice advocacy through their employment, or putting forth explicit company goals rooted in community empowerment. In this sense, marked professionalism expands the range of identities and values expressed by workers in ways that resonate with growing calls to "diversify" today's workplaces and promote DEI initiatives. This points to how enacting a degree of social difference can be strategic for some workers' careers. However, the expression of social difference most likely to be advantageous for a given worker's career is one that seamlessly complements preexisting goals of the organization or is minimally disruptive to the culture of the industry. For this very reason, I find that college-educated women and people of color are most successful in enacting marked professionalism by portraying themselves as sufficiently professional, comfortably "diverse," and well-attuned to the existing cultural logic of work.[24] Further, how key gatekeepers in this industry value marked professional identities among workers remains to be seen in the long run. Should managers seek those who embody or express diversity for jobs along subordinate career pathways while favoring those who enact pure passion for craft beer when hiring or promoting for positions of creative authority, this would uphold existing social hierarchies in the industry while simultaneously limiting the gains associated with expressing racialized and gendered work identities for minoritized workers.[25]

For workers, part of the value and viability of expressing a marked professional identity comes from the changing composition of the industry they are a part of. Industry context matters for how distinct kinds of work identities are enabled or constrained. In essence, what it means to be a "professional" in an emerging industry such as craft beer is still being worked out. Due to the value industry workers place on authenticity, individuals may have greater ability to stake new claims to an authentic work identity that incorporates their social identities. Similarly, given the recent "reckoning" of race and gender issues in this industry, marked professional identities that play up nondominant statuses are more likely to find a receptive audience within the industry today than in the past. DEI initiatives are currently widely supported in craft beer. But the institutionalization of these values are less clear in the long term. The changing nature of work in industries such as craft beer can cut both ways, and there is always the possibility that recent threats to an industry's status quo will prove temporary or limited in nature. As of this writing, several breweries that had put in place DEI programs or hired DEI managers have since put a freeze on these efforts, citing the need to cut costs.[26] Others have encountered stumbling blocks in implementing these initiatives. For example, one Black woman working as a "diversity officer" for a prominent brewery resigned while also releasing a statement that read: "Your actions have explicitly shown you are more interested in the optics of my face than the impact of my voice. I have dedicated myself to a life and career of equity, ethics, integrity, and morals. I cannot represent a company who doesn't stand for the same."[27] Clearly, the flexible structure of small, passion-driven business operations alone does not ensure that these workplaces will champion progressive visions for the workplace or support minoritized workers who voice marked professional identities—especially those that do not align with the goals of the companies these workers are embedded within.

A New Pathway in the Making?

Throughout this book we have met several workers, such as Esteban and Erica—the "Chief Experience Officer" described in chapter 5—who are forging open-ended and highly entrepreneurial careers in ways that draw on their marked professional identities. Some of these workers are also reimagining industry spaces by and for communities who, historically, they weren't meant for. But do these scattered stories indicate the emergence of new and more inclusive career pathway or just contingent opportunities for a small number of minoritized workers?

The prospect of an expanded *social equity pathway* within an industry like craft beer is similar to what some scholars refer to as the "diversity pathway," in which large institutions implement initiatives designed to support—or at least signal support for—members of minoritized groups.[28] In principle, the expansion of a social equity pathway would highlight linked job opportunities for workers who would traditionally find themselves confined to subordinate, racialized, and gendered career pathways or excluded from these workplaces entirely. However, we should not assume that organizational initiatives will necessarily result in viable, expanded career pathways for minoritized workers in the long term. For example, hiring or appointing a point person for DEI offers powerful symbolism and has been shown to marginally improve diversity in the workplace.[29] But these initiatives can also be of little use to rank-and-file workers and their career prospects when nothing is done to disrupt the cumulative effects of racialized networks, cultural norms steeped in whiteness, and informal practices that dictate who can access the most desirable positions in the company.[30] In craft beer, as in other work settings dominated by white men and their values, there will always be those who seek to reinforce the gilded position of "traditional" pathways to success, regardless of the slanted playing field these pathways are set on.

Nonetheless, a small but growing number of craft beer workers who are women and people of color appear to be forging job opportunities in ways that highlight their social identities, home communities, or social justice advocacy efforts.[31] This hints at the viability of a social equity pathway for these workers and, sometimes, made by them as well. If so, opportunities along this pathway may vary by region, shaped by specific kinds of local politics, industry dynamics, and demographics. For example, during the pandemic, a college-educated Latino brewery owner in Los Angeles described an unexpected silver lining for his company: "To be honest, there were a lot of grants and funding that the government made available [to small businesses and minority-owned businesses] that we applied for and received over the last two years. That is what funded all this new equipment, really. The canning line was $70,000, which we paid for all with grant money." Here, the financial life supports this business owner received during the pandemic functioned as a vital source of funds during an extraordinarily challenging time for the entire industry, especially its minoritized workers and minority-owned businesses without other resources to draw on. This also shows how the social equity pathway relies on contingent opportunities that, relative to opportunities for more privileged workers along well-established and desirable pathways such as the creative pathway, must be constantly renewed rather than expected.

Ultimately, the prospect of building and sustaining a *social equity pathway* for workers remains to be seen. Not everyone agrees that fostering this kind of socially marked employment is a move in the right direction for either companies or individual workers seeking to get their careers off the ground.[32] As sociologist Laura Garbes reminds us, "without rethinking modern professional standards in American organizational fields—often created by well-educated white men in an era of legalized racial segregation—organizational attempts at racial inclusion shall continue to be merely invitations into a white-dominant world, contingent on white discretion."[33] As a case in point, in craft beer, several companies have already retracted or delayed indefinitely their grants, fellowships, and job positions dedicated to promoting diversity and social inclusivity, citing economic challenges brought on by the pandemic.[34] Similarly, workers striving to forge careers along the equity pathway may find themselves asked to explain or justify to management the worth of supporting social justice. This serves as a sobering reminder: championing social issues rarely supersedes business considerations for most companies, particularly in an increasingly competitive capitalist market. For this reason, I suspect that the most sustainable opportunities for workers along the equity pathway will represent "both/and" opportunities rather than "either/or" ones, where supporting a worker's growth must complement a company's existing values and profit-oriented goals.

CRAFTING AUTHENTIC CAREERS OF QUALITY

> The end goal is clear. The road isn't. I don't know how I'm going to get there. I just know that I'm going to get there and the journey is clouded. I don't know what I'll be known for, I think that's the best way to put it. People will tell me what I'm known for.
> —Tony, a biracial (Latino, white) brewer talking about his newly launched craft beer company

Many people, including Tony, believe the craft beer industry is still a very desirable place to work. A recent industrywide poll found that a majority of all workers said they were happy with their jobs, and the two leading reasons for this were their relationships with coworkers followed closely by a "welcoming" and "collaborative" workplace and industry environment.[35] But, as Tony also indicates, workers are more ambivalent on whether their jobs will be sustainable work careers in the long run. When this same poll asked what would enhance workers' *future* happiness with their jobs—essentially, what would help improve their work lives—the leading responses from workers all had to do with improving the formal conditions of their employment: a raise to their base pay, having more growth opportunities, and increased benefits. Therein lies the double-edge reality of working in craft beer today, and one that is hardly unique to this industry.

Marginal job quality remains an issue that exists throughout this industry rather than one confined to its less desirable employment rungs. As sociologist Chris Land notes: "the credibility of being in a 'cool job' might contribute to a wider identity project and desirable lifestyle but pay for brewers and bar staff is rarely much above a living wage, and often minimum wage."[36] As people attempt to forge long-term careers in this industry, some view the trade-offs they incur at the expense of job security and earning potential to be unsustainable, as we saw last chapter with those who have taken the exit pathway. Ironically, marginal employment conditions in craft beer also help reserve these careers—especially those along the creative pathway that offer symbolic rewards—for workers from privileged backgrounds, not because these jobs are high-earning, but precisely because they are not. Only the affluent can afford the luxury of choosing to work "fun" and passion-rich jobs that make for relatively low-earning and unpredictable careers.

From a labor perspective, what we see in the craft beer industry is a snapshot of what a growing number of American workers face in the new economy: jobs that are highly atomized with little in the way of collective efforts to advocate on behalf of workers. This reality, however, may be at an inflection point if the recent uptick in labor union activity and rising worker power at both the industry and national level is any indication. Echoing and amplifying workers' concerns, I want to see a craft beer industry that prioritizes gainful career opportunities for those who work tirelessly behind the bar or over a brew kettle. Career opportunities that don't make workers choose between the appeals of the here-and-now at the expense of their future prospects. In order to ensure that employment in these settings is sustainable, jobs need to be restructured in ways that are less "cool" and higher *quality*. By "cool," I mean jobs that are imminently consumable, informal in nature, and sometimes intentionally un-work-like.[37] The ad hoc nature of many brewery workplaces and the informal atmosphere of employee-employer relations breed employment conditions over time that do not allow for clear pathways for worker advancement. They can also allow race and gender biases to creep into this process in the form of hiring friends from one's social circle or promoting workers based on informal and inconsistent criteria. To be sure, the appeal of pursuing careers in this industry that feel authentic and personally meaningful is not going away. A corporate-style restructure would likely register to workers as an unwelcomed overcorrection. Yet today's companies can reduce the strain of participating in this industry while also fostering career development by implementing clearer, more structured job roles, better-defined job expectations and ladders of promotion, and more attentive regulation of employee responsibilities.

Recall that some homebrewers mention that their enjoyment of homebrewing was premised on the fact that this activity did not double as their primary source of income. There may be a learning lesson as it pertains to improving the quality of employment for workers. Companies that employ workers who see their jobs as an extension of leisure activities ("I love craft beer, so I found a job in it") is convenient for management in that these workers may not be as concerned about marginal employment conditions. But it can lead to long-term issues for both parties, feeding into workers' perception that these same jobs are not the stuff of serious, long-term careers while management is left to contend with a revolving door of new hires. Essentially, the current structure of work in craft beer ushers in a peculiar type of burnout among workers not because the job is too serious and stressful but perhaps because it lacks a sense of structure and formality.[38] Too many jobs in craft beer feel like a cluster of activities that center passion and play without a clear way to advance in one's career—especially for minoritized workers along subordinate pathways of work.

Building the infrastructure necessary to foster gainful work careers could start with establishing industry groups, organizations, and support networks aimed at developing industry skills, sharing employment knowledge, and other career-focused advice. On the other end of the spectrum, as Kelly Rowe and other industry veterans have asserted, it may also be the case that too many people try to get into emerging industries as business owners thinking that this will be a quick way to make money and have fun while doing so. The reality is usually far more sobering. That said, structural improvements to working conditions in these types of industries will inevitably prove difficult for small and under-resourced companies to implement themselves, particularly in a work landscape that is constantly changing underfoot. Here is where industry associations, trade guilds, and worker resource centers can provide crucial forms of support. Ideally, some of these organizations would specialize in assisting employers in building employee-centered and inclusive workplaces. Others would assist workers in planning for career development and building skills that could make them better suited to thrive in new opportunities—and along career pathways of their choosing.

As with craft beer, workplaces in the new economy continue to struggle to foster a diverse workforce. They often end up with just the opposite. As we have seen, there are complex reasons for the persistence of racialized workplaces in emerging industry settings that reinforce whiteness as well as class privilege, patriarchy, and heteronormativity. However, there are also a growing number of organizations that seek to incubate career development for minoritized workers with the goal of fostering more equitable opportunities. For example, in craft beer, veteran brewmaster Garrett Oliver's scholarship is geared toward creating more career "pipelines" for Black and brown people within the industry; it aims to provide support to these individuals earlier and more often as they prepare to enter into and proceed upward along career pathways in this industry. For good reason, Oliver and his scholarship are admittedly most focused on improving access to what I have called the creative pathway. But not everyone in craft beer wishes to become a head brewer or brewery owner: even if racialized, classed, and gendered barriers of access are chipped away, workers will continue to differ in what they want to get out of their long-term careers.

Many of the working-class men employed along the hard labor pathway say they want a work life grounded in job stability and the ability to provide for their families. They seek a well-defined job that they can do with dignity while contributing to a company where their coworkers and managers appreciate what they have to offer. These career interests may seem universal and basic. Yet in an industry that prizes its aspirational and passion-driven qualities—and rewards the workers who embody them—they consistently get overlooked. Companies thus need to be intentional. Industry organizations supporting workers need to be flexible. The opportunity for high-quality careers must be extended to those who continue to build their careers in less visible roles, taking pride in being the "glue"—as one worker put it—that binds these companies together.

In the wake of the Great Resignation, stories abound of people who leave unremarkable jobs in search of fresh new chapters to their work lives that align with their personal passions and individual interests. Mike, Sheila, and Esteban have already found—and in some cases, lost—the kinds of jobs that make up handcrafted careers, albeit along divergent and unequal pathways. Yet where each of these workers go from here has yet to be written.

Acknowledgments

I want to thank all the amazing people in the craft beer industry who were kind enough to let me hang out with them at work and share their perspectives on what they do for a living. I found these conversations engrossing, highly enjoyable, and sometimes downright whimsical in the best sense. I am especially indebted to those I met with on multiple occasions over the course of this three-year research process. I am humbled to have had the opportunity to celebrate job promotions and positive life events with these extraordinary individuals—and occasionally commiserate moments of hard luck within this rough-and-tumble industry. To everyone in craft beer I am now proud to call my friend: it is hardly an understatement to say that this book couldn't have been written without you.

Several breweries and other beer companies were extremely generous in agreeing to open their doors to this research and allow me an insider's look into the daily rhythms of work behind the scenes. In each case, specific people within these companies (you know who you are!) were instrumental in making this happen, and often, happen again when I proclaimed there was too much fascinating detail to appreciate with just one visit. Thank you for believing in what I was there to do. It is true that this book does not shy from some hard questions about what occurs within craft beer spaces. Yet I hope that it also does justice to the dedication, hard work, and warm emotion that I know so many workers infuse into their jobs every day.

I would like to express my gratitude to my colleagues in the Department of Sociology and Criminology at the University of New Mexico. After arriving at my new intellectual home in 2018, I spent the bulk of my time as a junior faculty researching this project and writing this book. Surely some of my colleagues were left scratching their heads about how I was able to utter "craft beer" and "sociological research" in the same sentence with a straight face. Yet I can truly say I felt nothing but support. A special thanks to the following colleagues who were instrumental in helping me refine my thinking on key portions of this book: Maricarmen Hernandez, Elizabeth Korver-Glenn, Nancy Lopez, Ranita Ray, Owen Whooley, and Rich Wood. I am also fortunate to have arrived at UNM under the leadership of two outstanding department chairs, Sharon Nepstad and Lisa Broidy, both of whom made sure I was abreast of funding opportunities and research development workshops. Between 2019 and 2023, I was fortunate to receive funding support from the College of Arts and Science as well as the Research Allocations Committee at UNM.

University of California Press has been the perfect home for this project. Special thanks to my book editor, Kate Marshall, who welcomed this project from the moment I first described it over a Zoom meeting. Her enthusiasm was infectious. Kate helped remind me why expending so much effort to craft a single quality product—whether a beer or a new book—is totally worth it in the end. I also appreciate Chad Attenborough, an editorial assistant at the press, and Dawn Hall, an excellent copyeditor, for looking out for this manuscript and pointing out areas that needed attention before I tripped over them myself. I am also grateful to the three anonymous peer reviewers who were instrumental in helping me sharpen several key ideas of this book.

Throughout the writing of *Handcrafted Careers*, a number of (very) rough drafts have either been saved from certain embarrassment or brought into a vastly improved state with the help of many friends and colleagues. For their invaluable feedback on drafts of one or more chapters, I want to thank Sharan Mehta, Ellen Meiser, Richard Ocejo, Michael Ramirez, Michael Siciliano, Rachel Skaggs, and Ruben Hernandez-Leon. Additionally, Odul Bozkurt, Erin Cech, and Victor Ray each offered thoughtful comments on the writing and ideas that eventually made its way into this book. I am also grateful to my research collaborators who worked with me on various portions of this project over the years: Nate Chapman, Aaron Delgaty, Slade Lellock, and Asa Stone. Finally, mahalo nui loa to Ruben Hernandez-Leon, Nancy Lopez, and Roger Waldinger, each of whom continues to be mentor figures and wise friends just a phone call away (or a walk down the department hallway).

People say the secret to writing is to develop consistent writing routines. I'd like to add that for me, being able to receive consistent, quality feedback has also been essential to helping me produce halfway *decent* writing. My longtime writing partners, Phi Hong Su, Deisy del Real, Hajar Yazdiha, Amy Zhou—each a formidable scholar in their own right—deserve special recognition for having read, commented, and discussed many chapter drafts of this book from the early idea stage through to copyediting. You all continue to be my writing metronome.

Lastly, I'd like to raise a pint to my family for their unbending support. To my parents Christine and Scott, it is the ultimate luxury to have access to a trove of wisdom and wit so close to home. While writing this book, I frequently sought their honest critique ("Is this too much?" "How can I make this sound smarter??"). This was especially true in the case of my mother, the brilliant and now-emeritus cultural anthropologist. Her usual feedback was a smiling reminder to stay curious about the lives of others, follow unexpected leads, and be grateful for the unique job opportunity that we in academia call field work. Finally, to my wife Laura: through it all—the twists and turns of research, the pandemic disruptions, the small milestones and celebrations—you were there, generous with your time and love. Thank you for continuing to leave an indelible signature on my craftsmanship.

Researching Uncertainty

This project did not come together as originally planned. Starting in the early months of 2020, one year after beginning my research on craft beer workers, I, like everyone else, had to contend with the unavoidable disruptions and evolving health hazards brought on by the coronavirus pandemic. My research was frozen in place, no longer the immediate concern or interest. Forged during this turbulent moment in history, what *Handcrafted Careers* eventually became was different than I anticipated—far less smoothly produced, more analytically tangled, and only loosely bound to a single theoretical framework. But I also believe that this book gained new synergies between the research process and the real-life circumstances of the people whose stories fill this book. The twists and turns that went into this research ended up resembling the emergent work careers that I sought to study in the first place.

What follows is one part methodological note and one part research reflection. The first section charts the specific qualitative methods and the decisions behind them that went into this book, both of which evolved over time. I place special emphasis on how I chose to deal with unexpected developments over the course of this roughly four-year project when it became clear that "staying the course" was untenable. The second section lays out the strengths, as well as some potential challenges, of engaging in an open-ended research process driven by intellectual curiosity and fitted with an adaptable research tool kit. I hope to show the reader that adopting an open-ended approach to qualitative research can be particularly well-suited for dealing with unexpected developments in one's research as well as examining social processes defined by uncertainty.

THE DISRUPTED RESEARCH ARC

My initial idea for this research was straightforward enough: I was interested in understanding how people navigate their employment in types of jobs that lack a clear blueprint for how to do this. I would pay special attention to how social inequalities along the lines of race, class, and gender shape this process. I planned to use tried-and-true ethnographic techniques to approach this research, which involve, as sociologist Mario Small puts it: "travel to a site, observe interactions, talk to people, and take notes."[1] I also knew that I wanted to focus on workers in the craft beer industry both for theoretical reasons—craft beer is a prime example of the kind of "artisanal" work that is on the rise today—and methodological advantages, given that I had personally worked in this industry myself prior to graduate school and still had social connections I could tap into.

I began my research in the spring of 2019 by reaching out to a handful of existing craft beer industry contacts in Los Angeles and Albuquerque. These two cities, which became my primary settings for this study, made for an interesting comparison. Both were home to fast-growing craft beer industries. Both had ethnoracially diverse populations. At the same time, these two cities differed in size, wealth, and cultural prominence. I wanted to see how these differences might shape the kinds of job opportunities available to craft beer workers. My initial outreach efforts to former coworkers and industry colleagues proved fruitful. Soon after securing IRB approval from my home institution (University of New Mexico), I was able to line up opportunities to conduct field research in several different Albuquerque-based craft beer workplaces. During these visits, I shadowed brewers and taproom workers, toured backroom facilities, and talked informally to dozens of people familiar with the industry. This early data collection gave me a sense of the wide range of jobs within craft beer, which had expanded considerably since I left the industry ten years ago. Admittedly, these outreach efforts followed a path of least resistance for me as a researcher and mostly consisted of the recruitment of white men. This reflected my own positionality and social networks within the industry as a function of being a college-educated, white-appearing man who had previously held jobs that continue to be disproportionately held by white people, such as sales, taproom management, and brewing.[2] Cognizant of these issues, I had begun to actively recruit more demographically diverse participants into my study using snowball sampling by the end of 2019. My field research was otherwise proceeding smoothly and expanding in multiple directions. Better yet, workers seemed very receptive to talking to me about their employment experiences; several interviews and field visits had stretched into longer and more informal conversations that felt more like "hanging out" and talking about things of mutual interest.[3] I was also excited by initial patterns I was seeing in the data, which pointed to a far more complex employment landscape and varied career pathways than I anticipated. In the spring of 2020, I had a full schedule of site visits planned to breweries, distributor warehouses, industry group meetings, and craft beer festivals. COVID-19 had yet to become a global public health concern. All of that quickly changed.

The day the governor of New Mexico announced that food and drink establishments were required to close their in-person operations due to risk to public health—March 11, 2020—I was at a local brewery helping the head brewer dump 55-pound bags of specialty malt into the brew kettle. We were laughing at just how "low-tech" and unglamorous this so-called artisanal brewing process was ("if only those beer geeks knew . . . !"). The sudden shutdown of brewpubs and brewery taprooms in New Mexico and California, along with most of the country, started in the early spring of 2020. These shutdowns were a direct blow to many of the workers I had just gotten to know.[4] Some immediately lost their jobs or had them "temporarily suspended," while others took on completely new tasks in order to remain employed for their companies, such as driving around making house deliveries of packaged beer. Many workers told me they knew people who had decided to leave the industry; several said they had recently questioned their own career choice to get into craft beer in the first place.

Of course, the pandemic-related workplace shutdowns also brought my ethnographic research to its knees. In March 2020 alone, I was forced to cancel a week-long research trip to Los Angeles in which I was scheduled to observe full workdays at two different breweries, tour a beer distribution facility, attend a homebrew club meeting, and conduct a half-dozen interviews with workers. Halfway through this project's original timeline and with no end to pandemic-related closures in sight, I was forced to rethink all aspects of my research strategy. I knew I did not want to discard the ethnographic data I already had, which had proved extremely insightful about daily working life within craft beer.[5] But I struggled to conceptualize how to do "fieldwork without the field."[6] I decided to reshuffle the key pieces of my research, letting go of the notion that the heart of my data collection would be immersive fieldwork spent alongside workers in their labor settings. This difficult decision was about more than just "waiting out" the pandemic— which was initially projected to last a matter of weeks!—and hoping for a return to normalcy.[7] The prospect of doing in-person fieldwork during such hazardous times presented thorny methodological and ethical dilemmas. Foremost, this was because face-to-face meetings involved health and safety risks for everyone involved. Even inquiring about meeting up with workers to interview them did not seem right, given how many of their livelihoods had been thrust into turmoil.

For much of the spring and summer of 2020, I turned to other research activities that I could do remotely. I began regularly documenting news stories as well as social media posts that had to do with worker issues and workplace culture in craft beer. The pivot to focusing on this kind of online data did not match the richness of in-person ethnography—the sights, sounds, and spontaneity of it all. But it did turn out to be an unexpectedly productive form of data collection in other ways, allowing me to track evolving conversations taking place online within craft beer communities during this turbulent moment. At the time, craft beer was going through a groundswell of change with regard to conversations about race and gender equity issues as well as the need for greater diversity, equity, and inclusion (DEI) awareness in the industry, particularly in the aftermath of the murder of George Floyd at the hands of Minneapolis police.[8] These stories dominated coverage of the craft beer industry on websites such as Good Beer Hunting, Hop Culture, and Vine Pair. They were also the topics of numerous blogs, Reddit threads, and social media posts among craft beer workers themselves. These online-based conversations illustrated a side of what it meant to work in craft beer that I had not seen while immersed in fieldwork the previous year, as new voices found their footing in virtual spaces amid a changing cultural moment within the industry as well as the country at large. I was able to infuse these insights back into my research as emergent themes that I would continue to explore until the end of this project.[9] In effect, the sudden halt to my in-person research, which was a blow to my planned fieldwork, came with a silver lining: it allowed me to pivot to online-based data collection that offered a unique vantage on what workers were thinking and experiencing in the industry, especially during such a profoundly uncertain moment in history.

It took me until the fall of 2020 to develop a new strategy for fieldwork amid lingering health risks, worker layoffs, and business closures. The popularization of Zoom, the video conferencing service, proved a key development. I was initially very wary of conducting interviews over video chat rather than in person. Could I *really* get someone I had never met to agree to a video interview? Could I foster enough warmth and rapport with them necessary to have in-depth discussions while looking through a computer screen? Indeed, other scholars have noted these kinds of challenges and frustrations with virtual interviews when compared to in-person alternatives.[10] To my surprise, most workers I reached out to were open to the idea of conducting an interview over Zoom. The quality of our conversations, which lasted about an hour on average—the same as my in-person interviews—exceeded my expectations.[11] I ended up conducting more than a dozen interviews on Zoom by the end of 2020. I continued offering my interviewees the option to hold the interview virtually for the rest of this study.

The strategy of holding interviews on Zoom pushed my research forward in two inter-related ways. First, the ability to conduct interviews with people anywhere with an internet connection allowed me the possibility of following leads with workers located throughout the country. Recall that early on, my project focused exclusively on workers in two localized settings, Los Angeles and Albuquerque. But as the comparative analysis between these locales proved less fruit-ful than anticipated (turns out craft beer workers in both cities share many simi-lar joys and frustrations), I began to be more interested in loosening geographical parameters to speak with anyone willing to share personal insights into the nature of work careers, job aspirations, and day-to-day work life from all corners of craft beer. Just as importantly, the prospect of engaging in video-based inter-views allowed me to incorporate a wider range of workers in my research who were linked together through online communities rather than in-person ones. In particular, video-based interviewing expanded my ability to recruit women, people of color, and other minoritized workers who would have otherwise been difficult to locate and meet with.

Second, traditional in-person interviews and scheduled events require not only time and resources but also substantial coordination leading up to the event itself.[12] By contrast, I found Zoom-based interviews and other virtual research engagements extraordinarily convenient in that they more easily fit into existing schedules for all parties. At the suggestion of my interviewees, I met up virtually with workers while they were taking their lunch breaks or driving home from work (audio only). I scheduled interviews on Zoom between teaching my classes at the University of New Mexico and sometimes on weekends. In all, I was able to conduct two, or occasionally even three, Zoom-based interviews in a day—far more than I would have been able to do in person. Seeing the success of these virtual interviews, I sought out other opportunities to engage in online-based fieldwork, sometimes called "digital ethnography."[13] For instance, in 2020, I managed to attend a national craft beer industry conference that had been moved online to feature virtual panels, speaker events, and happy hours. I also attended a national beer festival with similar online interactive opportunities for participants.

Starting in the spring of 2021, as pandemic-related restrictions eased, I began to reincorporate in-person interviews. By this time, however, the core of my data collection for this research had shifted away from workplace-based ethnographic field notes to in-depth interview transcripts with workers. This presented new strengths and limitations. It was clear that I was not able to observe craft beer workers in their everyday workplaces as much as was originally planned before the pandemic. This meant that I missed out on the kinds of routine occurrences that patterns people's work lives and interactions in situ, the kind of data that animated my previous research about the shopfloor dynamics that reproduce social inequality in restaurants.[14] My unanticipated reliance on in-depth inter-views for this study helped me center other interesting insights about how work-ers reflected on their work lives. For instance, by asking workers open-ended questions such as "tell me about the first time you got interested in craft beer," then following up with questions like, "was that also when you knew you would enter this industry? Why or why not?" I was able to capture nuanced stories about how workers attributed meaning and value to their employment by linking together their past experiences with their present employment and future aspirations.[15] Moreover, focusing on worker interviews allowed me to hear how people bundled their discussions of employment together with other aspects of their lives that were not directly tied to work, such as homebrewing hobbies or having to make decisions about moving to another state because of their partner or another member of their family.

Much of what my interviewees described implicitly or explicitly involved a time-order context to their career developments. For this reason, I decided to try and interview as many workers as I could a second time to see how their employment circumstances and career perspectives may have changed. In all, I engaged in follow-up contact, either in the form of interviews or more casual contact such as back-and-forth text message exchanges and informal conversations with forty workers that I had originally interviewed at least one year prior.[16] About half of these workers had switched jobs or employers and spoke to me at length about the circumstances surrounding their respective employment microtransitions. These follow-up interviews, while conducted nonrandomly, gave me greater insight into the interplay of uncertainty and inequality shaping the lives of the workers I had gotten to know.

In sum, for each unexpected methodological deviation from the original study plan, new avenues for empirical and theoretical insight presented themselves. These were not the result of planned actions but rather an *open-ended research process*, one that leaves ample room to embrace change as needed. In what follows, I describe three main components of an open-ended research approach that I believe could be of use to qualitative researchers, especially those interested in studying how lives and social processes unfold amid uncertain contexts.

Embracing Not-Knowing

Embracing analytical and methodological not-knowing can be a strategic element of one's research design. By "not-knowing," I do not mean unreflective naivete but rather, leaving space for continual surprise and discovery about what affects the social phenomena you are most interested in. From an analytical standpoint, not-knowing aligns with the basic principles of grounded theory and inductive analysis. Researchers are encouraged to avoid a theoretical straitjacket upfront that could unduly narrow their scope of analysis.[17] Analytical not-knowing requires treating the research journey as an intellectually open-ended and emergent process.[18] Doing so allows one's research to capture a wider range of insights into the "stuff" that makes up people's everyday realities. This includes keeping an open mind about what informs people's interactions with others in a given setting, just as it can also mean considering a range of possibilities about how people engage in "representations, classification systems, boundary work, identity, imagined realities and cultural ideals, as well as emotional states."[19] Appreciating the layered and complex nature of any one person's lived experience and worldview demands that we hold in check our assumptions about what we should expect to find a priori; we shouldn't necessarily know how far down we'll need to dig the hole before we start.

Methodological not-knowing leaves open the possibility that a variety of research tools may be needed to inspect a given research question from different angles. This aspect of not-knowing seeks to avoid limiting a study to a narrow set of preordained research methods, especially early on in the research process. Here I echo sociologists Michèle Lamont and Ann Swidler's call for greater "methodological pluralism," though I also emphasize how methodological not-knowing can involve adapting during the research process to follow unexpected leads. I learned this accidentally. Early on while researching this book I was focused entirely on in-person ethnographic data collection. For this reason, I was completely stymied, and a good deal dismayed, by the pandemic-related closures of taprooms and other industry workplaces. Had I ended up putting all research activities on hold indefinitely, I would have missed out on the growing forms of community and conversations taking place online among workers in the industry, particularly among those from minoritized backgrounds. These conversations had not made it into the workplaces that I visited up to that point, and it is entirely possible that I would have missed these trends entirely should I have ended my data collection early or taken years to resume in-person fieldwork. It took pivoting my research methods and being open to the changing nature of data leads to begin to document these patterns.

Treating the research process as a draft able to be rewritten and revised keeps the focus on capturing what is most relevant for answering key research queries. This kind of not-knowing can also help researchers triangulate data insights from multiple angles. For instance, what people describe about their lives during an interview tends to involve at least some degree of rearranging of the facts—or recounting certain events—in ways that suit them. That is, when being interviewed, some people voice more control and agency over their individual circumstances than is often the case given structural circumstances (one obvious example would be a wealthy person recounting how he or she gained a high-earning job merely through hard work and smart choices). A researcher aiming to understand more about a given study participant could try to talk to other people who know that person or by observing them in settings they frequent. They could also contact the interviewee multiple times or access records on file, such as company employment records to double-check spoken accounts of events. What I am advocating here about methodological not-knowing involves using different methodological tools to reexamine data from different angles rather than simply assuming certain methodological limitations and moving on.

This is not without practical limitations. How should a researcher do this amid very real constraints of time, resources, and prior methodological training? As Annette Lareau reminds us, listening to ourselves—our personal interests, skills, and life obligations—is an essential part of the research process that complements listening to others.[20] One way to approach methodological not-knowing could be by using different research tools that vary situationally and based on one's personal qualities. Sociologist Victoria Reyes argues that drawing on one's "strategic positionality" in the field can result in richer insights and points of access for qualitative researchers. By strategic positionality, Reyes emphasizes how aspects of one's social position, such as one's race, class, gender, sexuality, age, and life experiences—prior jobs, childhood memories, multilinguistic abilities—can be strategically leveraged as a part of one's methodological tools. Strategic positionality can help build rapport with study participants from a particular background or generate other kinds of unique insights about the field. For example, while researching craft beer workers, I found it useful to have certain interviewees "read" me as a "bearded white guy" to put them at ease and signal my unspoken belonging in brewery spaces.[21] Alternately, with other interviewees I found it useful to verbalize my mixed-race background and present a more "off-white" or ambiguous racial position. I did something similar with my status as a former industry worker too, selectively drawing attention to the fact that I was relatively well-versed with craft beer or "merely" a sociology researcher who needed to be explained the basics of industry jobs and titles depending on the situation. *Who* one is as a researcher is a classic tenet of positionality in the research process; how one can draw on these intersecting social statuses and organizational roles can help them better approach novel scenarios through methodological not-knowing.

Studying Change through Change

In qualitative research, trying to pin down a through line of analysis in light of changing circumstances is always difficult. Meeting these circumstances using a flexible approach to research gives us the best chance to produce an analysis that will feel timely and real, one where motion, fluidity, and change-over-time are part of the story.[22] Over the course of researching this book, identifying sociological patterns in the unpredictable work lives of craft beer workers was a challenging task even *before* the pandemic. For example, some of the people I talked to grappled with the fact that their careers were in constant flux at a time when their perspectives on what constituted a "good" career was changing; others aspired to stay in the industry and "move up" but did not know what that would even look like long-term. This led me to realize that change and uncertainty were a key part of the story of these people's work lives rather than something to try and stamp out of the research process.

Figure 12. Hanging out in the field.

Taking time to reflect on change can also place into sharp relief the people and processes that are, in fact, *not* changing—or at least not with the same velocity or impact. This was the case when I began to assess the employment realities of workers in subordinate roles in breweries, particularly working-class men of color. In an industry where most of their colleagues celebrate aspirational pursuits of passion for craft beer and highly mobile, entrepreneurial careers, it was all the more striking that these men did not voice this same relationship to their jobs and found themselves in jobs defined by *im*mobility. The story of career dynamism in the new economy is one that centers change, but it is also mediated by racialized and classed privilege in important ways.

Some may say that research that grapples with too much unpredictability risks yielding an empirical scatterplot rather than a tight story. This, I believe, is a real risk. But also one well worth taking. Two strategies can help researchers approach change in systematic ways: talking with multiple study participants about the same situation and talking to the same person more than once at different times. The former involves asking multiple people to recount the same situation—one they inevitably saw and experienced from slightly different perspectives. This exercise not only helps corroborate key details about a given event, it also reveals important differences about how people understand their realities and frame them with distinct kinds of values, ideals, sensitivities, and symbolic boundaries.[23] To offer an example from my own research: I asked three different workers at an Albuquerque-based brewery to share their thoughts on a taproom-based event on Cinco de Mayo featuring a Mexican-themed character. Two of these workers, both white men, laughed about the whimsical creativity that went into this event and its crowd-sourced taproom decorations decked out in colorful green, yellow, and red. The other worker, a Hispanic woman, drew attention to the tone-deaf actions of her white coworkers surrounding an event that she felt veered uncomfortably close to cultural appropriation and racism. Keying in on how these three people experienced a shared event illustrated an important point about the whiteness of many brewery workplaces that allowed workers (and customers) to feel a sense of comfort and ease not shared by others.

Engaging in follow-up contact with the same individual can also be a productive way to capture changing material realities as well as how individuals make sense of these changes. We are able to learn more about how people contend with uncertain futures, just as it can draw out complex and sometimes contradictory elements of their thinking.[24] For example, it was only through repeated conversations with craft beer workers spaced at least one year apart that I gained insight into the conflicted relationship workers have with the cultural logic of work in craft beer. Over time, some of the white men who got into the industry because of their *pure passion* for craft beer struggled to make sense of the employment precarity that these careers often came with over time. In sum, the ability to meet changing data with changeable qualitative methods allows for a richer and more dynamic analysis that might otherwise be flattened out.

Linking Talk, Meaning, and Action

In the appendix to *On the Fireline*, sociologist Matt Desmond argues for a "habitus-driven approach" to doing ethnographic research, one that focuses on describing "specific links connecting personal histories with present-day social contexts."[25] Desmond contends that this approach helps bridge microlevel processes to macrosocial issues by focusing on the ways people's everyday lives are shaped by and within social structures. The open-ended research approach I advocate here shares much in common with Desmond's in that it seeks to link talk, meaning, and action together. The difference is a matter of emphasis: where this really shines is in studying contexts of uncertainty and change. In moments where study participants are facing an unclear future, whether due to large-scale disruptions like a global pandemic or more personal situations such as the loss of a job, being attentive to how people attempt to navigate and make sense of their circumstances using resources available to them can be highly revealing about who they are and what shapes their respective social worlds.

When taken alone, talk can be "cheap." That is, the extent to which people's talk of action corresponds to "real" actions and behaviors should be treated with a grain of salt, as has been well covered in recent methodological debates.[26] But if researchers are interested in determining how people approach and manage uncertainty in their lives, their talk on the subject can be highly informative. As Lamont and Swidler note, examining what people say gives us insight into "whether, how, and how much action is empowered by vocabularies, symbolic boundaries, cultural scripts and repertoires."[27] These aspects of people's talk points to cognitive processes and cultural worldviews that remain relatively consistent despite changing material realities. What people say about their lives—and what has meaning in their lives—is also implicitly longitudinal. People construct a narrative of their past in ways that draw connections to their present and anticipated futures. To be sure, these narratives tend to be overly tidy and coherent as people stitch together past realities that were often more inchoate in real time.[28] But these narratives should be engaged by researchers rather than ignored, especially in light of circumstances that do not present themselves in linear ways. As sociologist Iddo Tavory notes: "interviewers too rarely ask about the paths not taken—the near-misses and the plausible turns that could have been—that our interlocutors are often well aware of."[29] I personally found that one of the most fruitful lines of inquiry when interviewing craft beer workers for this book was to ask these individuals to tell me what *they* thought would have been different about their careers had something changed in their past. Some responded by mentioning jobs that they did or didn't get and people they did or didn't meet. Others framed their past employment situations in comparison to coworkers who now occupied more decorated jobs than themselves. In other words, workers talked me through what they personally experienced by linking these experiences to specific situations, then noting how these situations affected them. Clearly, these stories remain imperfect and fragmentary. But in drawing attention to what participants themselves see as key pivot points in their lives that carry with them both vivid memories and material consequences, research-ers give participants the opportunity to help them understand how these events made an impact on who and where they are today.

The reflections I offer here lay out open-ended research strategies that allow us to give focus to the blurred motion of people's messy lives. This can be particularly useful for those who study social processes defined by uncertainty and change, which are not only the subjects but the action verbs of our modern world. I don't know for sure if my research approach to *Handcrafted Careers* has been completely effective. I can't know if the specific methodological pivots I made considering the global pandemic were the right ones. I do know that a firm embrace of not-knowing was at the core of this research process as it unfolded.

ABBREVIATIONS USED BELOW IN THE LIST
OF KEY CHARACTERS

Education codes (highest level of education):

HS (high school); SC (some college); AA (Associates or brewing professional degree); COL (College); GRAD (Graduate degree); UNKN (unknown, not discussed).

Job Position Codes (with examples):

BOH, "back of the house" (cellarperson, draft technician); BREW (brewhouse worker); BREW-HOME (homebrewer, amateur); SALES-DSTR (sales representative, distribution); SALES-BREW (sales representative, brewery); FOH, "front of the house" (taproom server, beertender); OWNER/MGMT (owner, general manager); DISTR-DISTR (delivery driver, warehouse operator); DISTR-BREW (delivery driver, canning & packaging operator); MISC (consultant, brewery marketing firm, guild worker).

List of Key Characters

Name	Race	Age	Gender	Education	Years in Industry	Job Position
Aaron	white	33	male	COL	2	OWNER/MGMT
Alfred	white	35	male	GRAD	5	BREW
Amber	mixed	25	female	COL	4	FOH
Anthony	Latinx	43	male	HS	19	BREW
Ariana	Latinx	28	female	COL	4	FOH
Arnold	white	31	male	COL	8	OWNER/MGMT
Arturo	Latinx	32	male	COL	1	OWNER/MGMT
Bert	white	30	male	COL	9	SALES-DSTR
Bobby	Native Am	33	male	SC	5	DISTR-BREW
*Brad**	white	late 20s	male	COL	4	BOH
Brandon	white	43	male	BREW	6	BREW
Britney	white	30	female	SC	10	BREW
Carly	white	40	female	GRAD	6	OWNER
Chandra	Black	41	female	GRAD	6	SALES-DSTR
Charlie	white	40	male	COL	14	OWNER/MGMT
*Clint**	white	50	male	GRAD	15	OWNER/MGMT
Daniel	latinx	33	male	SC	2	DISTR-BREW
Derrick	Black	64	male	COL	8	OWNER
Drew	white	33	male	COL	6	BREW
Emmett	white	30	male	GRAD	n/a	BREW-HOME
Enrique	Latinx	29	nonbinary	SC	6	FOH
Erica	Latinx	31	female	COL	7	OWNER/MGMT
Esteban	Latinx	42	male	SC	2	OWNER/MGMT
Fernando	Latinx	42	male	COL	4	BREW
Francine	white	43	female	COL	13	CONSULT
Grant	white	28	male	COL	4	FOH
Gustavo	Latinx	39	male	COL	10	MISC
Henry	white	45	male	GRAD	6	MISC
Ignacio	Latinx	39	male	SC	2	OWNER/MGMT
Ishmael	Latinx	45	male	SC	2	OWNER/MGMT
Jack	white	39	male	SC	1	BREW
Jeremy	white	41	male	COL	10	SALES-BREW
Jerome	Black	34	male	COL	10	SALES-BREW
Jerry	white	50	male	GRAD	4	OWNER/MGMT
Jonah	white	38	male	COL	15	BREW
Jonathan	white	34	male	SC	8	BREW

Jordyn	white	35	female	COL	10	BREW
Jorge	Latinx	23	male	SC	1	DISTR-BREW
Josiah	Native Am	26	male	HS	5	BREW
Kenneth	white	58	male	HS	n/a	BREW-HOME
*Lalo**	Latinx	late 20s	male	UNKN	unknown	BOH
Lamar	Native Am	26	male	SC	2	DISTR-BREW
Lauren	white	39	female	GRAD	12	OWNER/MGMT
Maya	mixed	39	female	COL	15	SALES-BREW
Lucy	white	42	female	COL	9	FOH (former)
Luis	Latinx	33	male	AA	7	BREW
Manuel	Latinx	55	male	COL	4	FOH
Marisa	Asian	40	female	GRAD	n/a	MISC
Marisol	Latinx	31	female	COL	5	BREW
Marne	white	22	female	HS	2	FOH
Mike	white	36	male	GRAD	6	OWNER/MGMT
Mirabel	Latinx	35	female	SC	6	BREW
Mona	white	28	female	GRAD	2	FOH
Orlando	Latinx	35	male	COL	10	FOH
Paco	Latinx	53	male	HS	27	BREW
Paul	white	30	male	COL	7	SALES-BREW
Peter	white	35	male	GRAD	3	OWNER/MGMT
Quinn	mixed	55	female	SC	n/a	BREW-HOME
*Randall**	white	early 30s	male	UNKN	unknown	BREW
Ricardo	Latinx	36	male	SC	2	OWNER/MGMT
*Ricky**	white	late 20s	male	COL	unknown	SALES-BREW/ FOH
Samesh	Indian	28	male	COL	6	MISC
Santiago	Latinx	42	male	GRAD	8	OWNER/MGMT
Sheila	mixed	34	female	SC	9	SALES-DSTR
Sheldon	Asian	33	male	COL	6	SALES-DSTR
Sonny	white	56	male	SC	7	DISTR-BREW
Tony	mixed	31	male	COL	2	OWNER
Troy	Latinx	35	male	COL	8	BREW-LAB
Ty	Black	32	male	GRAD	3	OWNER/MGMT
Yareli	Latina	32	female	COL	8	FOH

* Informal conversation

APPENDIX C Demographic Characteristics of Interviewees

(N = 128)

	median or n	range or %
Age	36	22–64
Gender		
Men	94	73.4%
Women	32	25.0%
Nonbinary	2	1.6%
Race (self-identified)		
White	78	60.9%
Black	5	3.9%
Latinx	33	25.8%
Asian	3	2.3%
Native American	4	3.1%
Mixed Race*	5	3.9%
Education		
Graduate Degree	22	17.2%
Bachelor's Degree	59	46.1%
Brewing Certificate/AA	4	3.1%
Some College	28	21.9%
High School	15	11.7%

(continued)

	median or n	*range or %*
Job Position		
Ownership	28	*21.9%*
Brewhouse	32	*25.0%*
Taproom	18	*14.1%*
Sales and Distribution	25	*19.5%*
Misc. Jobs	14	*10.9%*
Homebrewer (amateur)	8	*6.3%*

NOTES: Age is median age; percentages are rounded and do not always add up to 100%.

* Self-identified as "mixed race," indicating no primary racial category.

Notes

PREFACE

1. I became a "Certified Cicerone," the beer industry equivalent of a wine sommelier, in 2009.

2. Du Bois (1904, 85). Sociologists José Itzigsohn and Karida Brown (2020, 104–5) note of W. E. B. Du Bois's sociology: "[Du Bois] saw in sociology the potential to analyze, with exacting scientific measurement, the scope of people's ability to shape their lives—which he called Chance—within all of the various historical constraints—which he called Law."

INTRODUCTION

1. All names and specific companies in this book are pseudonyms in order to preserve confidentiality. I have also selectively modified some identifying details about the people and businesses described throughout for similar reasons.

2. Throughout this book I describe people using the racial and ethnic categories they self-identify with. In Sheila's case, while "Persian" is not a widely accepted racial category in the United States, it does reflect how Sheila describes herself, at least in part, given her racial identity and given her mixed race background.

3. I base these industry statistics on a recent Brewers Association (2022) report.

4. The notion of workers as "free agents" was popularized by Daniel Pink's (2002) best-selling book *Free Agent Nation*. For more on this topic see Gershon 2017; Ross 2009; and Vallas and Christin 2017.

5. Halpin and Smith 2017; Pugh 2015.

6. Alegria 2019; Wingfield and Alston 2014.

7. Acker 2006; Ray 2019; Wooten and Couloute 2017.

8. For more on boundaryless careers, see Tams and Arthur 2010.

9. For example, many have observed that the careers of artists and other creative workers are highly uncertain given the nature of their respective industries (see Giuffre 2007; Menger 1999; Reilly 2017). Yet this scholarship does not give explicit attention to how these career dynamics are shaped by social inequalities, or how career pathways in uncertain labor markets are racialized, classed, and gendered.

10. See Halpin and Smith (2017) on "employment management work."

11. Giddens 1991. On the connection between socialized disposition, identity, and work, see Desmond 2007: 266.

12. See Skeggs 2004.

13. Kalleberg and Vallas 2018; Smith 2001.

14. Halpin 2015; Kalleberg 2000. Research shows that a growing proportion of workers rely on compensation that is structured piecemeal, contingent on customers (e.g., tips), or based on computer algorithms, as companies stretch the legal limits of independent labor contracts and "right to work" employment arrangements. See: Barley and Kunda 2004; Ravenelle 2020; Ross 2009; Smith 1997.

15. Kalleberg 2009, 2011; Ross 2009.

16. Pugh 2015; Smith 1997.

17. Cech 2021; Kalleberg 2009; Terkel 1974.

18. Barley and Kunda 2004; Cech 2021; Gershon 2017; Ross 2009.

19. Bunderson and Thompson 2007; Cech 2021; DePalma 2021.

20. Cech 2021; DePalma 2021. In her research, Cech (2021) finds that college students prioritize careers that align with their passions over those that promise employment security or high wages.

21. For more on the new spirit of capitalism, see Boltanski and Chiapello 2006.

22. These trends are more readily apparent among workers from socially privileged backgrounds, though Cech (2021) notes that they cut across demographics to reflect a broader shift in the culture of work today. See also: Rao and Tobias-Neely 2019.

23. Barley and Kunda 2004; Besen-Cassino 2014.

24. DePalma 2021; Duffy 2017; Mears 2015; Williams and Connell 2010. On creative jobs and precarious employment, see Frenette (2013); Menger 1999.

25. For more on work identity, see Ashcraft et al. 2012; Brady 2018; Brown 2015; Evetts 2013; Giazitzoglu and Muzio 2021; Holvino 2010; Ibarra 1999; Ibarra and Barbulescu 2010; Petriglieri 2011.

26. Amis, Mair, Munir 2019; Ray 2019; Roscigno and Wilson 2014; Tomaskovic-Devey and Avent-Holt 2019.

27. In their review of this literature, management scholars Amis, Mair, Munir (2019) identify five major types of organizational practices—hiring, role allocation, promotion, compensation, and structuring—that are central to the reproduction of social inequality within organizations.

28. Acker 1990, 2006.

29. Castilla 2008; Byron and Roscigno 2019; Tomaskovic-Devey and Avent-Holt 2020; Wingfield and Alston 2014.

30. To be clear, blatantly discriminatory and prejudicial forms of social exclusion at work do still exist, though they are far less pervasive and socially accepted than in a past era.

31. Pager and Quillian 2005.

32. Ray 2019; see also Moore 2008.

33. Waldinger and Lichter 2003; Williams 2006; Wilson 2021; Wingfield 2019; Wingfield and Alston 2014; Zamudio and Lichter 2008.

34. Ray 2019. For more on how favoritism reproduces racial inequality in organizations, see DiTomaso 2015.

35. This is consistent with what sociologists Kramer, Ray, and Bonilla-Silva (forthcoming) conceptualize as the "racism of omission."

36. Rivera 2015.

37. For more on how a worker's perceived "cultural fit" can reproduce inequality in companies, see Rivera 2012. In customer-service settings, such as restaurants, bars, and retail stores, research shows that managers often favor young, white, educated men and women who they perceive to embody the right "look," feel, and tastes for their brand. Wilson 2016; Williams and Connell 2010; Wright 2005.

38. Halpin and Smith 2018.

39. Granovetter 1973, 1985.

40. For good examples of how socially stratified networks result in job channeling, see Gomberg-Munoz 2011; Royster 2003; Wilson 2021.

41. Nelson and Vallas 2021; Wilson 2021.

42. Cech 2013.

43. Bourdieu 1984, 2011 [1986].

44. Desmond 2007.

45. See Cech 2013; Ridgway 2011.

46. I use the expression "bearded white guys" throughout this book for several reasons. First, it is a familiar trope to anyone with knowledge of the craft beer industry, one commonly used by workers and brewery patrons alike. Second, while "white guys"—as well as whiteness and masculinity—are central to this book's argument about inequality, "bearded" is also noteworthy. Men with beards working in craft beer has become a cliché and the object of satire (as illustrated

by the TV show *Portlandia*'s sketch "The Dream of the 1890s"). This suggests that beards, too, help mediate white male homosociality in ways that underwrite the dominant status of white men in craft beer.

47. See Correll 2017.

48. Hatmaker 2013; Kumra and Vinnicombe 2008; Rydzik, Ellis, Vowles 2019. For similar research from an intersectional lens that includes race, see Alegria 2019.

49. Hatmaker (2013) finds that women working as engineers use two primary strategies—impression management tactics and coping strategies—that selectively play up or subvert their gender at work. Similarly, the working-class white men in professional service firms must learn to perform cultural capital in order to attempt to fit in, though doing so can inflict hidden injuries of class and alienate them from their home communities (Giazitzoglu and Muzio 2021). See also Abad 2019.

50. Other variations of this trend involve chefs at farm-to-table restaurants (Leschzinger 2015) and artisanal cheese makers (see Paxson 2012).

51. Ocejo 2017; see also Thurnell-Read 2014; Wallace 2019.

52. Chapman and Koontz 2017; Thurnell-Read 2014.

53. Paxson 2012, 6; Thurnell-Read 2014.

54. Gandini 2019; Land 2018; Scott 2017.

55. Currid-Halkett 2017: chapter 5. See also Paxson 2012; Scott 2017.

56. According to the Brewers Association's (BA) definition, a craft brewery must produce less than six million barrels of beer annually and be less than 25 percent corporate owned. In 2019, the BA dropped the requirement that craft breweries must also use "traditional" brewing ingredients in their flagship brand, such as malted barley, wheat, and hops.

57. Wilson and Stone 2022.

58. For example, craft beer frequently makes appearances in mainstream movies, receives coverage in major news publications, and can be found on tap at professional ballgames. Craft breweries are also associated with efforts to "revitalize" (or more critically, gentrify) older neighborhoods with trendy commercial establishments. For more, see Chapman, Lellock, Lippard 2017; Wilson and Stone 2022.

59. Brewers Association 2022.

60. Carroll and Swaminathan 2000; Wilson and Stone 2022.

61. For recent explorations on this topic, see Koontz and Chapman 2019; Roberts and Desoucey 2023.

62. Describing the rise of craft breweries amid corporate consolidation, Carroll and Swaminathan (2000) argue that this dual trend follows a model of "resource partitioning" in the beer industry, in which small producers were able to survive because they occupied a niche market segment. For more on corporate buyouts of craft breweries, see Noel 2019. See also Wilson and Stone 2022.

63. I base this salary range on Payscale's 2023 data for Brewer (payscale.com). According to a recent survey by the Brewers Association, the average annual

salary for an assistant brewer is $27,615 (for a brewery making under 500 barrels) and $31,157 (for a brewery making between 501 and 1,000 barrels).

64. In 2018, the industry news outlet *Good Beer Hunting* produced a four-part series called "Will Work for Beer" that examined worker issues in the craft beer industry. Among the most prominent issues covered are the insufficient pay and benefits that workers face, and the widespread assumption that these labor conditions are treated as normal within the industry.

65. One of Miller's (2019) respondents referred to brewers as "glorified janitors." See also Delgaty and Wilson 2023.

66. Brewers Association 2022.

67. Borer 2019; Elliot 2019. I borrow the expression "'cool' jobs in 'hot' industries" from Neff, Wissinger, and Zukin 2005.

68. Chapman and Brunsma 2020; Wilson and Stone 2022; Withers 2017.

69. Chapman and Brunsma 2020.

70. Jordan 2020.

71. Chapman and Brunsma 2020, chapter 5.

72. Chapman and Brunsma 2020; for more, see the excellent edited volume *Untapped: Exploring the Cultural Dimensions of Craft Beer*, edited by Chapman, Lellock, and Lippard (2017).

73. There is some evidence that the patterns described in this paragraph can also be found in other small and craft-focused companies such as third wave coffee shops and gourmet butcheries, see Ocejo 2017.

74. For the Brewers Association's report of industry demographics, see Hertz 2019.

75. For more on this study's methodology, please see Appendix A. The coronavirus pandemic disrupted planned ethnographic data collection that would have occurred after March 2020. At that time, government-mandated temporary shutdowns led to brewery closures and worker layoffs that made in-person research both impractical and unethical. While I discuss the ongoing consequences of the pandemic on labor in this industry elsewhere, this subject is beyond the scope of this book.

76. See appendix A for more information on research methods.

77. I also talked with a handful of amateur homebrewers, former workers, and beer writers to get a better sense of the industry from people who were positioned around or just outside it (see chapter 6).

78. Berkelaar and Buzzanell 2015, 157. For a similar approach, see Bozkurt and Cohen 2018.

79. I am of a biracial background (half Asian, half white). For a more detailed discussion of my positionality while in the field, see the Appendix A.

80. It is worth noting that while Albuquerque and Los Angeles have sizable nonwhite populations, the African American population in both cities is

considerably lower than the national average of 13.6 percent, according to the most recent US Census.

81. Jackson 2017.

82. New Mexico Magazine 2019.

83. I base demographic information for both these cities on 2022 population estimates from the US Census (census.gov). I could not locate reliable, region-specific industry demographic information for Albuquerque or Los Angeles.

84. Los Angeles County Brewers Guild 2020.

CHAPTER 1. GOING DOWN THE RABBIT HOLE: CAREER PATHWAYS AND MICROTRANSITIONS

1. The "Lab" is a reference to a well-known, Albuquerque-based national laboratory that employs over 10,000 people, most of them highly educated, in a variety of science and engineering capacities.

2. For an overview on race and gender inequality within workplaces, see Tomaskovic-Devey 1993. Recent examples of ethnographic studies that describe socially segregated workplaces include Ribas 2015; Sherman 2009; Williams 2005, Wilson 2021.

3. Acker 2006; Maume 1999; Tomaskovic-Devey and Avent-Holt 2020; Wilson 2021.

4. Ray 2019. See also Tomaskovic-Devey and Avent-Holt 2020.

5. For more on how people plan actions based on imagined futures, see Tavory and Eliasoph 2013.

6. Beckhy 2006; Halpin and Smith 2017.

7. Borer 2019, 205. Similarly, Elliot (2023) describes the typical pathway to employment in craft beer based on how consumers become producers.

8. According to 2019 industry statistics released by the Brewers Association, less than 1 percent of all craft breweries are Black-owned.

9. Withers 2017.

10. A similar social organization of labor to this has been described by Williams 2004; Wilson 2021.

11. A large body of literature describes how customer service jobs involve emotional, "aesthetic," and sexualized forms of labor, particularly in male-dominated spaces. See Erickson 2007; Hall 1993; Hochschild 1983; Williams and Connell 2011.

12. Jones (1996) characterizes the career stages of creative professionals in a similar way: (1) beginning a career; (2) crafting the career; (3) navigating the career; and (4) maintaining the career. I build on this framework by examining how a similar process occurs that also involves job channeling based on intersecting social statuses.

13. Sociologist Alice Goffman (2019) notes that parties are settings that can facilitate unexpected new social connections and experiences that can be potentially meaningful for one's life course.

14. Chapman and Brunsma (2020) note that craft beer is less available in Black and brown communities in part because sales representatives operate on assumptions that these products won't sell well there.

15. Rodgers and Taves (2017) use the term "epistemic culture" to describe the shared culture of knowledge production between craft brewers and homebrewers.

16. An official "membership" at this brewery costs an annual fee and grants members access to discounted beer and merchandise as well as invitations to special events.

17. See Besen-Cassino 2014; Wilson 2019. For more on close relations between "regulars" and workers, see Erickson 2009.

18. Borer 2019.

19. Waldinger and Lichter 2003; Wilson 2021; Wingfield and Alston 2014.

20. Cosmic Brews is a pseudonym.

21. Katherine Giuffre (1999) also describes how social networks, especially diffuse, loosely connected ones, help prop up the careers of artists amid uncertain conditions.

22. Some of these workers seek out front-of-the-house jobs as short-term or part-time employment opportunities. Correspondingly, establishments that offer these jobs, such as restaurants, cafés, and bars, tend to structure them as contingent employment. See Besen-Cassino 2014; Shigihara 2015; Wilson 2019.

23. Cech 2003.

CHAPTER 2. CAREERS OF THE HEART: PURSUING PASSION IN THE BREWHOUSE

1. Vandenengel 2016.

2. The idea of cultural logics of work borrows from institutional logics, meaning organizing principles within institutions that provide social actors with motives and meaning for their actions. For more on institutional logics, see Friedland and Alford 1991; Haveman and Rao 1997; Thornton and Ocasio 2008.

3. Cech 2021; DePalma 2021.

4. This mission statement was first quoted in Bell et al. 2018, 4. It has since been taken down from Brewdog's website.

5. Cech 2021; DePalma 2021; Gershon 2017. As sociologist Erin Cech notes, the 1970 publication of Richard Bolles's *What Color Is Your Parachute?* marked the emergence of a new approach to employment: the first known usage of personal passion as a rationale for career choice.

6. Gershon 2017.

7. Some research by social psychologists suggests that employees who describe themselves as passionate about their work tend to be more proactive on the job and entrepreneurial than their less passionate peers (see Cardon et al. 2009; Ho et al. 2011). That said, workers who are passionate about their jobs also risk becoming overly obsessed about work and experience negative health and social outcomes; see Vallerand and Houlfort 2003, 2014.

8. Bellah et al. 1996.

9. Besen-Cassino 2014; Cech 2021; Ritzer et al., 2012; Wilson 2019.

10. Cech 2021.

11. Cech 2021; McCallum 2020; Kim et al. 2020.

12. DePalma 2021; Duffy 2017; Fleming and Sturdy 2011; Kim et al. 2020. For other examples of how exploitative labor conditions can double as fun and enjoyable opportunities, see Frenette 2013; Mears 2015; Siciliano 2021.

13. Lareau 2003, 2015; Seamster and Ray (2017) refer to this as racialized agency, in which the ability to structure one's time is unequally available to individuals based on racial privilege.

14. Rao and Tobias Neely 2019.

15. Cech 2013; Ridgeway 2011.

16. Shelly Correll and colleagues (2020) find that managers are more likely to evaluate men employees as "standout" or "genius" than women employees while also valuing the former's assertive behaviors in the workplace, such as "taking charge," more highly. See also Acker 2006; Brumley 2014; Cech 2013; Rivera and Tilcsik 2016.

17. Wingfield 2010.

18. Anderson 2015; Moore 2008.

19. Rao and Tobias Neely 2019.

20. The study of specific workplace cultures recalls sociologist Gary Fine's idea of "idiocultures" (2012, 116), or the shared systems of knowledge, beliefs, customs, and behaviors of a group that make up its shared social reality. Bringing this lens together with the study of social inequality can show how idiocultures are racialized, gendered, and classed, or how small group cultural dynamics found in workplaces like craft breweries can potentially deter minoritized individuals from fully participating in group life.

21. Prior conceptualizations of passion for work are implicitly binary—one is either passionate or not. By contrast, I argue that this cultural logic of work is better conceived as a *continuum,* from "pure" to "less pure" in ways that are inflected with race, class, gender, and other social statuses. These expressions of passion are accorded unequal value within a given industry.

22. Sociologist Melissa Abad (2019) uses a similar framework to describe how "ethnoracial logics" shape the occupational trajectories of women of color

whereby ideas about expertise are developed and differentiated along racial lines within organizations.

23. Connell 1995; Connell and Messerschimdt 2005; Messerschmidt and Messner 2018. For foundational scholarship on masculinity and "hegemonic masculinity," see Connell 1995. The gendering of work reflects the gender framing of social life more broadly, which exists alongside other kinds of intersecting statuses to create a range of expressions of masculinity also shaped by local contexts. See Messerschmidt and Messner 2018.

24. Desmond (2007, 26) writes that for working-class men employed as wildland firefighters: "the decision to fight fire was not a bold leap into a new world but a small step into familiar territory."

25. Giazitzoglu and Muzio 2021.

26. For more on masculinity and modern craft work, see Bozkurt and Cohen 2018; Gandini and Gambrose 2022; Land 2018; Ocejo 2017.

27. Ocejo 2017, 20. The notion of "blended" masculinities also recalls Bridges and Pascoe's (2014) notion of "hybrid masculinities," which selectively incorporate performances and identities associated with marginalized and subordinated masculinities and femininities.

28. Artists and musicians also tend to locate their authentic selves in their work; see Grazian 2005; Ramirez 2018.

29. Sociologists Michael Ramirez (2018), writing on indie rock musicians, notes how men have an easier time than women making sense of their uncertain careers given how masculinity is normalized and idealized in the music industry. For more on authenticity and craftsmanship in "neo-craft" work, see Gandini and Gerosa 2021.

30. Blair-Loy 2009; Correll et al. 2014; Mickey 2022; Turco 2010; Williams 2000.

31. For more on commitment devices in "bad" jobs that do not necessarily offer high wages or conventional status, see Adler 2021.

32. Bourdieu 1993.

33. Unsurprisingly, not all workers maintain this view over time, even those from privileged backgrounds.

34. Connell 1995.

35. I make a similar point about front-of-the-house restaurant workers in higher-end settings; see Wilson 2019.

36. Musicians and other creative workers also tend to see their work as central to their identities and lifestyles, see Ramirez 2018; Umney and Kretsos 2015.

37. Sennett 1997.

38. Besen-Cassino 2014.

39. Scholars note similar patterns among workers in some retail stores, restaurants, and other service establishments. See, for example, Besen-Cassino 2014 and Wilson 2021.

40. For more on "bottle shares" among craft beer enthusiasts, see Borer 2023.

41. See Withers 2017. For more on how gender and race get embedded within organizations, see Acker 2006; Ray 2019.

42. Koontz and Chapman 2019.

43. The appeal of "handcrafting" beers as these men do is similar to what Elizabeth Currid-Halkett (2017, chap. 5) calls "conspicuous production," where the process of making goods is transparent to consumers.

44. Sennett 2008.

45. Henson and Rogers 2001.

46. Stephen Shukaitis and Joanna Figiel (2020) refer to this as the psychological contract of work, particularly for workers in creative and cultural industries.

47. Lamont, Beljean, and Clair (2014) lay out how cultural processes can function as mechanisms of social inequality.

48. For more on identity work, see Brown 2015.

CHAPTER 3. WE LIKE TO HAVE FUN: CONSUMPTIVE CAREERS IN THE TAPROOM

1. For much of 2020–21, wearing face masks in indoor commercial establishments was mandated by state government in both California and New Mexico due to the COVID-19 pandemic.

2. Neff, Wissinger, and Zukin 2005.

3. For additional literature on this topic, see Besen-Cassino 2015; Hesmondhalgh and Baker 2009; Misra and Walters 2016; Neff, Wissinger, and Zukin 2005; Umney and Kretsos 2015; Wilson 2019.

4. Besen-Cassino 2015.

5. Wilson 2019. For more on how individuals manage their employment, see Halpin and Smith 2017.

6. Consumptive careers builds on and extends the notion of "consuming work" (Besen-Cassino 2015) by considering how workers' relationships to their jobs may change over time.

7. Hall 1992; Hochschild 1984; Macdonald and Sirianni 1996. Sociologist Helen Holmes (2015) notes that these gendered patterns of service work also exist in modern craft work settings.

8. Holmes 2015.

9. Campbell 2005; Elliot 2019; Thurnell-Read 2014. Gandini and Gerosa (2023) argue this form of "neo-craft" springs from hipster culture, as articulated by Scott 2017.

10. Johnston and Baumann 2014; Thurnell-Read 2014.

11. Ocejo 2017; Sherman 2011. Sociologist Elizabeth Currid-Halkett (2017) refers to this type of labor as "conspicuous production." Gandini and Gerosa

(2023) note that conveying a preference for craft beer as opposed to its mainstream counterparts allows hipster consumers to present themselves as culturally sophisticated beer drinkers.

12. Besen-Cassino 2015; Marshall 1986; Wilson 2019. How and whether individuals fit comfortably in particular institutional settings is also true beyond work. For instance, according to Hamilton and Armstrong (2014), socially privileged young women navigate the "party pathway" of public universities in the United States, characterized by relatively easy coursework and a high amount of extracurricular social activities.

13. Land 2018.

14. Writing on "hipster capitalism," sociologist Michael Scott describes hipsters as a new petite bourgeoisie of "credentialed cultural producer(s)" with a middle-class habitus, who possess some academic qualifications or otherwise institutionalized forms of cultural capital. Land (2018) and Gandini and Gerosa (2023) assert that working in craft breweries falls within this category of work.

15. Ocejo 2017.

16. Hochschild 1983; Williams and Connell 2010; Warhurst 2016; Warhurst, Tilly, and Gatta 2017.

17. Studying casual restaurants, sociologist Karla Erickson (2007) describes how front of the house workers, who are primarily women but not necessarily class privileged, help establish a workplace ambiance where customers can "consume familiarity."

18. Borer 2019; Withers 2017. In my prior research with restaurant workers (Wilson 2016), I refer to this type of customer service style as "proximal service," in which management seeks to produce an environment where workers interact with customers in peer-like ways rather than through deferential acts.

19. In comparing men's and women's career trajectories in fashion, sociologist Allyson Stokes (2017) argues that women's stories more often reflected long periods of struggle, while men described having "fallen into" their careers, how quickly their careers progressed.

20. This cluster of activities, which Scott describes as indicative of "hipster capitalism," can now be found in many urban commercial areas that have been developed, both intentionally or otherwise, around "new elites" drawn to creative lifestyles; see Lloyd 2010; Scott 2017.

21. Richard Ocejo makes a similar observation about high-end butchers in New York City: "Workers must learn the social and communication skills required for interacting with customers, the cultural knowledge of meat and cooking to guide their orders, and the meat philosophy that undergirds the shop's very existence."

22. I could not verify whether this was indeed the case. However, this sentiment is consistent in other ways, that taproom workers prioritize working for a passionate, craft company.

23. Ocejo notes that Aldo, a Mexican immigrant man, struggled with the full performance of his butcher shop job—that of communicating the cultural repertoire of what he is doing to customers. In lieu of being able to do this, Aldo's performance was "incomplete" (Ocejo 2017, 237–49).

24. Orlando claims the decision to fire him was racially motivated, and that he was told he didn't "fit the new direction the company was going for." This would clearly seem to signal the racialized character of craft service jobs in the industry and the process by which people of color are excluded from these opportunities. However, I would caution that I was unable to independently verify Orlando's specific claims.

25. For Marne, community-building is what she wants to continue to do with her career: "I want to run my own business. One day I would actually like to either open a bar or open up a small art-based shop and then I want to have a small sustainable farm on my dad's property," says Marne. It should be noted that the idea of "community"—which is widely used among craft breweries—can also be problematic in the way it implies social boundaries of membership.

26. Others have written about the deep connection between taprooms and "community" (see most recently, the edited collection by Harvey, Jones, and Chapman 2023). As beer journalist Phil Mellows notes, "in the evolution from satisfying the connoisseurship of the beer aficionado to constructing a family-based community, tap rooms have a genetic relationship with the craft ethos, a seriousness about beer that's more organoleptic than alcoholic." See Mellows 2021.

27. Wallace 2019.

28. This statement is similar to Thurnell-Read's (2019, 1460) notion of "biographical authenticity" (emphasizing the specific maker) and "oppositional authenticity" (made by a company that is not a corporate conglomerate). However, Thurnell-Read does not attend to how workers nod to community, rather than the product, as the core motivation of their jobs as craft service workers.

29. Other studies have described this binary categorization of work among other service and retail workers, see Huddleston 2011; Shigihara 2015; Wilson 2021.

30. Ayala-Hurtado 2022.

31. For similar findings on men working "women's" jobs, see Henson and Rogers 2001; Williams 1989.

CHAPTER 4. EMBRACE THE SHIT! PRIDE AND COMMITMENT ALONG THE HARD LABOR PATHWAY

1. When we talked in 2019, Bobby had recently earned an associate degree in accounting from an Albuquerque-based community college.

2. Mountain Brewing had been around for eleven years at the time of Bobby's interview.

3. It should be noted that distribution workers are not the only workers in the industry who engage in routine, physical tasks. For example, in her study of Oregon-based brewers, sociologist Chloe Fox Miller (2019) finds that many of the daily chores that workers do in brewhouses are mundane rather than creative, and that workers sometimes feel they are "glorified janitors" rather than creative craftspeople.

4. In small-production breweries, such as "nanobreweries" producing less than 15,000 barrels of beer annually, the same worker or workers might do distribution labor tasks alongside all other tasks that need to get done—think about a brewer-owner cleaning kegs and mopping floors after a brew day and then serving customers in the tasting room in the evening. For more on the division of restaurant labor into distinct worker subgroups, see Fine 1996; Wilson 2021.

5. These statistics are based on 2019 survey results from the Brewers Association.

6. Williams 2006; Wilson 2021; Wingfield 2019; Wingfield and Alston 2015. Many restaurants and retail stores also feature a racially segmented division of labor in which the least desirable jobs are filled by people of color, especially those from lower-class backgrounds.

7. Waldinger and Lichter 2003.

8. Zamudio and Lichter 2008.

9. Zamudio and Lichter 2008; Waldinger and Lichter 2003; see also Neckerman and Kirchenman 1991; Moss and Tilly 2001.

10. For more on how workers justify their work using "occupational rhetorics," see Fine 1996. Moreover, in studying temporary workers who seem to enjoy their structurally precarious jobs, sociologist Vicki Smith (2001, 106–7) writes that this can be "explained by their own occupational trajectories—where they have been, where they hope to go, and what they perceive as possible."

11. Chinoy 1955; Hodson 2001; Lamont 2000.

12. See Desmond 2008.

13. Lamont 2000. This is consistent with other studies on working-class men, see Desmond 2008; Lamont 2000; Wilson 2021, chap. 4.

14. Rydzik and Ellis-Vowles 2019.

15. Harris and Giuffre 2015 make a similar point about the challenge women chefs face in professional kitchens.

16. In their study of cleaners, Tweedie and Holly (2016) note that these workers remain committed to "working well" on the job and sometimes subvert managerial controls and marginal work conditions that might otherwise disincentivize this behavior.

17. Lamont 2000.

18. I use the term "Hispanic" here because that is how Paco self identifies.

19. It is worth noting that while Paco appears to describe this man in ways that relate to his own work philosophy, Paco is also in a position of authority to

make hiring decisions based on who he perceives to be "good soldiers," which can perpetuate race and class biases. See Zamudio and Lichter 2008.

20. Our first interview took place in 2019. Sadly, when I texted Jorge a year later in the middle of 2020, he told me he had been laid off from the brewery due to the pandemic, when business had plummeted. Jorge remained upbeat about this experience: "I still miss that place. I wish I could go back!"

21. Smith 2001, 106–7.

CHAPTER 5. IT COULD NEVER BE JUST ABOUT BEER: RACE, GENDER, AND MARKED PROFESSIONAL IDENTITY

1. Beer Judge Certification Program.

2. Giazitzoglu and Muzio 2021; Holvino 2010.

3. Acker 1990; Brady 2018; Watkins-Hayes 2009; Wingfield 2019.

4. The term "racialized equity labor" comes from Lerma et al. 2019. See also Wingfield and Alston 2014.

5. Cech 2014; Hatmaker 2013; Rydzik and Ellis-Vowles 2019; see also Denissen 2010.

6. Correll 2017; Holvino 2010; Williams, Muller, and Kilanski 2012; Watkins-Hayes 2009; Wingfield 2019.

7. Ballakrishnen 2017.

8. See Ellen Berrey's (2015) work on diversity initiatives within universities and large corporations.

9. I borrow the concept of "marked" from Peggy Phelan (1994), who argues that what is visible is always defined by the invisible ("unmarked") position and wrapped up in issues of power.

10. The concept of marked professionalism parallels Celeste Watkins-Hayes's (2009, 287) notion of "racialized professionalism," whereby workers "integrate race into the understanding and operationalization of their work and their goals for what it should accomplish." I build on this idea by drawing attention to how the "marking" process of work identity extends in multiple directions: work identities are racialized (as well as gendered and classed) by others and also asserted by workers as strategic points of distinction. For a similar approach, sociologist Oneya Okuwobi (2021) shows how pastors in multiracial churches do strategic kinds of "biographical work," by drawing attention to certain aspects of their personal backgrounds that align opportunistically with their organization's mission to support diversity.

11. The "social equity pathway" shares some commonalities with what other scholars have called the "diversity pathway" within large organizations, which usually involves job positions such as "diversity officer," or targeted opportunity

hires, which take into explicit consideration one's status as a member of a minoritized group. By contrast, the equity pathway centers workers and their career microtransitions through a wider range of job opportunities, including entrepreneurship. For more on the "diversity pathway" within large organizations, such as universities and corporate workplaces, see Berry 2015; Rivera 2015.

12. Journalist Dave Infante's 2015 article for *Thrillist* helped to draw attention to the white and male character of the industry—something readily apparent to many workers in the industry from marginalized groups.

13. These conversations were particularly prominent in the wake of national protests surrounding the murder of George Floyd at the hands of a white police officer in 2020. For instance, many craft breweries made public statements in support of social justice movements such as Black Lives Matter. See Boyce 2020; Chapman and Brunsma 2020; Wilson 2022a.

14. Jordan 2020.

15. Based on author's calculations.

16. Punchdrink, https://punchdrink.com/articles/craft-beer-already-imagined-better-inclusive-equitable-future/).

17. A growing number of companies today invest in so-called diversity, equity, and inclusion (DEI) initiatives despite mixed evidence on the efficacy of these initiatives in helping women, people of color, and other workers from minoritized status groups improve their standing in their respective workplaces. On the one hand, research indicates that adopting formal procedures can reduce inequalities by way of curbing managerial bias in evaluating candidates for hiring and promotion (Reskin 2000). Organizational efforts to get managers to support workplace diversity can have positive effects on the likelihood that they will hire women and people of color (Dobbin, Schrage, and Kalev 2015). On the other hand, critical race scholars argue that most DEI initiatives are unlikely to produce lasting change within workplaces that otherwise remain dominated by white men in leadership and cultural standards of whiteness and masculinity. This is because diversity initiatives largely fail to address systemic issues of racism and sexism in organizations (Berry 2015; Mayorga-Gallo 2019; Okuwobi 2021). For these reasons, management-led initiatives superficially aimed at promoting diversity within the workplace may end up reproducing or even exacerbating existing social hierarchies among workers (Acker 1990, 2000; Evans and Moore 2015, 444; Ray 2019; Williams, Muller, and Kilanski 2014).

18. Gorman 2015, 138.

19. In an attempt to classify and evaluate DEI initiatives in corporations, sociologists Kalev, Dobbin, and Kelly (2006) identify three popular types of programs: training programs that seek to eliminate stereotype-based bias, targeted mentoring and networking programs for female and minority employees, and specialized positions or departments focused on diversity. They found the most effective diversity programs appear to involve hiring a clear diversity leader,

engaging management to get behind this initiative, and making broader hiring decisions and the criteria that they are based on more transparent. See also Dobbin, Schrage, Kalev (2015, 1034).

20. Williams, Kilanski, and Muller 2014. These researchers noted that diversity training within the company may actually exacerbate these biases.

21. Kaiser et al 2013. Diversity and work-family policies risk "backlash" effects: in one study women were more likely to report being bullied by their supervisors in workplaces that use these programs than in workplaces that did not, especially when their supervisors were men (Rainey and Melzer 2021).

22. Berrey 2015; Embrick 2011; Mayorga-Gallo 2019. For this reason, some critical race scholars argue that diversity initiatives function as the newest expression of institutionalized white supremacy, one that largely deflects systemic efforts at reapportioning opportunities in a more equitable manner. For example, sociologist Oneya Okuwobi (2021) argues that diversity initiatives are not only likely to fail within most organizations, they were never intended to succeed in changing company culture in the first place. Seen from this perspective, organizations that prioritize "diversity talk" can end up silencing other kinds of conversations geared toward addressing persistent social inequality (Bell and Hartmann 2007).

23. Acker 2000, 2006.

24. Wingfield 2019; Lerma et al. 2019; Moore 2008; Ray 2019. See also Gorman 2016.

25. Ashcraft et al. 2012; Giazitzoglu and Muzio 2020.

26. Moore 2008. A similar pattern has been noted among women in male-dominated professions: Hatmaker (2013) describes how engineers who are women must grapple with their gender qualifier work identity.

27. For more on social entrepreneurship among Los Angeles–based Latinx workers, see Vallejo and Canizales 2018. For more on craft work and entrepreneurship, see Solomon and Mathias 2018.

28. See Cicerone.org.

29. According to Carly, her company is formally an L3C tax organization, which is low profit limited liability company.

30. Evans and Moore 2014.

31. For similar findings in other industries, see Brady 2018; Correll 2017.

32. For similar findings in other industries, see Risse 2021.

33. See Cech 2015; Watkins-Hayes 2009.

34. This was the case for roughly one out of every four women and people of color working in craft beer that I talked to.

35. See Kanter 1977 on women's token employment in predominantly male workplaces.

36. Okuwobi 2019. On "whitening" résumés, see Kang et al. 2016.

37. See Cech and Blair-Loy 2014.

38. Vega (2019) notes how "conservative rationales" can develop among immigrants with restrictionist mentalities toward immigration policy.

39. This is similar to sociologist Amy Wilkins's notion of "moderate Blackness" performed by college-going Black men. Wilkins (2012, 37) argues that, for these men, performing moderate Blackness is a strategy for crafting upwardly mobile identities that makes many of their feelings and experiences more tolerable while also signifying them as easygoing Black people who aren't "out to start a revolution."

40. Watkins-Hayes (2009, 299) notes how Black and Latinx bureaucrats must also consider their own institutional and economic standing as they manage their racialized professional identities. As one such respondent explained: "I have to keep a job too."

41. See also Land, Sutherland, and Taylor 2018.

42. For more on authenticity discourse in craft beer, see Thurnell-Read 2014, 2019. For more on the importance of organizational context on identity work, see Brown 2015.

43. In my interview with her, Erica explained how her explicit support for social justice causes in the community complements values that already existed at River Bend Brewery:

Our mission statement is to enhance the New Mexico story by providing genuine experiences. A lot of that is through craft beverages and food but also through community-building. We're really community-minded, and I think that can be cliché in a lot of ways, saying, "Oh, we're doing these things for the community." But for us, it's like, "Put your money where your mouth is. What are you actually doing for the community?" We have, in each location, relationships that are established unique to that location.

CHAPTER 6. PATHS LESS TRAVELED: SIDE
PATHWAYS, HOBBYIST CAREERS, AND DEAD ENDS

1. Munro and O'Kane 2022.

2. I draw loosely on the approach of "deviant case" or "negative case" methodology (see Emigh 1997), in which researchers faced with anomalous findings do not dismiss them as exceptions but expand the range of the explanation to account for the anomalous finding.

3. Here I borrow from Becker's (1982, 1) notion of "art worlds," which he uses to describe the "joint activity" of a large number of people and businesses in a given industry.

4. Here I define "former workers" as those who spent at least one year in the industry before leaving, either by choice or because of getting let go.

5. Many of the workers described here resemble a category of brewery owners that Andrew Wallace (2019, 955) calls "beer entrepreneurs," focused more on business opportunities within a growing industry rather than love of "neo-artisanal" production.

6. Barley and Kunda 2004.

7. Rodgers and Taves 2017.

8. Rodgers and Taves 2017. Sociologist Pat Reilly (2016) makes a similar point regarding stand-up comedians, who periodically return to prior "layers" of their career (such as smaller comedy venues) in order to remain connected to these scenes. See also Robert Stebbins's (2001) work on "serious leisure."

9. Land (2018) also notes the relatively low compensation of brewing jobs and questions whether brewing jobs can be considered stable employment with good pay.

10. For a similar discussion of the tensions of career commitment among musicians, see Ramirez 2018.

11. Mears (2015) makes a similar observation about how the "girls" who participate in the VIP club scene who are not formally paid do sometimes enjoy the temporal pleasures and fun that comes with having exclusive access to these spaces. As with Jerome, many of these "girls" also know they can't do this forever.

12. I thank Michael Siciliano for the term *willful disentanglement*.

13. Barley and Kunda (2004) note how the high-skilled contractors they talked with traded stability for the potential for greater contract-based income and schedule flexibility. Importantly, what allows the most successful of these individuals to do so is well-established industry networks that reduce the likelihood of unwanted bouts of unemployment.

14. Katherine Giuffre (1999) has similarly written about the importance of social networks for the ongoing careers of artists.

15. Ocejo 2017, 255. This also resembles "portfolio"-style careers as described by a large body of literature; see Hesmondhalgh and Baker 2011.

16. For more on "hobbyists," see Bozkurt and Cohen 2018; Fine 2003.

17. Other scholars have noted the gendered nature of tinkering as a hobby and its connection to a masculine identity, particularly for middle-class men. See Katsuno 2011.

18. As another example, Quinn and her husband split batches of fermenting beer into two vessels, known as "carboys," in order to add different fruits to each and observe the difference.

19. It should be noted that Rowe's comments occurred after a period when many breweries had been closed or reduced to package sales due to public health concerns surrounding the COVID-19 pandemic. Rowe also explained that he is defining profitability as a company that is coming out in the black net of prior capital investments and outstanding loans.

20. Frenette and Ocejo 2017. On successful and marginal side paths, see Barley and Kunda (2004) on consultants; Ravenelle (2020) on gig workers. It is worth underscoring that this kind of ongoing career flexibility is buffered by having the right skills and sources of racialized social and cultural capital.

21. Homebrewers I interviewed tended to be slightly older than industry workers. However, given a nonrepresentative sample, I could not confirm this as a larger pattern differentiating these two groups.

CONCLUSION

1. Esteban and I spoke in the late summer of 2022.

2. I tried reaching out to Mike several times after I found out the news about Renegade's closing but received no response back. Ironically, my last visit to the brewery, where I ran into Mike, was while accompanying another LA-based brewer who was looking to buy equipment for his own brewery.

3. See Royster 2003 on how white men reproduce their advantage in the labor market through racialized social networks.

4. Chapman and Brunsma 2020; Darwin 2018; Withers 2017.

5. Land 2018.

6. See Currid-Halkett 2017.

7. Acker 1990, 2006; Ray 2019; Wilson 2021; Wingfield and Alston 2015; Wooten and Couloute 2017. See also Amis, Mair, and Munir 2020.

8. To be clear, this is not to say that overt racism does not exist in the craft beer industry. One need look no further than the steady stream of accusations of racial harassment by workers of color over the last few years (see Boyce 2020).

9. See Barley, Beckhy, and Miliken 2017; Halpin and Smith 2017. Scholars of "boundary-less" careers are particularly keen in noting how workers engage in job moves across multiple work settings throughout their careers. For an overview, see Tams and Arthur 2010.

10. I adapt this phrase from Katherine Giuffre's (1999) useful metaphor of artists' careers as "sandpiles," in which "each actor's attempts to reach the top change the shape of the climb."

11. Amis, Mair, and Munir 2020; Rao and Tobias-Neely 2019; Rivera 2015; Royster 2003; Tomaskovic-Devey and Avent-Holt 2020.

12. For a similar approach, see Abad 2019.

13. A similar point is made in Wilson and Stone 2022, chap. 3.

14. Bernot 2020.

15. It is worth underscoring here that my argument is not that minoritized workers do not have passions for work, but rather, that their passions are less valued in an industry that is otherwise dominated by the privileged tastes and norms of white men.

16. For more on "ideal workers" and their connection to gender inequality in the workplace, see Blair-Loy 2009; Brumley 2014; Turco 2010.

17. Ray 2019, 47.

18. Michele Lamont and colleagues (2014) call for research on how cultural processes lead to social inequality, linking micro- and macroprocesses.

19. Cartwright 2022; Ocejo 2017; Thurnell-Read 2014.

20. For research focused on these types of settings, see Bozkhurt and Cohen 2019; McRobbie 2018.

21. On "authentic" careers, see Svejenova 2005. For more on precarious yet personally meaningful jobs today, see Bunderson and Thompson 2009; Frenette 2013; Menger 1999; Umney and Kretsos 2015.

22. I use "professional" the way study respondents deploy this term to talk about their work identity. Thus, while this study concerns issues of social and symbolic exclusion within an industry, strategies of professional closure (Abbot 1988) are beyond the scope of this study.

23. I borrow the concept of "marked" from Peggy Phelan (1994), who argues that what is visible is always defined by the invisible ("unmarked") position and wrapped up in issues of power.

24. Berry 2015; Cartwright 2022. The notion of well-assimilated people of color buttressing whiteness is also consistent with Bonilla-Silva's notion of "honorary whites" in a triracial hierarchy with whites remaining on top. That said, one difference is that those who incorporate social justice messages into their (marked) professional identities and platforms do not necessarily hold an integrationist standpoint with dominant ideals coded in whiteness and masculinity.

25. See Acker 2006; Amis, Mair, and Munir 2020; Watkins-Hayes 2009.

26. The pandemic-related closures of 2020 and 2021 significantly affected the revenue flow of many craft breweries.

27. Boyce 2020.

28. As a point of distinction between these concepts, the social equity pathway, like other career pathways I describe in this book, emphasizes the kinds of employment microtransitions workers engage in over time that lead to socially stratified jobs and job opportunities.

29. Dobbin and Kalev 2022.

30. Ray (2019, 33–34) and Collins (1997) make this point about "diversity consultants"; scholars such as Collins (1997) and Ray (2019, 33–34) note how organizational resources can be systematically "decoupled" from diversity initiatives, which can dilute their ability to improve opportunities for minoritized workers. See also Berry 2015.

31. Support for a social equity pathway has been generally well received in craft beer. In an era of rising race and gender equity and inclusion discourse, hundreds of companies have issued statements supporting DEI, and many have also launched in-house programs in line with this goal, treating these programs

as a needed corrective to the industry's increasingly unpalatable demographic homogeneity (see Chapman and Brunsma 2020; Wilson and Stone 2022).

32. See Vallejo and Canizales 2022. One beer writer, who is a Latina woman, writes: "I mean, Henry and Adriana at Monkish, if you think about it, that's the most successful brewery in LA that is owned by people of color. I mean, he is Vietnamese and she is Puerto Rican or something. They are hood from Gardena. He is a hip-hop head, she is a Chola. Like, you know. They are Gardena hood through and through and yet they own the most popular brewery in LA. *They've never leaned into that. They've never pushed that at all*" (my emphasis).

33. Garbes 2022, 92.

34. Boyce 2020.

35. This report was conducted in 2022 by the industry platform Craft Beer Professionals. It was based on self-reporting by 228 industry employees. See Coplon and Varda 2022.

36. Land 2018.

37. This insight is adapted from Delgaty and Wilson 2023.

38. See Williams and Connell 2011; Wilson 2021.

APPENDIX A: RESEARCHING UNCERTAINTY

1. Small 2022, 478.

2. It is worth noting that I am biracial (Asian-white), though my physical appearance is light-skinned with Euro-American physical features.

3. For more on "ride alongs" and "hanging out" as methodological strategies, see Kusenbach 2003.

4. A nationwide industry poll conducted in the early summer of 2020 found that one out of every three craft brewery owners would have to consider shutting down their operation if government mandated taproom and indoor dining closures were kept in effect for two more months. The situation appeared to be dire. Fortunately, at the time of this writing in 2022, only a fraction of these companies did end up folding permanently during the pandemic.

5. I recognize that this runs the risk of "cameo appearances," as noted by Hancock, Sykes, and Verma (2018), which can potentially miss (and misconstrue) ground-level dynamics that would be more fully apparent to longer-term observers and inhabitants of a given space. I tried hard to work around this pitfall by triangulating my data descriptions from multiple sources, across multiple field sites, and to some extent, across time. I also returned to the field again intermittently, particularly in the summers of 2021 and 2022.

6. See Galloux et al. 2022.

7. By the summer of 2021, with COVID cases declining nationally and health restrictions easing, I was able to engage in a final round of in-person fieldwork.

These data served as a re-joiner to field research begun pre-pandemic. However, given newly emergent research themes, I chose to expand data collection beyond the two original industry locales. In all, I ended up visiting workplaces and meeting industry contacts across the country, such as Seattle, San Francisco, San Jose, Asheville, and Raleigh.

8. I write about these social justice movements, as well as their pushback, elsewhere (Wilson and Stone 2022). For more on using new technologies to enrich ethnography, see Fine and Hancock 2017.

9. Several pieces of writing I completed during this era also explore these themes: see Wilson 2022; Wilson and Stone 2022.

10. See Lareau 2021.

11. Other researchers have noted the positive, if unexpected, benefits to online-based interviews, citing the ease with which interviews are able to take place in private and at a location and time that is optimal for interviewees (see Howlett 2022, 393).

12. For this reason, Annette Lareau suggests that conducting one in-person interview per day, and just two or three in a week, should be considered a job well done.

13. Digital ethnography is an increasingly recognized alternative to in-person or "analog" ethnography (see Forberg and Schilt 2023; Small 2022).

14. *Front of the House, Back of the House* involved nearly six years of ethnographic research, including firsthand research while working in the industry. For more on the relative strengths of participant-observation versus interviewing, see Lamont and Swidler 2014.

15. Ayala-Hurtado 2022. See also Lamont and Swidler 2014; Tavory 2020.

16. In all, I contacted about sixty workers for follow-up conversations.

17. Charmaz 2004; Glaser and Strauss 1999. There is considerable debate about the relative merits of grounded theory versus a more "abductive" approach, which is beyond the scope of this discussion. See Timmermans and Tavory 2012.

18. For more on this point, see Lareau 2022.

19. Lamont and Swidler 2014.

20. Lareau 2022.

21. Withers 2017.

22. I follow Gailloux et al. (2022) in noting the advantages of continually adapting to unpredictable and changing circumstances for researchers.

23. Lamont and Swidler 2014, 157.

24. Ayala-Hurtado 2022; Pugh 2015.

25. Desmond 2007, 269.

26. There are some instances where we can be reasonably certain that what people are saying corresponds to the truth, especially if researchers focus on what sociologist Iddo Tavory calls "process-oriented" interview questions, such as asking people about how, what, when, and where something occurred instead

of asking them to provide an explanation of *why* it occurred. See Katz 2001; Tavory 2020.

27. Lamont and Swidler 2014, 156. See also Tavory 2020. For more on cultural processes, see Lamont, Beljean, and Clair 2014.

28. Lamont and Swidler 2014; Tavory 2020.

29. Tavory 2020, 452.

References

Abad, Melissa V. 2019. "Race, Knowledge, and Tasks: Racialized Occupational Trajectories." *Research in the Sociology of Organizations* 60: 111–30.

Abbott, Andrew. 1988. *The System of Professions: An Essay on the Division of Expert Labor.* Chicago: University of Chicago Press.

Acitelli, Tom. 2013. *The Audacity of Hops: The History of America's Craft Beer Revolution.* Chicago: Chicago Review Press.

Acker, Joan. 1990. "Hierarchies, Jobs, Bodies: A Theory of Gendered Organizations." *Gender & Society* 4: 139–58.

———. 2006. "Inequality Regimes: Gender, Class, and Race in Organizations." *Gender & Society* 20: 441–64.

Adler, Laura. 2021. "Choosing Bad Jobs: The Use of Nonstandard Work as a Commitment Device." *Work and Occupations* 48, no. 2: 2017–242.

Alegria, Sharla. 2019. "Escalator or Step Stool? Gendered Labor and Token Processes in Tech Work." *Gender & Society* 33, no. 5: 722–45.

Amis, John, Johanna Mair, and Kamala Munir. 2020. "The Organizational Reproduction of Inequality." *Academy of Management Annals* 14, no. 1: 1–36.

Anteby, Michael, and Beth A. Bechky. 2016. "Book Review: Editorial Essay: How Workplace Ethnographies Can Inform the Study of Work and Employment Relations." *ILR Review* 69, no. 2: 501–5.

Ashcraft, Karen Lee, Sara Louise Muhr, Jens Rennstam, and Katie Sullivan. 2012. "Professionalization as a Branding Activity: Occupational Identity and the Dialectic of Inclusivity-Exclusivity." *Gender, Work & Organization* 19, no. 5: 467–88.

Ayala-Hurtado, Elena. 2022. "Narrative Continuity/Rupture: Projected Professional Futures amid Pervasive Employment Precarity." *Work and Occupations* 49, no. 1: 45–78.

Ballakrishnen, Svetha. 2017. "'She gets the job done': Entrenched Gender Meanings and New Returns to Essentialism in India's Elite Professional Firms." *Journal of Professions and Organization* 4: 324–42.

Barley, Stephen, Beth A. Bechky, and Frences J. Miliken. 2017. "The Changing Nature of Work: Careers, Identities, and Work Lives in the 21st Century." *Academy of Management Discoveries* 3, no. 2: 111–15.

Barley, Stephen, and Gideon Kunda. 2004. *Gurus, Hired Guns, and Warm Bodies: Itinerant Experts in a Knowledge Economy.* Princeton, NJ: Princeton University Press.

Becker, Howard. 1982. *Art Worlds.* Berkeley: University of California Press.

Bell, Emma, Gianluigi Mangia, Scott Taylor, and Maria L. Toraldo, eds. 2018. *The Organization of Craft Work: Identities, Meanings, and Materiality.* New York: Routledge.

Bell, Joyce, and Douglas Hartmann. 2008. "Diversity in Everyday Discourse: The Cultural Ambiguities and Consequences of 'Happy Talk.'" *American Sociological Review* 72: 895–914.

Bellah, Robert Neelly, Richard Madsen, William M. Sullivan, Ann Swidler, and Steven M. Tipton. 1985. *Habits of the Heart: Individualism and Commitment in American Life.* New York: Harper & Row.

Berkelaar, Brenda L., and Patrice M. Buzzanell. 2015. "Bait and Switch or Double-Edged Sword? The (Sometimes) Failed Promises of Calling." *Human Relations* 68, no. 1: 157–78.

Bernot, Kate. 2020. "Say It Out Loud—Who Do Breweries Talk About When They Talk About 'Community'?" *Good Beer Hunting.* Accessed April 5, 2021, www.goodbeerhunting.com/sightlines/2020/6/5/who-do-breweries-talk -about-when-they-talk-about-community.

Berrey, Ellen. 2015. *The Enigma of Diversity: The Language of Race and the Limits of Racial Justice.* Chicago: University of Chicago Press.

Besen-Cassino, Yasemin. 2014. *Consuming Work: Youth Labor in America.* Philadelphia: Temple University Press.

Bettie, Julie. 2014. *Women without Class: Girls, Race, and Identity.* Berkeley: University of California Press.

Blair-Loy, Mary. 2009. *Competing Devotions: Career and Family among Women Executives.* Cambridge, MA: Harvard University Press.

Bolles, Richard. 1970. *What Color Is Your Parachute? Your Guide to a Lifetime of Meaningful Work and Career Success.* Berkeley, CA: Ten Speed Press.

Boltanski, Luc, and Eve Chiapello. 2005. "The New Spirit of Capitalism." *International Journal of Politics, Culture, and Society* 18, no. 3: 161–88.

Borer, Michael I. 2019. *Vegas Brews: Craft Beer and the Birth of a Local Scene.* New York: New York University Press.

Bourdieu, Pierre. 1977. *Outline of a Theory of Practice.* Cambridge: Cambridge University Press.

———. 1984. *Distinction: A Social Critique of the Judgment of Taste.* Cambridge, MA: Harvard University Press.

———. 1993. *The Field of Cultural Production: Essays on Art and Literature.* New York: Columbia University Press.

———. 2011. "The Forms of Capital" (1986). In *Cultural Theory: An Anthology,* edited by Imre Szeman and Timothy Kaposy, part 1: 81–93. Malden, MA: Wiley.

Boyce, Toni. 2020. "The Time Is Now, Part Two—Why Beer's Culture and Workplace Practices Must Change." *Good Beer Hunting.* Accessed April 5, 2021, www.goodbeerhunting.com/blog/2020/8/10/the-time-is-now-part-two-why-beers-culture-and-workplace-practices-must-change.

Bozkurt, Odul. 2015. "The Punctuation of Mundane Jobs with Extreme Work: Christmas at the Supermarket Deli Counter." *Organization* 22, no. 4: 476–92.

Bozkurt, Odul, and Rachel L. Cohen. 2018. "Repair Work as Good Work: Craft and Love in Classic Car Restoration Training." *Human Relations* 72, no. 6: 1105–28.

Brady, Jennifer. 2018. "Toward a Critical, Feminist Sociology of Expertise." *Journal of Professions and Organization* 5: 123–38.

Brewers Association. 2021. "Small & Independent U.S. Craft Brewer Annual Production Report." Accessed October 28, 2022, www.brewersassociation.org/press-releases/2020-craft-brewing-industry-production-report/.

———. 2022. "National Beer Sales & Production Data." Accessed October 28, 2022, www.brewersassociation.org/statistics-and-data/national-beer-stats/.

Bridges, Tristan, and C. J. Pascoe. 2014. "Hybrid Masculinities: New Directions in the Sociology of Men and Masculinities." *Sociology Compass* 8, no. 3: 246–58.

Brown, Andrew D. 2015. "Identities and Identity Work in Organizations." *International Journal of Management Reviews* 17, no. 1: 20–40.

Browne, Irene, and Joya Misra. 2003. "The Intersection of Gender and Race in the Labor Market." *Annual Review of Sociology* 29: 487–513.

Brumley, Krista. 2014. "The Gendered Ideal Worker Narrative: Professional Women's and Men's Work Experiences in the New Economy at a Mexican Company." *Gender & Society* 28, no. 6: 799–823.

Byron, Reginald, and Vincent Roscigno. 2019. "Bureaucracy, Discrimination, and the Racialized Character of Organizational Life." In *Race, Organizations, and the Organizing Process*, edited by Melissa Wooten. Bingley, UK: Emerald Publishing.

Bunderson, J. Stuart, and Jeffrey A. Thompson. 2009. "The Call of the Wild: Zookeepers, Callings, and the Double-Edged Sword of Deeply Meaningful Work." *Administrative Science Quarterly* 54, no. 1(: 32–57.

Campbell, Colin. 2005. "The Craft Consumer: Culture, Craft and Consumption in a Postmodern Society." *Journal of Consumer Culture* 5, no. 1: 23–42.

Cardon, Melissa S., Joakim Wincent, Jagdip Sing, and Mateja Drnovsek. 2009. "The Nature and Experience of Entrepreneurial Passion." *Academy of Management Review* 34, no. 3: 511–32.

Carroll, Glenn, and Anand Swaminathan. 2000. "Why the Microbrewery Movement? Organizational Dynamics of Resource Partitioning in the U.S. Brewing Industry." *American Journal of Sociology* 106, no. 3: 715–62.

Cartwright, Ashleigh. 2022. "A Theory of Racialized Cultural Capital." *Sociological Inquiry* 92, no. 2: 317–40.

Castilla, Emilio J. 2008. "Gender, Race, and Meritocracy in Organizational Careers." *American Journal of Sociology* 113: 1479–526.

Cech, Erin A. 2013. "The Self-Expressive Edge of Occupational Sex Segregation." *American Journal of Sociology* 119: 747–89.

———. 2015. "Engineers and Engineeresses? Self-Conceptions and the Development of Gendered Professional Identities." *Sociological Perspectives* 58, no. 1: 56–77.

———. 2021. *The Trouble with Passion: How Searching for Fulfillment at Work Fosters Inequality*. Berkeley: University of California Press.

Cech, Erin A., and Mary Blair-Loy. 2014. "Perceiving Glass Ceilings? Meritocratic versus Structural Explanations of Gender Inequality among Women in Science and Technology." *Social Problems* 57, no. 3: 371–97.

Chapman, Nathaniel G., and David L. Brunsma. 2020. *Beer and Racism: How Beer Became White, Why It Matters, and the Movements to Change It.* Bristol, UK: Bristol University Press.

Chapman, Nathaniel G., J. Slade Lellock, and Cameron Lippard. 2017. *Untapped: Exploring the Cultural Dimensions of Craft Beer*. Morgantown: Western Virginia University Press.

Charmaz, Kathy. 2004. "Grounded Theory," In *Approaches to Qualitative Research: A Reader on Theory and Practice*, edited by Sharlene Nagy Hesse-Biber, and Patricia Leavy, 155–79. New York: Oxford University Press.

Chinoy, Ely. 1955. *Automobile Workers and the American Dream*. New York: Doubleday.

Chong, Phillipa K. 2021. "Dilemma Work: Problem-Solving Multiple Work Roles into One Work Life." *Work and Occupations* 48, no. 4: 432–69.

Connell, Richard W. 1995. *Masculinities: Knowledge, Power, and Social Change.* Berkeley: University of California Press.

Connell, Robert W., and James W. Messerschmidt. 2005. "Hegemonic Masculinity: Rethinking the Concept." Gender & Society 19, no. 6: 829–59.

Coplon and Varda. 2022. *2022 Employee Satisfaction Report.* Craft Beer Professionals and Craft Beer Advisory Services.

Correll, Shelley J. 2017. "Reducing Gender Biases in Modern Workplaces: A Small Wins Approach to Organizational Change." *Gender & Society* 31, no. 6: 725–50.

Correll, Shelley J., Erin L. Kelly, L. T. O'Connor, and J. C. Williams. 2014. "Redesigning, Redefining Work." *Work and Occupations* 41: 3–17.

Correll, Shelley J., Katherine R. Weisshaar, Alison T. Wynn, and JoAnne Delfino Wehner. 2020. "Inside the Black Box of Organizational Life: The Gendered Language of Performance Assessment." *American Sociological Review* 85, no. 6: 1022–50.

Currid-Halkett, Elizabeth. 2017. *The Sum of Small Things.* Princeton, NJ: Princeton University Press.

Darwin, Helana. 2018. "Omnivorous Masculinity: Gender Capital and Cultural Legitimacy in Craft Beer Culture." *Social Currents* 5, no. 3: 301–16.

Delgaty, Aaron, and Eli R. Wilson. 2023. "The Hidden Strains of 'Cool' Jobs." *Sociology.* DOI: 0.17.7/00380385231172129.

Demetry, Daphne. 2017. "Pop-Up to Professional: Emerging Entrepreneurial Identity and Evolving Vocabularies of Motive." *Academy of Management Discoveries* 3, no. 2: 187–207.

Denissen, Amy. 2010. "The Right Tools for the Job: Constructing Gender Meanings and Identities in the Male-Dominated Building Trades." *Human Relations* 63, no. 7: 1051–69.

DePalma, Lindsay. 2020. "The Passion Paradigm: Professional Adherence to and Consequences of the Ideology of 'Do What You Love.'" *Sociological Forum* 36, no. 1: 134–58.

Desmond, Matthew. 2007. *On the Fireline: Living and Dying with Wildland Firefighters.* Chicago: University of Chicago Press.

———. 2014. "Relational Ethnography." *Theoretical Sociology* 43: 547–79.

DiMaggio, Paul J., and Walter W. Powell. 1983. "The Iron Cage Revisited: Institutional Isomorphism and Collective Rationality." *American Sociological Review* 48: 147–60.

DiTomaso, Nancy. 2015. "Racism and Discrimination versus Advantage and Favoritism: Bias For versus Bias Against." *Research in Organizational Behavior* 35: 57–77.

Dobbin, Frank, and Alexandra Kalev. 2022. *Getting to Diversity: What Works and What Doesn't.* Cambridge, MA: Harvard University Press.

Dobbin, Frank, Alexandra Kalev, and Erin L. Kelly. 2007. "Diversity Management in Corporate America." *Contexts* 6, no. 4: 21–28.

Dobbin, Frank, Daniel Schrage, and Alexandra Kalev. 2015. "Rage against the Iron Cage: The Varied Effects of Bureaucratic Personnel Reforms on Diversity." *American Sociological Review* 80, no. 5: 1014–44.

Du Bois, W. E. B. 1904. "Atlanta Conferences." *Voice of the Negro* 1: 85–90.

Duffy, Brooke E. 2017. *(Not) Getting Paid to Do What You Love: Gender, Social Media, and Aspirational Work.* New Haven, CT: Yale University Press.

Elliot, Christopher S. 2019. "Consuming Craft: The Intersection of Production and Consumption in North Carolina Craft Beer Markets." PhD diss., University of North Carolina at Chapel Hill.

———. 2023. "From Consumer to Producer: Pathways to Working in Craft Beer." In *Beer Places,* edited by Daina Cheyenne Harvey, Ellis Jones, and Nathaniel G. Chapman. Fayetteville: University of Arkansas Press.

Embrick, David G. 2011. "The Diversity Ideology in the Business World: A New Oppression for a New Age." *Critical Sociology* 37, no. 5: 541–56.

Emigh, Rebecca Jean. 1997. "The Power of Negative Thinking: The Use of Negative Case Methodology in the Development of Sociological Theory." *Theory and Society* 26, no. 5: 649–84.

Emirbayer, Mustafa, and Ann Mische. 1998. "What Is Agency?" *American Journal of Sociology* 103, no. 4: 962–1023.

Endrissat Nada, Gazi Islam, and Claus Noppeney. 2015. "Enchanting Work: New Spirits of Service Work in an Organic Supermarket." *Organization Studies* 36, no. 11: 1555–76.

Erickson, Karla A. 2009. *The Hungry Cowboy: Service and Community in a Neighborhood Restaurant.* Jackson: University Press of Mississippi.

Evans, Louwanda, and Wendy Leo Moore. 2015. "Impossible Burdens: White Institutions, Emotional Labor, and Micro-Resistance." *Social Problems* 62: 439–54.

Evetts, Julie. 2013. "Professionalism: Value and Ideology." *Current Sociology Review* 61, no. 5–6: 778–96.

Ezzy Douglas. 1997. "Subjectivity and the Labour Process: Conceptualising Good Work." *Sociology* 31. no. 3: 427–44.

Fine, Gary A. 1996. *Kitchens: The Culture of Restaurant Work.* Berkeley: University of California Press.

———. 2003. "Crafting Authenticity: The Validation of Identity in Self-Taught Art." *Theory and Society* 32, no. 2: 153–80.

———. 2009. *Kitchens: The Culture of Restaurant Work,* updated edition with a new preface. Berkeley: University of California Press.

———. 2012. "Group Culture and the Interaction Order: Local Sociology on the Meso-Level." *Annual Review of Sociology* 38: 159–79.

Fine, Gary Alan, and Black Hawk Hancock. 2017. "The New Ethnographer at Work." *Qualitative Research* 17: 260–68. DOI:10.1177/1468794116656725.

Fleming, Peter, and Andrew Sturdy. 2011. "'Being Yourself' in the Electronic Sweatshop: New Forms of Normative Control." *Human Relations* 64, no. 2: 177–200.

Forberg, P., and K. Schilt. 2023. "What Is Ethnographic about Digital Ethnography? A Sociological Perspective." *Frontiers in Sociology* 8: 1156776. DOI: 10.3389/fsoc.2023.1156776.

Fox Miller, Chloe. 2019. "'Glorified Janitors': Creativity, Cachet, and Everyday Experiences of Work in Portland, Oregon's Craft Brewing Sector." *Geoforum* 106: 78–86.

Frenette, Alexandre. 2013. "Making the Intern Economy: Role and Career Challenges of the Music Industry Intern." *Work and Occupations* 40, no. 4: 364–97.

Frenette, Alexandre, and Richard E. Ocejo. 2018. "Sustaining Enchantment: How Cultural Workers Manage Precariousness and Routine." In *Race, Identity, and Work: Research in the Sociology of Work*, vol. 32, edited by E. L. Mickey and A. H. Wingfield, 35–60. Bingley, UK: Emerald Publishing.

Friedland, Roger, and R. Robert Alford. 1991. "Bringing Society Back In: Symbols, Practices, and Institutional Contradictions. In *The New Institutionalism in Organizational Analysis,* edited by Walter W. Powell and Paul J. DiMaggio, 232–63. Chicago: University of Chicago Press.

Gailloux, Chantal, Walter W. Furness, Colleen C. Myles, Delorean S. Wiley, and Kourtney Collins. 2022. "Fieldwork without the Field: Navigating Qualitative Research in Pandemic Times." *Frontiers in Sustainable Food Systems* 6: 750409.

Gandini, Alessandro, and Alessandro Gerosa. 2023. "What is 'Neo-Craft' Work, and Why it Matters." *Organization Studies*: 1–19. DOI: 10.1177/01708406231213963.

Garbes, Laura. 2022. "When the 'Blank Slate' Is a White One: White Institutional Isomorphism in the Birth of National Public Radio." *Sociology of Race and Ethnicity* 8, no. 1: 79–94.

George, Molly. 2008. "Interactions in Expert Service Work: Demonstrating Professionalism in Personal Training." *Journal of Contemporary Ethnography* 37, no. 1: 108–31.

Gershon, Ilana. 2017. *Down and Out in the New Economy*. Chicago: University of Chicago Press.

Giazitzoglu, Andreas, and Daniel Muzio. 2021. "Learning the Rules of the Game: How Is Corporate Masculinity Learned and Enacted by Male

Professionals from Nonprivileged Backgrounds?" *Gender Work Organization* 28: 67–84.

Giddens, Anthony. 1991. *Modernity and Self-Identity: Self and Society in the Late Modern Age*. Palo Alto, CA: Stanford University Press.

Giuffre, Katherine. 1999. "Sandpiles of Opportunity: Success in the Art World." *Social Forces* 77, no. 3: 815–32.

Glaser, Barney, and Anselm Strauss. 1999. *Discovery of Grounded Theory: Strategies for Qualitative Research*. New York: Routledge.

Goffman, Alice. 2019. "Go to More Parties?" *Social Psychology Quarterly* 82, no. 1: 51–74.

Gomberg-Muñoz, Ruth. 2011. *Labor and Legality: An Ethnography of a Mexican Immigrant Network*. New York: Oxford University Press.

Gompers, Paul, and Silpa Kovvali. 2018. "The Other Diversity Dividend." *Harvard Business Review* (July–August): 72–77.

Good Beer Hunting. 2018. "Will Work for Beer, Pt. 1—The Dollars and Sense of the Industry." Accessed November 15, 2023, www.goodbeerhunting.com /sightlines/2018/4/26/will-work-for-beer-pt-1-the-dollars-and-sense-of-the-industry.

Gorman, Elizabeth H. 2015. "Getting Ahead in Professional Organizations: Individual Qualities, Socioeconomic Background, and Organizational Context." *Journal of Professions and Organization* 2, no. 2: 122–47.

Granovetter, Mark. 1985. "Economic Action and Social Structure: The Problem of Embeddedness." *American Journal of Sociology* 91: 481–510.

———. 1995 [1974]. *Getting a Job: A Study of Contacts and Careers*. 2nd ed. Chicago: University of Chicago Press.

Grazian, David. 2005. *Blue Chicago: The Search for Authenticity in Urban Blues Clubs*. Chicago: University of Chicago Press.

Hall, Elaine. 1993. "Smiling, Deferring, and Flirting: Doing Gender by Giving 'Good Service.'" *Work and Occupations* 20, no. 4: 452–71.

Halpin, Brian W., and Vicki Smith. 2017. "Employment Management Work: A Case Study and Theoretical Framework." *Work and Occupations* 44, no. 4: 339–75.

Hamilton, Laura, and Elizabeth Armstrong. 2014. *Paying for the Party: How College Maintains Inequality*. Cambridge, MA: Harvard University Press.

Hancock, Black Hawk, Bryan L. Sykes, and Anjuli Verma. 2018. "The Problem of 'Cameo Appearances' in Mixed-Methods Research: Implications for Twenty-First-Century Ethnography." *Sociological Perspectives* 61, no. 2: 314–34.

Harris, Deborah, and Patti Giuffre. 2015. *Taking the Heat: Women Chefs and Gender Inequality in the Professional Kitchen*. New Brunswick, NJ: Rutgers University Press.

Harvey, Daina Cheyenne, Ellis Jones, and Nathaniel G. Chapman, eds. 2023. *Beer Places: The Microgeographies of Craft Beer.* Fayetteville: University of Arkansas Press.

Hatmaker, Deneen. 2013. "Engineering Identity: Gender and Professional Identity Negotiation among Women Engineers." *Gender, Work & Organisation* 20, no. 4: 382–96.

Haveman, Heather A., and Rao Hayagreeva. 1997. "Structuring a Theory of Moral Sentiments: Institutional and Organizational Coevolution in the Early Thrift Industry." *American Journal of Sociology* 102, no. 6: 1606–51.

Henson, Kevin D., and Jackie Krasas Rogers. 2001. "'Why Marcia You've Changed!' Male Clerical Temporary Workers Doing Masculinity in a Feminized Occupation." *Gender & Society* 15, no. 2: 218–38.

Hertz, Julie. 2019. "The Diversity Data Is In: Craft Breweries Have Room and Resources for Improvement." *Brewer's Association.* Accessed November 1, 2020, www.brewersassociation.org/communicating-craft/the-diversity-data-is-in-craft-breweries-have-room-and-resources-for-improvement/.

Hesmondhalgh, David, and Sarah Baker. 2011. *Creative Labour: Media Work in Three Cultural Industries.* New York: Routledge.

Hitlin, Steven, and Monica K. Johnson. 2015. "Reconceptualizing Agency within the Life Course: The Power of Looking Ahead." *American Journal of Sociology* 120, no. 5: 1429–72.

Ho, Violet T., Sze-Sze Wong, and Chay Hoon Lee. 2011. "A Tale of Passion: Linking Job Passion and Cognitive Engagement to Employee Work Performance." *Journal of Management Studies* 48, no.1: 26–47.

Hochschild, Arlie. 1983. *The Managed Heart.* Berkeley: University of California Press.

Hodson, Randy. 2001. *Dignity at Work.* Cambridge: Cambridge University Press.

Holmes, Helen. 2015. "Transient Craft: Reclaiming the Contemporary Craft Worker." *Work, Employment, and Society* 29, no. 3: 479–95.

Holvino, Evangelina. 2010. "Intersections: The Simultaneity of Race, Gender, and Class in Organizational Studies." *Gender, Work, and Organization* 17, no. 3: 248–77.

Howlett, Marnie. 2022. "Looking at the 'Field' through a Zoom Lens: Methodological Reflections on Conducting Online Research during a Global Pandemic." *Qualitative Research* 22, no. 3: 387–402.

Huddleston, Prue. 2011. "'It's All Right for Saturdays, but Not Forever': The Employment of Part-Time Student Staff in the Retail Sector." In *Retail Work,* edited by Irene Grugulis and Odul Bozkurt, 109–27. New York: Palgrave Macmillan.

Hughes, Everett C. 1958. "Cycles, Turning Points, and Careers." In *Men and Their Work,* edited by Everett Hughes, 111–22. Glencoe, IL: Free Press.

Ibarra, Herminia, and Roxana Barbulescu. 2010. "Identity as Narrative: Prevalence, Effectiveness, and Consequences of Narrative Identity Work in Macro Work Role Transitions." *Academy of Management Review* 35, no. 1: 135–54.

Infante, Dave. 2015. "There Are Almost No Black People Brewing Craft Beer. Here's Why." Thrillist. Accessed May 10, 2021, www.thrillist.com/drink /nation/there-are-almost-no-black-people-brewing-craft-beer-heres-why.

Itzigsohn, José, and Karida Brown 2020. *The Sociology of W. E. B. Du Bois*. New York: New York University Press.

Jackson, Chris. 2017. *Albuquerque Beer: Duke City History on Tap*. Mount Pleasant, SC: History Press.

Jerolmack, Colin, and Shamus Khan. 2014. "Talk Is Cheap: Ethnography and the Attitudinal Fallacy." *Sociological Methods & Research*, 43, no. 2: 178–209.

Johnston, Josée, and Shyon Baumann. 2014. *Foodies: Democracy and Distinction in the Gourmet Foodscape*. New York: Routledge.

Jordan, Mike. 2020. "The Time Is Now, Part One—Understanding the Origins of Beer's Inequity." August 11, 2020. Good Beer Hunting. Accessed June 1, 2020, www.goodbeerhunting.com/blog/2020/8/10/the-time-is-now-part-one-understanding-the-origins-of-beers-inequity.

Kaiser, Cheryl R., Brenda Major, Ines Jurcevic, Tessa L. Dover, Laura M. Brady, and Jenessa R. Shapiro. 2013. "Presumed Fair: Ironic Effects of Organizational Diversity Structures." *Journal of Personality and Social Psychology* 104, no. 3: 504–19.

Kalev, Alexandra, Frank Dobbin, and Erin L. Kelly. 2006. "Best Practices or Best Guesses? Assessing the Efficacy of Corporate Affirmative Action and Diversity Policies." *American Sociological Review* 71: 589–617.

Kalleberg, Arne. 2009. "Precarious Work, Insecure Workers: Employment Relations in Transition." *American Sociological Review* 74: 1–22.

———. 2011 *Good Jobs, Bad Jobs: The Rise of Polarized and Precarious Employment Systems in the United States, 1970s–2000s*. New York: Russell Sage Foundation.

Kalleberg, Arne, and Steven P. Vallas. 2018. "Probing Precarious Work: Theory, Research, and Politics." *Research in the Sociology of Work* 31, no. 1: 1–30.

Kang, Sonia K., Katherine A. DeCelles, András Tilcsik, and Sora Jun. 2016. "Whitened Resumes: Race and Self-Presentation in the Labor Market." *Administrative Science Quarterly* 61: 1–34.

Kanter, Rosabeth M. 1977. *Men and Women of the Corporation*. New York: Basic Books.

Katsuno, Hirofumi. 2011. "The Robot's Heart: Tinkering with Humanity and Intimacy in Robot-Building." *Japanese Studies* 31, no. 1: 93–109.

Katz, Jack. 1997. "Ethnography's Warrants." *Sociological Methods and Research* 25, no. 4: 391–423.

———. 2001. "From How to Why: Luminous Description and Causal Inference in Ethnography, Part 1." *Ethnography* 2, no. 4: 443–73.

Kim, Jae Y., Troy H. Campbell, Steven Shepherd, and Aaron Kay. 2020. "Understanding Contemporary Forms of Exploitation: Attributions of Passion Serve to Legitimize the Poor Treatment of Workers." *Journal of Personality and Social Psychology* 118, no. 1: 121–48.

Koontz, Amanda, and Nathaniel Chapman. 2019. "About Us: Authenticating Identity Claims in the Craft Beer Industry." *Journal of Popular Culture* 52, no. 2: 351–72.

Kramer, Rory, Victor Ray, and Eduardo Bonilla-Silva. Forthcoming. "Introduction: Racism of Omission." *Social Problems*.

Kroezen, Jochem, Davide Ravasi, Innan Sasaki, Monika Żebrowska, and Roy Suddaby. 2021. "Configurations of Craft: Alternative Models for Organizing Work." *Academy of Management Annals* 15, no. 2: 502–36.

Kumra, Savita, and Susan Vinnicombe. 2008. "A Study of the Promotion to Partner Process in a Professional Services Firm: How Women Are Disadvantaged." *British Journal of Management* 19: 65–74.

Kusenbach, Margarethe. 2003. "Street Phenomenology: The Go-Along as Ethnographic Research Tool." *Ethnography* 4, no. 3: 455–85.

Lamont, Michèle. 2000. *The Dignity of Working Men.* Cambridge, MA: Harvard University Press.

Lamont, Michèle, Stefan Beljean, and Matthew Clair. 2014. "What Is Missing? Cultural Processes and Causal Pathways to Inequality." *Socio-Economic Review* 12: 573–608.

Lamont, Michèle, and Ann Swidler. 2014. "Methodological Pluralism and the Possibilities and Limits of Interviewing." *Qualitative Sociology* 37, no. 2: 153–71.

Land, Chris. 2018. "Back to the Future: Re-imagining Work through Craft." *Futures of Work.* Available at https://futuresofwork.co.uk/2018/11/19/back-to-the-future-re-imagining-work-through-craft/. Last accessed February 14, 2022.

Land, Chris, Neil Sutherland, and Scott Taylor. 2018. "Back to the Brewster: Craft Brewing, Gender, and the Dialectical Interplay of Re-traditionalisation and Innovation." In *The Organization of Craft Work: Identities, Meanings, and Materiality,* edited by Emma Bell, Gianluigi Mangia, Scott Taylor, and Maria Laura Toraldo. New York: Routledge.

Lareau, Annette. 2021. *Listening to People: A Practical Guide to Interviewing, Participant Observation, Data Analysis, and Writing It All Up.* Chicago: University of Chicago Press.

Lerma, Veronica, Laura T. Hamilton, and Kelly Nielson. 2019. "Racialized Equity Labor, University Appropriation, and Student Resistance." *Social Problems* 67: 287–303.

Lloyd, Richard. 2010. *Neo-bohemia: Art and Commerce in the Postindustrial City*. New York: Routledge.

Los Angeles County Brewers Guild. 2020. Accessed March 1, 2022, https://labrewersguild.org/.

Macdonald, Cameron L., and Carmen Sirianni, eds. 1996. *Working in the Service Society*. Philadelphia: Temple University Press.

Maguire, Jennifer S. 2018. "Wine, the Authenticity Taste Regime, and Rendering Craft." In *The Organization of Craft Work*, edited by Emma Bell, Gianluigi Mangia, Scott Taylor, and Maria Laura Toraldo, 60–78. New York: Routledge.

Marshall, Gordon. 1986. "The Workplace Culture of a Licensed Restaurant." *Theory, Culture & Society* 3, no. 1: 33–47.

Maume, David J., Jr. 1998. " Glass Ceilings and Glass Escalators: Occupational Segregation and Race and Sex Differences in Managerial Promotions." *Work & Occupations* 26, no. 4: 483–509.

Mayorga-Gallo, Sarah. 2019. "The White-Centering Logic of Diversity Ideology." *American Behavioral Scientist* 63, no. 13: 1789–809.

McCallum, Jamie K. 2020. *Worked Over: How Round-the-Clock Work Is Killing the American Dream*. New York: Basic Books.

McClain, Noah, and Ashley Mears. 2012. "Free to Those Who Can Afford It: The Everyday Affordance of Privilege." *Poetics* 40: 133–49.

McRobbie, Angela. 2018. *Be Creative: Making a Living in the New Culture Industries*. Cambridge: Wiley.

Mears, Ashley. 2015. "Working for Free in the VIP: Relational Work and the Production of Consent." *American Sociological Review* 80, no. 6: 1099–122.

Mellows, Phil. 2021. "From Connoisseurship to Community: The Evolution of the Brewery Tap Room." In *Researching Craft Beer: Understanding Production, Community, and Culture in an Evolving Sector*, edited by Daniel Clarke, Vaughan Ellis, Holly Patrick-Thomson, and David Weir, 165–71. Bingley, UK: Emerald Publishing.

Menger, Pierre M. 1999. "Artistic Labor Markets and Careers." *Annual Review of Sociology* 25, no. 1: 541–74.

Messerschmidt, James W., and Michael A. Messner. 2018. "Hegemonic, Nonhegemonic, and 'New' Masculinities." *Gender Reckonings: New Social Theory and Research*: 35–56.

Mickey, Ethel L. 2019. "When Gendered Logics Collide: Going Public and Restructuring in a High-Tech Organization." *Gender & Society*, no.4: 509–33.

———. 2022. "The Organization of Networking and Gender Inequality in the New Economy: Evidence from the Tech Industry." *Work and Occupations* 49, no. 4: 383–420.

Misra, Joya, and Kyla Walters. 2016. "All Fun and Cool Clothes? Youth Workers' Consumer Identity in Clothing Retail." *Work and Occupations* 43, no. 3: 294–325.

Moore, Wendy Leo. 2008. *Reproducing Racism: White Space, Elite Law Schools, and Racial Inequality.* Lanham, MD: Rowman and Littlefield.

Moss, Philip, and Chris Tilly. 2001. *Stories Employers Tell: Race, Skill, and Hiring in America.* New York: Russell Sage Foundation.

Munro, Kristin, and Chris O'Kane. 2022. "The Artisan Economy and the New Spirit of Capitalism." *Critical Sociology* 48, no. 1: 37–53.

Neckerman, Kathryn, and Joleen Kirschenman. 1991. "Hiring Strategies, Racial Bias, and Inner-City Workers." *Social Problems* 38, no. 4: 433–47.

Neff, Gina, Elizabeth Wissinger, and Sharon Zukin. 2005. "Entrepreneurial Labor among Culture Producers: 'Cool' Jobs in 'Hot' Industries." *Social Semiotics* 15, no. 3: 307–34.

Nelson, Jennifer, and Steven Vallas. 2021. "Race and Inequality at Work: An Occupational Perspective." *Sociology Compass* 15, no. 10, e12926, https://doi.org/10.1111/soc4.12926.

New Mexico Magazine. "The Ultimate Craft Beer Guide to New Mexico." July 17, 2019. Accessed November 17, 2023, www.newmexicomagazine.org/blog/post/new-mexico-beer-guide/.

Ocejo, R. 2017. *Masters of Craft: Old Jobs in the New Urban Economy.* Princeton, NJ: Princeton University Press.

Okuwobi, Oneya. 2019. "'Everything That I've Done Has Always Been Multiethnic': Biographical Work among Leaders of Multiracial Churches." *Sociology of Religion: A Quarterly Review* 80, no. 4: 478–95.

———. 2021."Broadening the Conversation about Racism in Research on Organizations, Occupations, and Work." May 3. Organized by the Organizations, Occupations, and Work section, American Sociological Association.

O'Mahony, Siobhan, and Beth Bechky. 2006. "Stretchwork: Managing the Career Progression Paradox in External Labor Markets." *Academy of Management Journal* 49, no. 5: 918–41.

Ortner, Sherry B. 1997. "Thick Resistance: Death and the Cultural Construction of Agency in Himalayan Mountaineering." *Representations* 59: 135–62.

Pager, Devah, and Lincoln Quillian. "Walking the Talk? What Employers Say versus What They Do." *American Sociological Review* 70, no. 3: 355–80.

Paxson, Heather. 2012. *The Life of Cheese: Crafting Food and Value in America.* Berkeley: University of California Press.

Peterson, Richard, and N. Anand. 2004. "The Production of Culture Perspective." *Annual Review of Sociology* 30: 311–34.

Peterson, Richard A., and Roger M. Kern. 1996. "Changing Highbrow Taste: From Snob to Omnivore." *American Sociological Review* 61: 900–907.

Peterson, Richard. 2005. "In Search of Authenticity." *Journal of Management Studies* 42, no. 5: 1083–98.

Petriglieri, Jennifer. 2011. "'Under Threat: Responses to and the Consequences of Threats to Individuals' Identities." *Academy of Management Review* 36, no. 4: 641–62.

Phelan, Peggy. 1994. *Unmarked: The Politics of Performance*. New York: Routledge.

Phillips, Katherine W., Douglas Medin, Carol D. Lee, Megan Bang, Steven Bishop, and D. N. Lee. 2014. "How Diversity Works." *Scientific American* 311, no. 4: 42–47.

Pierce, Jennifer. 1996. *Gender Trials: Emotional Lives in Contemporary Law Firms*. Berkeley: University of California Press.

Pink, Daniel. 2001. *Free Agent Nation: The Future of Working for Yourself*. New York: Warner Books.

Pugh, Allison J. 2015. *The Tumbleweed Society: Working and Caring in an Age of Insecurity*. New York: Oxford University Press.

Rainey, Anthony, and Silvia Maja Melzer. 2021. "The Organizational Context of Supervisory Bullying: Diversity/Equity and Work-Family Policies." *Work and Occupations* 48, no. 3: 285–319.

Ramirez, Michael. 2018. *Destined for Greatness: Passions, Dreams, and Aspirations in a College Music Town*. New Brunswick, NJ: Rutgers University Press.

Rao, Aliya H., and Megan Tobias Neely. 2019. "What's Love Got to Do with It? Passion and Inequality in White-Collar Work." *Sociology Compass* 13, no. 12: 1–14.

Ravenelle, Alexandrea J. 2019. *Hustle and Gig*. Berkeley: University of California Press.

Ray, Victor. 2019. "A Theory of Racialized Organizations." *American Sociological Review* 84, no. 1: 26–53.

Reid, Erin. 2015. "Embracing, Passing, Revealing, and the Ideal Worker Image: How People Navigate Expected and Experienced Professional Identities." *Organization Science* 26: 997–1017.

Reilly, Patrick. 2016. "The Layers of a Clown: Career Development in Cultural Production Industries." *Academy of Management Discoveries* 3, no. 3: 145–64.

Reskin, Barbara F. 2000. "The Proximate Causes of Employment Discrimination." *Contemporary Sociology* 29, no. 2: 319–28.

Reyes, Victoria. 2020. "Ethnographic Toolkit: Strategic Positionality and Researchers' Visible and Invisible Tools in Field Research." *Ethnography* 21, no. 2: 220–40.

Ribas, Vanesa. 2016. *On the Line: Slaughterhouse Lives and the Making of the New South*. Berkeley: University of California Press.

Ridgeway, Cecilia L. 2011. *Framed by Gender: How Gender Inequality Persists in the Modern World*. New York: Oxford University Press.

Risse, Leonora. 2021. "The Gender Qualification Gap: Women 'Over-invest' in Workplace Capabilities." *The Conversation*. Accessed May 10, https://theconversation.com/the-gender-qualification-gap-women-over-invest-in-workplace-capabilities-105385.

Ritzer, George, Paul Dean, and Nathan Jurgenson. 2012. "The Coming of Age of the Prosumer." *American Behavioral Scientist* 56, no.4: 379–98.

Rivera, Lauren A. 2012. "Hiring as Cultural Matching: The Case of Elite Professional Service Firms." *American Sociological Review* 77, no. 6: 999–1022.

———. 2015. *Pedigree: How Elite Students Get Elite Jobs*. Princeton, NJ: Princeton University Press.

Rivera, Lauren A., and Andras Tilcsik. 2016. "Class Advantage, Commitment Penalty: The Gendered Effect of Social Class Signals in an Elite Labor Market." *American Sociological Review* 81: 1097–181.

Rodgers, Diane, and Ryan Taves. 2017. "The Epistemic Culture of Homebrewers and Microbrewers." *Sociological Spectrum* 37, no. 3: 127–48.

Roscigno, Vincent J., and George Wilson. 2014. "The Relational Foundations of Inequality at Work I: Status, Interaction, and Culture." *American Behavioral Scientist* 58, no. 2: 219–27.

Ross, Andrew. 2004. *No-Collar: The Humane Workplace and Its Hidden Costs*. Philadelphia: Temple University Press.

Royster, Diedre A. 2003. *Race and the Invisible Hand: How White Networks Exclude Black Men from Blue-Collar Jobs*. Berkeley: University of California Press.

Rydzik, Agnieszka, and Victoria Ellis-Vowles. 2019. "Don't Use the 'Weak' Word: Women Brewers, Identities, and Gendered Territories of Embodied Work." *Work, Employment, Society* 33, no. 3: 483–99.

Sayer, Aaron. 2007. "Dignity at Work: Broadening the Agenda." *Organization* 14, no. 4: 565–81.

Scott, Michael. 2017. "'Hipster Capitalism' in the Age of Austerity? Polanyi Meets Bourdieu's New Petite Bourgeoisie." *Cultural Sociology* 11, no. 1: 60–76.

Seamster, Louise, and Victor Ray. 2018. "Against Teleology in the Study of Race: Toward the Abolition of the Progress Paradigm." *Sociological Theory* 36, no. 4: 315–42.

Sennett, Richard. 1997. *The Craftsman*. New Haven, CT: Yale University Press.

Sherman, Rachel. 2011. "The Production of Distinctions: Class, Gender, and Taste Work in the Lifestyle Management Industry." *Qualitative Sociology* 34, no. 1: 201–19.

Shigihara, Amanda. 2015. "'Strategic Adulthood': A Case Study of Restaurant Workers Negotiating Non-traditional Life Course Development." *Advances in Life Course Research* 26: 32–43.

Shukaitis, Stephen, and Joanna Figiel. 2020. "Knows No Weekend: The Psychological Contract of Cultural Work in Precarious Times." *Journal of Cultural Economy* 13, no. 3: 290–302.

Siciliano, Michael. 2021. *Creative Control: The Ambivalence of Work in the Culture Industries.* New York: Columbia University Press.

Skeggs, Beverly. 2004. "Exchange, Value, and Affect: Bourdieu and 'the Self.'" *Sociological Review* 52, no. 2: 75–95.

Small, Mario. 2009. "'How Many Cases Do I Need?' On Science and the Logic of Case Selection in Field-Based Research." *Ethnography* 10, no. 1: 5–38.

———. 2022. "Ethnography Upgraded." *Qualitative Sociology* 45: 477–82.

Smith, Vicki. 1997. "New Forms of Work Organization." *Annual Review of Sociology* 23, no. 1: 315–39.

Solomon, Shelby, and Blake Mathias. 2018. "Crafted in America: From Culture to Profession." In *The Organization of Craft: Identities, Meanings, and Materiality*, edited by E. Bell, G. Mangia, S. Taylor, and M. L. Toraldo, 41–59. New York: Routledge.

Stebbins, Robert A. 2001. "Serious Leisure." *Society* 38, no. 4: 53–57.

Stokes, Allyson. 2017. "Fashioning Gender: The Gendered Organization of Cultural Work." *Social Currents* 4, no. 6: 518–34.

Svejenova, Silviya. 2005. "'The Path with the Heart': Creating the Authentic Career." *Journal of Management Studies* 42, no. 5: 947–74.

Tams, Svenja, and Michael B. Arthur. 2010. "New Directions for Boundaryless Careers: Agency and Interdependence in a Changing World." *Journal of Organizational Behavior* 31: 629–46.

Tavory, Iddo. 2020. "Interviews and Inference: Making Sense of Interview Data in Qualitative Research." *Qualitative Sociology* 43, no. 4: 449–65.

Tavory, Iddo, and Nina Eliasoph. 2013. "Coordinating Futures: Toward a Theory of Anticipation." *American Journal of Sociology* 118, no. 4: 908–42.

Terkel, Studs. 1974. *Working.* New York: New Press.

Thornton, Patricia H., and William Ocasio. 2008. "Institutional Logics." *Sage Handbook of Organizational Institutionalism* 840: 99–128.

Thurnell-Read, Thomas. 2014. "Craft, Tangibility, and Affect at Work in the Microbrewery." *Emotion, Space, and Society* 13: 46–54.

———. 2019. "A Thirst for the Authentic: Craft Drinks Producers and the Narration of Authenticity." *British Journal of Sociology* 70, no. 4: 1448–1468.

Timmermans, Stefan, and Iddo Tavory. 2012. "Theory Construction in Qualitative Research: From Grounded Theory to Abductive Analysis." *Sociological Theory* 30, no. 3: 167–86.

Tomaskovic-Devey, Donald. 1993. *Gender and Racial Inequality at Work: The Sources and Consequences of Job Segregation.* Ithaca, NY: Cornell University Press.

Tomaskovic-Devey, Donald, and Dustin Avent-Holt. 2019. *Relational Inequalities: An Organizational Approach.* New York: Oxford University Press.

Turco, Christine J. 2010. "Cultural Foundations of Tokenism: Evidence from the Leveraged Buyout Industry." *American Sociological Review* 75, no. 6: 894–913.

Umney, Charles, and Lefteris Kretsos. 2015. "'That's the Experience': Passion, Work Precarity, and Life Transitions among London Jazz Musicians." *Work and Occupations* 42, no. 3: 313–34.

Vallas, Steven Peter. 2001. "Symbolic Boundaries and the New Division of Labor: Engineers, Workers, and the Restructuring of Factory Life." *Research in Social Stratification and Mobility* 18: 3–37.

Vallas, Steven P., and Angèle Christin. 2018. "Work and Identity in an Era of Precarious Employment: How Workers Respond to 'Personal Branding' Discourse." *Work and Occupations* 45, no. 1: 3–37.

Vallejo, Jody Agius, and Stephanie L. Canizales. 2018. "Latino/a Professionals as Entrepreneurs: How Race, Class, and Gender Shape Entrepreneurial Incorporation." In *Intersectionality and Ethnic Entrepreneurship*, 85–104. New York: Routledge.

Vallerand, Robert J., and Nathalie Houlfort. 2003. Passion at Work: Toward a New Conceptualization. In *Social Issues in Management*, vol. 3, edited by D. Skarlicki, S. Gilliland, and D. Steiner, 175–204. Greenwich, CT: Information Age Publishing.

Vallerand, Robert J., Celine Blanchard, Genevieve A. Mageau, Richard Koestner, Catherine Ratelle, Maude Leonard, and Marylene Gagne, et al. 2003. "Les Passions de l'Âme: On Obsessive and Harmonious Passion." *Journal of Personality and Social Psychology* 85, no. 4: 756–67.

Vandenengel, Heather. "Turning a Passion into a Career." *Beer and Brewing.* Accessed November 16, 2023, https://beerandbrewing.com/turning-a-passion-into-a-career/.

Waldinger, Roger, and Michael Lichter. 2003. *How the Other Half Works.* Berkeley: University of California Press.

Wallace, Andrew. 2019. "'Brewing the Truth': Craft Beer, Class and Place in Contemporary London." *Sociology* 53, no. 5: 951–66.

Warhurst, Chris. 2016. "From Invisible Work to Invisible Workers: The Impact of Service Employers' Speech Demands on the Working Class." In *Invisible Labor: Hidden Work in the Contemporary World*, edited by Marion Crain, Winifred Poster, and Miriam Cherry, 214–36. Berkeley: University of California Press.

Warhurst, Chris, Chris Tilly, and Mary Gatta. 2017. "A New Social Construction of Skill." In *The Oxford Handbook of Skills and Training*, edited by John

Buchanan, David Finegold, Ken Mayhew, and Chris Warhurst, 72–91. New York: Oxford University Press.

Watkins-Hayes, Celeste. 2009. "Race-ing the Bootstrap Climb: Black and Latino Bureaucrats in Post-Reform Welfare Offices." *Social Problems* 56, no. 2: 285–310.

Williams, Christine L. 1989. *Gender Differences at Work: Women and Men in Non-Traditional Occupations.* Berkeley: University of California Press.

———. 2006. *Inside Toyland: Working, Shopping, and Social Inequality.* Berkeley,: University of California Press.

Williams, Christine, and Catherine Connell. 2010. " 'Looking Good and Sounding Right': Aesthetic Labor and Social Inequality in the Retail Industry." *Work and Occupations* 37, no. 3: 349–77.

Williams, Christine L., Kristine Kilanski, and Chandra Muller. 2014. "Corporate Diversity Programs and Gender Inequality in the Oil and Gas Industry." *Work and Occupations* 41, no. 4: 440–76.

Williams, Christine L., Chandra Muller, and Kristine Kilanski. 2012. "Gendered Organizations in the New Economy." *Gender & Society* 26: 549–73.

Wilson, Eli R. 2016. "Matching Up: Producing Proximal Service in a Los Angeles Restaurant." *Research in the Sociology of Work* 29: 99–124.

———. 2021. *Front of the House, Back of the House: Race and Inequality in the Lives of Restaurant Workers.* New York: New York University Press.

———. 2022a. " 'It Could Never Be Just about Beer': Race, Gender, and Marked Professional Identity in the US Craft Beer Industry." *Journal of Professions and Organization* 9, no. 2: 232–45.

———. 2022b. "Privileging Passion: How the Cultural Logic of Work Perpetuates Social Inequality in the Craft Beer Industry." *Socius* 8: 1–12.

Wilson, Eli R., and Asa B. Stone. 2022. *Beer and Society: How We make Beer and Beer Makes Us.* Lanham, MD: Lexington Books.

Wingfield, Adia H. 2010. "Are Some Emotions Marked 'Whites Only'? Racialized Feeling Rules in Professional Workplaces." *Social Problems* 57(2): 251–68.

———. 2013. *No More Invisible Man: Race and Gender in Men's Work.* Philadelphia: Temple University Press.

———. 2019. *Flatlining: Race, Work, and Health Care in the New Economy.* Berkeley: University of California Press.

Wingfield, Adia H., and Renee S. Alston. 2014. "Maintaining Hierarchies in Predominantly White Organizations: A Theory of Racial Tasks." *American Behavioral Scientist* 58, no. 2: 274–87.

Withers, Erik. 2017. "Brewing Boundaries of White Middle-Class Maleness." In *Untapped: Exploring the Cultural Dimensions of Craft Beer*, edited by N. Chapman, J. S. Lellock, and C. Lippard, 236–60. Morgantown: West Virginia University Press.

Wooten, Melissa E., and Lucius Couloute. 2017. "The Production of Racial Inequality Within and Among Organizations." *Sociology Compass* 11, no. 1: e12446.

Wright, David. 2005. "Commodifying Respectability: Distinctions at Work in the Bookshop." *Journal of Consumer Culture* 5, no. 3: 295–314.

Zamudio, Margaret M., and Michael I. Lichter. 2008. "Bad Attitudes and Good Soldiers: Soft Skills as a Code for Tractability in the Hiring of Immigrant Latina/os over Native Blacks in the Hotel Industry." *Social Problems* 55, no. 4: 573–89.

Zukin, Sharon. 2008. "Consuming Authenticity." *Cultural Studies* 22, no. 5: 724–48.

Index

Abad, Melissa, 200n22
abstract passion, 56–57
achievement narrative, 85
Acker, Joan, 11–12, 116
aesthetic labor, 198n11
Albuquerque, New Mexico, 176; brewery growth in, 20–21; demographics of, 21
annual sales, 6
artisanal masculinity: authenticity and, 64; creative pathway and, 51, 62–66; framing, 62–66; gender and, 65–66; passion and, 67; physical expression of, 64–65; pride and, 63; privilege and, 64–65; race and, 65–66; self-identity and, 62–64
art worlds, 209n3
assistant brewers, 30
attitude, 93
authenticity, 16, 166–70; artisanal masculinity and, 64; biographical, 204n28; community and, 83; craftsmanship and, 15; economic disinterest and, 55; family and, 27; homebrewers and, 146–47; informality and, 27; marked professionalism and, 129; oppositional, 204n28; passion and, 55–56; performance of, 71–72; through rejection of conventional standards, 120; self-identity and, 51; Thurnell-Read on, 71–72, 204n28; value of, 161, 163
authority: informal, 125; proving, 124
Ayala-Hurtado, Elena, 85

bad jobs, 94
Barley, Stephen, 134
bearded white guy, 30, 40, 157; explanation of, 195n46; reinforcement of, 47, 160
Beer and Brewing, 46
beer brokering, 142
beer entrepreneurs, 210n5
beer styles: creativity and, 111–12; guidelines, 111
beertenders, 31
belonging: Cicerone certification and, 124; through privilege, 56–57; proving, 124; service pathway and, 73–76; work identity and, 118
Besen-Cassino, Yasemin, 70
Big Beer buyout, 16–17
biographical authenticity, 204n28
biographical work, 206n10; marked professionalism and, 127
Black Lives Matter, 207n13
blended masculinity, 201n27
Bolles, Richard, 199n5

237

Founded in 1893,
UNIVERSITY OF CALIFORNIA PRESS
publishes bold, progressive books and journals
on topics in the arts, humanities, social sciences,
and natural sciences—with a focus on social
justice issues—that inspire thought and action
among readers worldwide.

The UC PRESS FOUNDATION
raises funds to uphold the press's vital role
as an independent, nonprofit publisher, and
receives philanthropic support from a wide
range of individuals and institutions—and from
committed readers like you. To learn more, visit
ucpress.edu/supportus.

www.ingramcontent.com/pod-product-compliance
Lightning Source LLC
Chambersburg PA
CBHW020849270326
41928CB00006B/619